Through the World's Eye

Sir Zelman Cowen

As Governor General, I found that I could always rely on Michael's ability to distil, from a remarkable array of sources, some key insights and light up the course of my own thinking. In this book he demonstrates this extraordinary breadth of thought, humanity and insight into contemporary issues. No doubt he will stimulate the thoughts of his readers.

Mary Robinson, High Commissioner for the Office of the United Nations Commissioner for Human Rights

Michael Kirby's voice is one which richly deserves to be heard because of his deep knowledge of human rights issues, his leadership over many years in such bodies as the International Commission of Jurists, and his recognition of how international standards can help protect human rights at the national level.

Justice Edwin Cameron, Constitutional Court of South Africa

Through a sublime combination of intellectual brilliance, emotional depth and a nearly inexhaustible capacity for human engagement, Michael Kirby has become not only the world's most distinguished openly gay man, but its foremost voice on rationality and fairness in dealing with the AIDS epidemic.

Lord Cooke of Thorndon, New Zealand

It is appropriate that someone outside Australia should write a foreword to this book. Michael Kirby is a most distinguished citizen and servant of Australia. Yet it is his international impact that has most marked him out. He identifies profound modern concerns. He ransacks a wide range of materials with which we would not otherwise be familiar. There is not a paper in this book that can be read without interest and at least some degree of enlightenment. We can be disturbed but never bored.

Professor David Weisbrot, Australian Law Reform Commission

Justice Michael Kirby has an unparalleled reputation – based upon an unparalleled record of depth, breadth and achievement – amongst world law reformers. To use the technical term, he is a dead set legend.

Geoffrey Robertson QC

The wisdom in his words is audible, almost tangible. Where doctors have failed to relieve suffering, Michael Kirby has demonstrated that law really can be of help. He shows this time and again in the chapters of a book which makes you proud to be a lawyer or, if you aren't, might at least make you keen to become one, like its author.

Through the World's Eye

"Once we saw issues and problems through the prism of a village or nation-state, especially if we were lawyers. Now we see the challenges of our time through the world's eye."

Michael Kirby

The Federation Press
2000

Published in Sydney by

The Federation Press
PO Box 45, Annandale, NSW, 2038.
71 John St, Leichhardt, NSW, 2040.
Ph (02) 9552 2200. Fax (02) 9552 1681.
E-mail: info@fedpress.aust.com
Website: http://www.fedpress.aust.com

National Library of Australia cataloguing-in-publication
Kirby, MD (Michael Donald)
Through the world's eye.

Bibliography
Includes index.
ISBN 1 86287 347 X

1. Human rights – Australia. 2. Courts – Australia. 3. Law – Australia. I. Sampford, CJG (Charles JG). II. Blencowe, Sophie. III. Condlln, Suzanne. IV. Key Centre for Ethics, Law, Justice & Governance (Australia). V. Title.

340.1129004

Typeset by The Federation Press, Leichhardt, NSW.
Printed by Ligare Pty Ltd, Riverwood, NSW.

Through the World's Eye

speeches selected and edited by

Charles Sampford, Sophie Blencowe & Suzanne Condlln

of the

Key Centre for Ethics, Law, Justice and Governance

Griffith University

In late 1995, Justice Kirby agreed that the Centre's predecessor, the National Institute for Law, Ethics and Public Affairs, should consolidate some of his most important public speeches in a single volume. This process involved an editorial team of three: Charles Sampford, Sophie Blencowe and Suzanne Condlln. The team selected the topics and the most representative speeches, developed a book structure and then converted the speeches into essays. In many cases, this involved amalgamating several speeches into a single essay as the most complete and up-to-date statement of Justice Kirby's views on that subject. To assist the reader, summaries have been attached to each of the essays. Justice Kirby has, of course, been heavily involved throughout and has gone carefully through the edited texts to ensure that this book presents his views in his words.

The Key Centre for Ethics, Law, Justice and Governance

The Key Centre for Ethics, Law, Justice and Governance (KCELJAG) is the first nationally funded research centre in Law, Ethics, Governance or Criminology. It incorporates three centres – the Centre for Australian Public Sector Management, the Centre for Crime Policy and Public Safety and the National Institute for Law, Ethics and Public Affairs (NILEPA). It aims to provide a distinctive and significant response to the challenges to the values and institutions of liberal democracy posed by globalisation. It aims to do this through the application of the insights of academics and practitioners in law, ethics, politics and criminology. One of its prime publishing outputs is through the series Law, Ethics and Public Affairs. The patron of the Key Centre is His Excellency, Sir William Deane, AC, KBE, and the Chairman of the Advisory Board is Hon Justice Tony Fitzgerald. It is led by Professor Charles Sampford (Director) and Professors Pat Weller and Ross Homel (Deputy Directors). More information on the Centre is available on its website, <www.gu.edu.au>, and from the Centre Manager. One of the publication outlets is the series on Law, Ethics and Public Affairs, published by The Federation Press.

LAW, ETHICS AND PUBLIC AFFAIRS

General Editor: Charles Sampford

Interpreting Constitutions: Theories, Principles and Institutions
edited by Charles Sampford and Kim Preston

Rethinking Human Rights
edited by Brian Galligan and Charles Sampford

Justice for People with Disabilities: Legal and Institutional Issues
edited by Marge Hauritz, Charles Sampford and Sophie Blencowe

Ethics and Political Practice
edited by Noel Preston and Charles Sampford with C-A Bois

Beyond the Adversarial System
edited by Helen Stacy and Michael Lavarch

Educating Lawyers for a Less Adversarial System
edited by Charles Sampford, Suzanne Condlln and Sophie Blencowe

Through the World's Eye
Michael Kirby

Forthcoming titles

Local Government, Public Enterprise and Ethics
edited by Patrick Bishop and Noel Preston

Beyond the Republic
edited by Charles Sampford and Thomas Round

Table of Contents

Foreword

Lord Cooke of Thorndon

It is not inappropriate that someone from outside Australia should be invited to write a foreword to this book. That Michael Kirby is a most distinguished citizen and servant of Australia needs no underlining. It is enough to mention a few highlights of his career: President for nine years of the Australian Conciliation and Arbitration Commission, Chairman for nine years of the Australian Law Reform Commission, Judge of the Federal Court of Australia, President for twelve years of the New South Wales Court of Appeal, Justice of the High Court of Australia since 1996. All this he accomplished by the age of 58. Yet it is probably his international impact that has most marked him out from other Australian lawyers of the front rank.

Others have indeed been international figures. Apart from his enduring fame as an analytical jurist, Sir Owen Dixon is remembered for his service as wartime Envoy in Washington and as United Nations Mediator in Kashmir. Sir Zelman Cowen, basically an academic lawyer, rose to be Governor-General of Australia and justifiably occupies more than half a column of *Who's Who* (London), his many overseas distinctions including the Provostship of Oriel College, Oxford. Sir Ninian Stephen, although born in Scotland, must go down in history as a great Australian and, after serving as a Justice of the High Court and Governor-General, he has given much elsewhere in the world, including chairing Anglo-Irish Talks and holding office as a Judge of the International War Crimes Tribunal for the former Yugoslavia. Sir Anthony Mason, after his eminent (arguably pre-eminent) service as Chief Justice of Australia, almost immediately held the Arthur Goodhart Visiting Chair of Legal Science at Cambridge. The list could easily be lengthened, and even to mention those illustrious names is perhaps to be invidious.

I count myself fortunate to have been privileged by the personal friendship of the three last-named, while I feel that I know Dixon through hours of cogitating over his judgments and other writings and a much briefer exposure to the striking and surely penetrating portrait by Louis Kahan in the common room of the Melbourne Law School. But I claim Michael Kirby, too, as a personal friend and fellow judge; and it is safe to affirm that his international role has been altogether *sui generis.* Today professional judges, especially senior appellate judges, are expected by the community to deliver occasional public lectures and talks or to submit to media interviews. Most are prepared to undertake these extra-judicial activities from time to time, though a few take their stand either on the principle that the faithful discharge of judicial responsibilities is labour enough, or the principle that a judge should never compromise his or her appearance of impartiality by saying anything publicly about any subject possibly controversial.

Kirby is assuredly not of the latter school of thought. Acutely conscious of the power of the mass media and therefore of the need for some degree of judicial control (unspecified in detail) to curb the international might of monopolies, which he regards as a threat to the rule of law itself, he is nevertheless a champion of freedom of speech. He is above all a skilful exponent of it. Naturally he joined in the unanimous High Court decision in *Lange v Australian Broadcasting Corporation*,[1] holding, in refinement of earlier split decisions,[2] that the Constitution contains an implied freedom of communication on government and political matters, limited to what is necessary for representative and responsible government. The effect of the decision is to give a privilege in defamation law beyond the hitherto accepted (in Australia) extent of qualified privilege in English law; provided always that the defendant's conduct is reasonable. I hope that this is an accurate summary of what has been laid down. But his separate judgment in *Mann v O'Neill*[3] seems to carry hints that he might consider an even wider constitutional defence, although another possibility is that these observations were no more than precautionary. And he joined in the 'hands off' approach of the Australian Courts to the *Spycatcher* litigation.[4]

It is indeed Kirby's skill as a publicist, in the best sense of the word, which has given him a unique international standing and role. Both within Australia and in many other countries he has demonstrated an unequalled capacity for providing a flow of informed and informative lectures and addresses on a range of subjects to which no limits have yet

---

1 (1997) 189 CLR 520.

2 *Theophanous v Herald & Weekly Times Ltd* (1994) 182 CLR 104; and *Stephens v West Australian Newspapers Ltd* (1994) 182 CLR 211. If I may respectfully say so, the Brennan court was at its best in its loyal and unanimous basic acceptance, but constructive development, of the controversial majority decisions of the Mason court. In the United Kingdom the common law has now been restated in terms not very different from the Australian solution: *Reynolds v Times Newspapers Ltd* [1999] 4 All ER 609.

3 (1997) 191 CLR 204 at 249-274.

4 See *Attorney-General (UK) v Heinemann Australia Ltd* (1987) 10 NSWLR 86; on appeal (1988) 165 CLR 10. Contrast the approach in *Attorney-General for United Kingdom v Wellington Newspapers Ltd* [1988] 1 NZLR 129. In brief, the Australian courts were altogether unwilling to lend any aid to the British government in enforcing a secret service agent's duty of confidentiality and preventing publication of Peter Wright's memoirs. The New Zealand Court of Appeal, however, would have thought it right to help but for the international extent of existing publication and the public interest of New Zealand, with its intelligence service influenced by the traditions of the British services.

become apparent. Some of the best of these are contained in this rich collection. In principle he appears to remain willing to travel to the ends of the earth to speak in return only for an economy airfare. Almost miraculously, he has managed this output without any evident prejudice to his judicial duties or the fullness of his judgments. Moreover, the liberal idealism running through all his work has by no means stopped at words. His practical contribution in Cambodia as Special Representative for Human Rights of the United Nations Secretary-General, involving arduous travelling and negotiations, and even physical danger, must exact the admiration of his sternest critics. His election as President of the International Commission of Jurists (ICJ), after holding office for some years in the more active post of Chairman of the Executive Committee of that multinational non-government human rights organisation, is a kind of summary of his status. In those roles, qualities of leadership, tact and self-control are demanded from time to time; and at ICJ meetings I have witnessed remarkable demonstrations of these by Michael Kirby. They are of a piece with the intellectual courage that he has displayed, for instance, in his continuing and (I believe) farsighted support of Lionel Murphy.

It would be largely artificial to try to distinguish Kirby the judge from Kirby the publicist. The same philosophy and the same approach to legal problems underlie his entire output. They are subject only to the differing technical disciplines of judgment writing on the one hand and public lecturing on the other. Critics, especially lawyers of the positivist school (although they themselves might be uneasy at that label), will assert that he is the less of a judge for that very reason. But that kind of criticism gives away, often unconsciously, its own uncandid approach. Especially at appellate level, most especially in Australia at the top appellate level of the High Court, the choice constantly facing the court requires in the ultimate a weighing of values.

At least since a general pre-condition of leave has been gained by the High Court for resort to its jurisdiction, one may suspect that the cases reaching there which turn primarily on analysis of prior decisions are the exception rather than the rule. At that level a judge who falls back on analysis alone may be doing only half – and often the easier half – of his or her judicial job. As they mature many, if not all, appellate judges acknowledge and avowedly practise this. Nowhere has the process of evolution been brought out more strikingly than in 'The Mason High Court: A Study of Change in Judicial Technique', to be found in this collection.[5] As Kirby on Mason it will, I predict, be one of the first of the papers to which Australian readers will turn.

---

5 See Kirby, Chapter 10.

Seldom has the process of deciding grey area cases by an open and particularised examination of conflicting policy considerations been better illustrated than by some of Kirby J's High Court judgments. A vintage specimen is in *Mann v O'Neill*,[6] where by a majority of six to one (McHugh J dissenting) the High Court denied absolute privilege for letters written by an unhappy litigant, a medical man, to the Commonwealth Attorney-General and the Minister of Justice questioning on medical grounds the mental capacity of a Special Magistrate. Although conforming to the High Court's traditional preference for thoroughness before liveliness, Kirby J's judgment may be said to compensate by its breadth of reference to materials and its frankness. If I dare say so, it is the most interesting of the judgments in that case. To compound presumption still further, I add that his dissenting judgment in the HIV discrimination case, *IW v City of Perth*,[7] shows an outstanding depth of realism and insight.

In contrast to the responsibilities of the judicial role, Kirby's lectures and addresses do not have to present concrete answers to problems. In them he rarely attempts as much; nor, within the scope of 45 or 50 minutes or so with an audience waiting to be entertained, does he essay much original thought. Rather he identifies profound modern issues and exhorts his audience to be sensitive to them and to reflect. He ransacks a wide range of materials, including in particular American publications with which we would not otherwise be familiar, and he is a master of spicing his discourse with extracts from these sources. No legal lecturer could be better at holding an audience's attention.

And none has such a repertoire. Much of it is the fruit of his Law Reform period, which led him down paths trodden by few lawyers in Australia or elsewhere in the Commonwealth of Nations. What other all-round lawyer could write with any vestige of authority about the Human Genome?[8] Being out of my depth, I thought it prudent to consult one of the world's leading scholars in the law of biotechnology, Dr Yvonne Cripps of Emmanuel College, Cambridge, as to the scientific accuracy of Kirby's approach to this subject. Her verdict is that the author knows what he is talking about.

Even on more familiar terrain he can present old themes attractively. There can hardly be anything more to be said about judicial activism, as is borne out by the fairly frequent hackneyed treatment of this subject in newspaper editorials, but Kirby relates it all beautifully to an Indian

---

6 (1997) 191 CLR 204.

7 (1997) 191 CLR 1 at 51-84. Toohey J also delivered a persuasive dissenting judgment at 26-34. But I agree that the majority judgments are also well reasoned.

8 See Kirby, Chapter 4.

context.[9] An example of his gift for bringing problems out in the open for the first time for many of his listeners is his discussion of judicial stress.[10] He may go a shade far, though, in apparently suggesting, possibly for the sake of dramatic emphasis, that such offences by judicial officers as threatened kidnapping, extortion, and falsifying claims for expenses could be put down partly to this cause.

Diverse as these papers are, they and his judgments have three constant themes. These are the function of the law in protecting disadvantaged groups and minorities (women, Aborigines, AIDS sufferers); the rendering of municipal law accountable to the growing force of international law, especially in human rights (note how often he bolsters a judgment by incorporating an international standard); and what he calls 'conceptualism' as distinct from a mechanical application of case decisions (perhaps another way of seeing law as a set of preferred values). In case those descriptions should sound portentous, let me add that there is not a paper in the book that can be read without interest and at least some degree of enlightenment. We can be disturbed but never bored.

Michael Kirby would not expect me to leave this foreword without some reference to his Achilles' heel. This has been his illusion about the powers of Parliament. In the past he has subscribed vehemently to the widely (but often perhaps unthinkingly) held Diceyan view that at common law Parliaments are supreme or sovereign, in the sense that literally nothing that they might do could be questioned in the courts. It is a view ultimately subversive of the principles of the rule of law and democracy which have a strong claim to be accepted as basic in evolved constitutional common law. Carried to extremes, it would presumably imply that the courts would uphold a statute unambiguously purporting to deprive them of their functions and to transfer all criminal and civil jurisdiction to a hierarchy of administrative tribunals whose members are to hold office at the pleasure of ministers. So, too, if a statute were to enact that no Parliament shall be summoned for three years and that during that time all such regulations as the executive may see fit may be promulgated by order in council. What answers Kirby would have given to such examples are unknown, for hitherto he has supplied none. Some account of his former thesis, and the friendly difference between us about it, will be found in his valued and entertaining contribution to a 1997 Auckland conference organised by the New Zealand Legal

---

9 See Kirby, Chapter 9.

10 See Kirby, Chapter 14. See also JB Thomas, 'Get Up Off the Ground' (1997) 71 *Australian Law Journal* 785 and M Kirby, 'Judicial Stress – A Reply' (1997) 71 *Australian Law Journal* 791, for some of the debate generated by this topic.

Research Foundation.[11] It should be read together with Sir Anthony Mason's foreword and a ringside description of proceedings at the conference by Patrick Downey.[12]

In 1986, Kirby P and colleagues in the New South Wales Court of Appeal expounded such views in *Building Construction Employees & Builders' Labourers Federation v Minister for Industrial Relations.*[13] They rather went out of their way to do so, however, for that case merely upheld a legislative cancellation of the registration of an industrial union which had already been held by a judge of the Supreme Court of New South Wales to have been validly achieved by a Minister's order under delegated authority. An appeal by the union from the judge's decision was pending. Certainly the new legislation put an end to the appeal and made provision about the costs of the litigation. But the argument for the union, alleging violation of constitutional fundamentals, was a desperate one. The union had duly had its day in court. No sense of constitutional propriety is offended by legislation putting beyond challenge a superior court's decision, reached after a full and fair hearing.

I have been writing in the past tense because the 1997 Deakin Oration within this book evidences some development in Kirby's position.[14] He now explains it as having been influenced by the premise that the Australian Constitution derives its authority from the Westminster Parliament. He discerns a movement in Australian judicial and other public thought towards acceptance of a different theoretical starting point, namely the sovereignty of the Australian people. That different approach he perceives as facilitating an assumption that there are some fundamental rights untouched and untouchable by the Constitution: they should be treated as having been implicitly reserved by the people. Scrupulously not committing himself to such a *volte-face*, he nevertheless quietly opens the door to it.

The idea that the very existence of human society implies the existence of some inalienable human rights, or natural law, is as old as it is persistent. Of course, to identify these rights is far from easy. In particular it would be a serious mistake to be preoccupied with rights generally recognised in western-style democracies. The traditions of the most populous countries on earth have to be taken into account as well.

---

11 M Kirby (1997) 'Lord Cooke and Fundamental Rights' in P Rishworth (ed) *The Struggle for Simplicity in the Law*, Butterworths, pp 351-354.

12 Sir A Mason (1997) 'Foreword' in P Rishworth (ed) *The Struggle for Simplicity in the Law,* Butterworths, pp ix-xiv; and PJ Downey, 'Simplicity, Fairness and Reasonable Expectations' [1997] *New Zealand Law Journal* 147.

13 (1986) 7 NSWLR 372.

14 See Kirby, Chapter 12.

But, at least in relation to the constitutional rules underlying western-style democracies, it may reasonably be said that the functioning of a legislature with a house elected by some form of general suffrage and the functioning of courts independent of the executive are two fundamentals. A third, intimately linked with the other two, is a respect for minority interests. The difficulty of acceptably defining the latter more precisely is huge; but this does not mean that the task has to be given up as hopeless. The general similarity in content of formal human rights declarations and instruments, broadly inspired in turn by the *Universal Declaration of Human Rights*,[15] represents progress towards a solution.

In western-style democracies the foregoing ideas are gradually gaining ground. Thus in the United Kingdom the shadow Conservative Lord Chancellor, Lord Kingsland QC, who hinted gently at his thinking while his party was in power,[16] is reported to have said more recently that the courts may have some residual jurisdiction to restrain abuses of power by a parliamentary majority.[17] The leading English administrative law counsel, Michael Beloff QC, has disclosed that there are other lawyers who may not have come out but in private think on the same lines:

> [A]s I discovered in private conversations, when a participant in a recent [New Zealand] conference ... Commonwealth judges from a wide variety of jurisdictions are sympathetic to the idea, as an insurance against a time when democracy declines into elective and even unelected dictatorship.[18]

Kirby's earlier position always was a strange one, in the light not only of the separation of powers embodied in the Australian Constitution but also of the accepted Australian orthodoxy that what Dixon called 'the British conception of the complete supremacy of Parliament' derives its authority from the common law.[19] The common

---

15 *Universal Declaration of Human Rights*, United Nations GA Res 217AA (III), 10 December 1948.

16 House of Lords Official Report, 15 June 1996, 572 HL Deb 1289.

17 The report in *The Times* of 6 November 1997 reads:

> Judges have the power to overturn statutes if democratic principles are at risk of being violated, the Shadow Lord Chancellor, Lord Kingsland, QC, said last night.
>
> Speaking on BBC Radio 4's *Analysis*, he said that it was not 'inconceivable' that in certain circumstances courts would 'step in'. They might do this, he said, to take account of the fact that 'in some circumstances governments that have been elected for a period of five years with large majorities can sometimes abuse that power'.

18 From a book review of Joshua Rozenberg's *Trial of Strength* in *The Times Literary Supplement*, 22 August 1997, p 14.

19 See the quotations from *Jesting Pilate* in the judgment of the High Court in *Lange v Australian Broadcasting Commission* (1997) 189 CLR 520 at 562.

law has never been immutable. There would appear to be no theoretical obstacle to a development on revised Kirby lines, whereby the common law of Australia might recognise some fundamental human rights as antecedent to and surviving the Constitution. An alternative approach, perhaps more practical, would be continuance of the process so strikingly demonstrated in some fields by both the Mason and the Brennan courts of extracting implied rights or freedoms from the Constitution. The incentive to move in one or other of these directions may be a little greater when, on the coming into force of the *Human Rights Act* 1998 in the United Kingdom, Australia is left alone among the common law countries of the Commonwealth in lacking any general human rights instrument at least partly enforceable in the courts.

I must not stray further into the realms of contemplation stimulated by the addresses here collected. Their publication is a major event in Australian legal history in that they largely represent the current state of Michael Kirby's thinking as he moves further into what should be one of the most productive and influential phases of his career. It is obvious that in the high office of Justice of the High Court he will be a significant figure, if occasionally perhaps a lonely one. Yet it would be a mistake to predict that even that office will necessarily mark the end of the services to Australia of this leading Australian citizen, who is also a citizen of the world.

Robin Cooke

House of Lords, Westminster
and Victoria University of Wellington, New Zealand

Foreword

Geoffrey Robertson QC

I was once, by happenstance, the observer of a significant moment in Australian legal history. I was taking morning tea with Michael Kirby, a recent appointment to the Australian Conciliation and Arbitration Commission, in some anonymous Commonwealth office block in Sydney, when the telephone rang. 'It's the Attorney,' said Michael, looking shaken. 'He says we should join him upstairs – he wants me to chair the Australian Law Reform Commission.' Lionel Murphy knew unerringly what was best for Australia (if not always for himself): he greeted us with a lop-sided grin and a bottle of champagne. Michael's demurrers (he thought he should stay longer at the Commission, and he was only 35) were interrupted by the Attorney-General's toast: 'To Justice Kirby – your first step to the High Court bench.'

That was 1974 and, however much water has flowed under the Harbour Bridge since, there was always an historical inevitability that Lionel's toast would one day ring true. Legal appointments in Australia are often a matter of luck: you are in the right place at the right time when your political or personal star-sign comes into alignment. In the regrettable absence (federally and in all States) of a proper and impartial judicial appointments commission, a few potentially great judges wither on the vine (or at the Bar) while some mediocrities are preferred beyond their merits. But there is no appointments system yet devised which could keep Michael Kirby from the highest court: his infant words were, I am sure, uttered judiciously, and his first steps taken in a measured and dignified stride.

It is easy to poke fun at serious and solemn people. At Sydney University in the sixties I observed Michael Kirby at work, obsessively protecting the rights of those who would have been first to take the mickey out of him and his profession.[1] As 'student solicitor,' his defence of the youthful author Bob Ellis, wrongly accused of burglary by his girlfriend's irate father, went down in literature (with the line 'the best burglars burgle naked'). His work in the *Tharunka* and *Oz* cases, defending dissident student magazines facing absurd obscenity charges, helped to change our repressive obscenity laws. As a leading light for civil liberties, he was a friend indeed to the many anti-Vietnam and anti-apartheid protesters, to Aborigines and underdogs who came before Sydney's irascible magistrates, several of whom were corrupt while two

1 See Kirby, Chapter 8.

were certifiably insane. What I observed – and as President of the Students' Representative Council I would burden him with many clients – was his utter devotion to them, 18 hours a day and invariably for free. His commitment and self-sacrifice made him almost too daunting to serve as a role model, but it was so conspicuous that our utterly irreverent student revues never made lawyer jokes.

It was unusual to have as a judge someone who had cut his legal teeth on civil liberties causes, and who had acted so frequently for the poor and oppressed. It was Lionel Murphy's genius to provide for the further education of young Michael by placing him at the helm of law reform. This was long overdue, for the common law – largely inherited from Britain – was not only unsuited in some cases to Australian needs, but was internally deficient. Britain's great Lord Chancellor, Gerald Gardiner, had recognised this a decade before by establishing a Law Reform Commission under the far-sighted guidance of Lord Scarman. Michael took the English model and improved upon it – most notably by involving the people in its business through public hearings and by presenting the issues to them in lectures and newspaper articles. Many of the essays in this book owe their inspiration, and certainly their depth, to Michael Kirby's law reform period (he chaired the Commission from 1975 to 1984), during which he dragged a lot of Australian law into the late twentieth century. The experience has fitted him uniquely for the task of nurturing and fertilising that constitutional garden which we leave in the care of the High Court of Australia.

The other extraordinary aspect of Michael's career which finds reflection in this book is his contribution to the development of international human rights law. He is the best known Australian lawyer outside Australia, through his Presidency of the International Commission of Jurists and his service to Organisation for Economic Co-operation and Development (OECD) committees on data protection, the United Nations Educational, Scientific and Cultural Organisation (UNESCO) work on the Human Genome Project and as United Nations Special Representative in Cambodia. What he has strived to achieve in fashioning Australian law, he has managed in some respects to repeat for a global community. But for all the revolution in communications brought about by the satellite and the fax machine, Australians who conquer the tyranny of distance must do so at severe personal cost. Those endless flights from Sydney for a lecture in London or a meeting in Geneva, often economy class (and always catching the tube rather than a taxi from Heathrow), must take their human toll on a man who has been tireless in the work of building a better world.

Robin Cooke provides an illuminating introduction to Kirby the judge. It seems to me that the business of judging, at appellate level, has changed quite significantly in recent years, certainly in terms of public expectations. No longer is it a privilege; it is a public position serving a democracy. It is not therefore enough to be a good lawyer (although that is a necessary condition): there must also be a fairly deft grasp of human rights principles, of the requirement of 'fairness' in all things, and a street wisdom which will not be learned from textbooks or law reports. It is more difficult in Australia, lacking a Bill of Rights and with politicians who cynically seek publicity by knocking the judiciary.[2] The American people are mostly proud of judicial activism, in defence of first principles which are valued because they once had to fight for them. In other countries, too, Supreme Courts are beginning to get the hang of human rights: there is some inspired jurisprudence emerging from South Africa and what the House of Lords will make of Britain's new Bill of Rights remains to be seen (Robin Cooke's presence there affords some reassurance). The Australian High Court has had to 'imply' fundamental rights into the Australian Constitution, a wonder of its age (Victorian) but an anachronistic and uninspiring document as we turn into the twenty-first century. We should be proud of Federation, but ashamed at the political laziness which has left its original blueprint largely unaltered.

I hope that Australians will soon come to understand the importance of keeping up with the advanced world by adopting a Bill of Rights. Then, our High Court will compete for a gold medal in jurisprudence with the top courts of other countries. These essays show how well equipped Justice Kirby is for the task of building on the recent work of Justices Mason, Deane and Gaudron, once he gets into his judicial stride. With slightly shorter steps, preferably: am I imagining it, or have the *Australian Law Journal's* High Court reports doubled in length since his accession to its bench?

My only regret about this book is that it is not accompanied by a CD of the author performing 'live'. These are the occasions when the wisdom in his words is audible, almost tangible, in the controlled passion of his utterance, leavened with topical (but invariably polite) jokes and snatches of poetry. The packed audience in St-Martin-in-the-Fields church, London, on World Aids Day 1995, will never forget his delivery from the pulpit, not of a sermon but of a charter for compassionate law reform. Where doctors have failed to relieve suffering, Michael Kirby has demonstrated that law really can be of help. He shows this time and again in the chapters of a book which makes you proud to be a lawyer or, if you aren't, might at least make you keen to become a lawyer, like its author.

Geoffrey Robertson QC
Doughty Street Chambers, London

2 See Kirby, Chapter 13.

Preface

Michael Kirby

When William Shakespeare referred in his 69th Sonnet to the world's eye, even his uniquely vivid imagination could not have conceived what we now know. He could not have imagined the radio telescopes that search the universe for unseeable galaxies. He could not have imagined how we would identify and manipulate the atom. How we would use computers to examine the basic elements of life. How we would walk on the moon and look back and see the world. How we would view our blue planet as an integrated entity and perceive all its marvels and problems through the world's eye.

Consider the twentieth century. What will history say of it? A time of terrible wars and unprecedented suffering. Of grotesque genocide and the Holocaust. Of astonishing technology often warped to the purposes of war. Of seemingly irrepressible nationalism and racial pride. Such menaces recur in an era when telecommunication makes us the inhabitants of a global village, when the human species claims space as its new frontier, and when the Genome Project offers the prospect of altering the make-up of human and animal life.

Amidst this worrying chronicle history will also record that ours was the time when people everywhere began to define their fundamental rights, struggled to achieve the rudimentary mechanisms of global government, co operated in responding to common problems (such as HIV/AIDS) and nurtured constitutionalism and the rule of law as the alternatives to anarchy and brute power. Science and technology, while misused by war lords, have had remarkable spin-offs for the world. New forms of informatics, such as the Internet, promise to revolutionise the nature of society. And the development of biological technology and genomic science heralds a long-term potential that may profoundly affect the very nature of the species that has given it birth. The universe existed before humanity. But humanity has become the intelligence that perceives and interprets that existence.

By a remarkable set of chances I have had opportunities to see at close hand many of the optimistic developments for which the twentieth century will be best remembered. In countless conferences I have learned with others and shared my thoughts. This book collects a few of the papers that I offered in such settings. The limitation of such a collection is that it lacks the coherence of a work written with a single unifying theme. Nevertheless, I hope that the energy and enthusiasm of the particular occasions when the speeches were presented may, in some way, stimulate the reader to a more profound consideration of global values.

The first part of these collected essays deals with themes relating to the defence of fundamental human rights. The need to find non-violent solutions to challenges to the peace and security of the world and its peoples. The need to respond to the predicament of the millions of refugees forced from their homes by war, chaos and disasters. The obligation to build the international institutions that will stimulate and defend the foundations of human rights in countries long deprived of them. The need to reflect, with humanity, upon the challenges of the genome and of cyberspace. The obligation to respond with enlightenment to new challenges to human rights (such as those presented by greater understanding of human sexuality) and the special problems presented by completely unexpected developments (such as the AIDS pandemic). These concerns enliven our obligation to participate in the struggle for human rights both internationally and in our own communities.

The beginning of the new millennium also coincides with the centenary of the federation of the Australian Commonwealth. It is therefore timely to scrutinise the values of the Australian courts and legal profession at this time. The second part of this collection contains essays on the law and its institutions in Australia. The issue of so-called judicial activism, for example, has raised the temperature of public discourse about the role of the judiciary. Attacks on judges have become a universal, and sometimes dangerous, phenomenon. As a profession the judiciary in Australia generally responds without complaint. But the judiciary is subjected to a great deal of stress today, and not only by the many ignorant attacks made upon it. Other significant issues in the law are discussed by special reference to the judicial work of two former Justices of the High Court of Australia: Chief Justice Anthony Mason and Justice Lionel Murphy. Both developed the unique capacity to view the law from 'outside' – to see it, if you like, through the world's eye.

Law has the potential to be a noble profession. This is precisely because it is not mechanical. It involves something more than an automatic application of pre-ordained rules. It calls forth judgment, evaluation and the exercise of discretion. It relies upon the will of a fellow human being to do justice according to law – the two inescapable attributes of a civilised legal system. The will to do justice is a strong motivation of the judiciary and the legal profession of Australia and other like countries. I hope that will always be so.

This collection of essays concludes with a reminder that law is not just another privatised commercial activity. Necessarily, it is part of the government of a country. It serves the attainment of justice for individuals and it sets the standard of fairness which makes the rule of law a cherished ideal and not an oppressive imposition.

I express my thanks to Professor Charles Sampford of the Key Centre for Ethics, Law, Justice and Governance of Griffith University, Queensland, Australia, for the encouragement to publish this book. To the publishers, The Federation Press, for their professional support in its publication. To Sophie Curzon Blencowe and Suzanne Condlln, also of Griffith University, for their painstaking editorial revisions. To Kingsley Siebel, for preparing the index. To my personal assistant, Janet Saleh, for her effort in retrieving and amending past speeches. To Jennifer Younan, Macgregor Duncan, Rebecca Craske, Joe Tan and Samantha Fradd, my law associates in the High Court for 1998-2000, for suggestions and for chasing up many tedious footnotes. And to the audiences who have sat through these and other addresses on thousands of occasions in the twenty-five years since my first appointment to public office in 1974.

In those twenty-five years the metaphor of looking back at the world and seeing its entirety has continued to influence the human imagination. Once we saw issues and problems through the prism of a village or nation-state, especially if we were lawyers. Now we see the challenges of our time through the world's eye.

Part I

LAW REFORM AND HUMAN RIGHTS

Part I of this collection looks at national and international challenges to fundamental human rights and reflects on strategies for responding to these challenges. One of the recurring themes in this part is Michael Kirby's belief in the role of international institutions, particularly the agencies of the United Nations, in building a better world through the recognition and defence of human rights. While he acknowledges that the UN has weaknesses, he believes that its institutions represent the most practical and effective way of responding to the challenges faced by the global community as it enters the new millennium.

In Chapter 1, Michael Kirby considers the Dalai Lama's philosophy of non-violence and the potential of this idea to bring about political change and lasting peace in Tibet, and in the resolution of international conflicts. He takes this as a paradigm for other like conflicts and their solution. In Chapter 2, he examines the problems faced by refugees in Australia and overseas. His message is that the underlying issues that give rise to the global tide of refugees – the unrequited right to self-determination, unchecked population growth and economic inequality – must be tackled before any meaningful and long-term change can take place. In Chapter 3, he records his experiences as Special Representative of the Secretary-General for Human Rights in Cambodia, a position he held from 1994 to 1996.

Chapters 4 and 5 deal with the ethical, social and legal implications of advances in science and technology, in particular in the areas of human genomic research and informatics. Michael Kirby reflects on the need to protect those human rights – privacy, confidentiality and dignity – that compete with scientific progress and the free flow of information. He suggests that what is lacking is an understanding of the relevance of scientific developments for the *concept* of human rights. He cautions against resignation that will allow 'science and technology to take our species where they will', and argues that ethical and legal responses must keep pace with technological advances.

In Chapter 6, Michael Kirby reflects on the progress of law reform in Australia in the area of sexual orientation. He outlines some of the positive developments that are taking place in the areas of property relations, migration law and employment benefits. He cautions that much remains to be done, however, and calls attention to the many legislative provisions that continue to discriminate on the basis of a person's sexual orientation. The lesson of Chapter 6 is that no one should accept unjustifiable discrimination in any form. This theme is continued in Chapter 7, an account of the various emotions experienced by people living with HIV/AIDS and their loved ones, and a call to break through the silence that continues to surround this epidemic.

In the final chapter of Part I, Michael Kirby recalls his early years as an impressionable young lawyer participating in the work of the New South Wales Council for Civil Liberties. He recalls the foresight of those who perceived the human rights issues of the future and concludes by posing the question – what issues do we not see today but which will be on the human rights agenda tomorrow?

Chapter 1

Non-Violence, Compassion and Visions for the Twenty-First Century

This speech was written for a symposium celebrating the 60th birthday of His Holiness the Dalai Lama, as part of the World Colloquium on Sciences, Spirituality and the Future, held in New Delhi, India, 4 July 1995. Michael Kirby discusses the evolution of the principle of non-violence and its role in the resolution of international conflicts, reminding us of the need to take a long-term approach to the resolution of human rights issues. He shares the Dalai Lama's belief that negotiation and compromise should be used rather than violence and brute force to achieve a lasting settlement of disputes. The Dalai Lama's message that most of humanity aspires to peaceful co-existence is reflected in the achievements of various international and regional bodies in implementing universal human rights standards. Michael Kirby views the Dalai Lama's philosophy as a powerful counterweight to values of materialism and greed and as presenting a challenge to the world's institutions, which will need to find new ways to solve the problems of the twenty-first century.

Non-Violence and Compassion

Non-violence or *Ahimsa* is not specifically an Asian phenomenon. Nor is it confined to Buddhist philosophy. The Reverend Martin Luther King Jr preached non-violence as a means of securing change in the racial laws and policies of the United States of America. Most of the gains won by Nelson Mandela and his followers in South Africa were achieved by the exercise of the tactics of non-violence.

Yet when we talk of non-violence today, our thoughts usually fly to Asia, to figures like Mahatma Gandhi, who made the powerful idea of non-violent protest familiar as a successful instrument of radical political change. And nowadays, we think of the Dalai Lama's insistence on non-violence as the only available strategy for achieving the rights of the Tibetan people to self-determination, promised to them by international law.

In response to critics of his philosophy, the Dalai Lama has stated:

> Non-violence ... is something more positive, more meaningful ... The true expression of non-violence is compassion. Some people seem to think that compassion is just a passive emotional response instead of

> rational stimulus to action: to experience compassion is to develop a feeling of closeness to others combined with a sense of responsibility for their welfare. ... Compassion compels us to reach out to all human beings, including our so-called enemies, those people who upset or hurt us.[1]

In approaching the subject matter of this contribution, it is useful to understand and develop these thoughts of the Dalai Lama. Sometimes they may seem antithetical to the common experience of humankind. The Dalai Lama, for example, rejects the commonly held view that human beings have a basically violent, aggressive character which must be controlled and tamed by force. According to him, human beings basically have a non-violent nature.[2] This theory rests upon a particular perspective of the basic drives in the nature of all of us:

> Irrespective of what [so-called enemies] do to you, if you remember that all beings like you are only trying to be happy, you will find it much easier to develop compassion towards them. Usually your sense of compassion is limited and biased. We extend such feelings only towards our family and friends or those who are helpful to us. People we perceive as enemies or others to whom we are indifferent are excluded from our concern. That is not genuine compassion. True compassion is universal in scope. It is accompanied by a feeling of responsibility. To act altruistically, concerned only for the welfare of others, with no selfish or ulterior motives, is to affirm a sense of universal responsibility. As a Buddhist monk, the cultivation of compassion is an important part of my daily practice.[3]

It might seem strange, and even faintly eccentric, to many in Western countries to hear such instruction from a person who, with his people, has been driven into exile, excluded from his homeland and reminded every day of wrongs done to the people left behind and to the environment. Yet this message has secured a rare global fascination and popular currency.

Many who observe his life and writings, however, ask whether by this means he, like Gandhi, Martin Luther King Jr, Nelson Mandela and others, can ever lead his people to the achievement of their objectives. Even amongst the Dalai Lama's own followers, there are some who are impatient with his strategy of non-violence and his seeming acceptance of the need to negotiate with China towards a position falling short of

---

1 HH The Dalai Lama, 'True Expression of Non-Violence is Compassion', *The Asian Age*, 1 January 1995, reprinted in the *Tibetan Bulletin*, January/February 1995, p 14.

2 HH The Dalai Lama (1995) *On the Environment*, Department of Information and International Relations, Central Tibetan Administration of HH The Dalai Lama, p 48.

3 HH The Dalai Lama (1995) *Tibetan Bulletin*, p 14.

total independence for Tibet. The Dalai Lama, recognising this impatience, in his statement on the 36th anniversary of the Tibetan National Uprising Day, said:

> Many Tibetans have voiced unprecedented criticism of my suggestion that we should compromise on the issue of total independence. Moreover, the failure of the Chinese government to respond positively to my conciliatory proposals has deepened the sense of impatience and frustration among my people. ... However, as long as I lead our freedom struggle, there will be no deviation from the path of non-violence.[4]

Some observers, and not only within Tibet, are profoundly pessimistic about the chances of a peaceful resolution of the Tibet problem. They suggest that with some opponents it is not easy to talk one's way to freedom or to persuade by non-violence and example alone. Gandhi ultimately was able to reach the conscience of the British people. Martin Luther King Jr inspired Americans of all races and encouraged the use of the independent lawmaking institutions of his country to help correct great national wrongs. Nelson Mandela found a compatriot of rare open-mindedness and realism in FW de Klerk. But critics of the Dalai Lama's message of non-violence and compassion point to the difficulty of succeeding with such a strategy against enemies such as Hitler, Stalin or Pol Pot. They ask whether some people are so unjust and wicked that they depart from the basic nature of humanity and require sanctions more powerful than argument, compassion and non-violence.

Some optimists suggested that Tibet's time would come on the passing of China's paramount leader, Deng Xiaoping.[5] Others placed emphasis upon the growth of diverse media outlets in China itself. They have suggested that technological changes in the spread of information throughout the world, and in China itself, will make the autocratic control of any country impossible to maintain in the century to come.[6]

The Dalai Lama does not deny the existence of irrational, cruel, uncompromising individuals and groups. Of course they exist. History, including recent history, teaches this. But the Dalai Lama's thesis is that such aberrations are exceptions to the basic instincts of humanity. Rationality, kindliness and the search for happiness and love are such

---

4 Statement by HH The Dalai Lama on the 36th Anniversary of the Tibetan National Uprising Day, 10 March 1995, printed in *Australia Tibet Council News*, February/March 1995, pp 2-3.

5 L Evans, 'Tibet Expects Changes When Deng Dies', *The Australian*, 1 March 1995, p 6. Deng Xiaoping died on 19 February 1997.

6 See 'NTU Co-Conference on Chinese Press in China', *The Straits Times*, 22 March 1995, p 3.

deep universal characteristics of the overwhelming mass of humankind that in the end, he teaches, these forces will win out against the exceptional people of violence and enmity. Those who take the 'middle way', the spirit of which has motivated the Dalai Lama's path, maintain a perspective of human events which is distinctly long term. They recognise that, in the end, justice usually prevails. Lasting peace and reconciliation are more likely to be brought about by non-violent means which tackle the fundamental disorders that beset humanity. Bombing problems away will frequently do little more than kill immediate opponents – devastating the environment and leaving it to angry descendants to take up the cause at a later time with ever-increasing violence.

To those who admire the philosophy of non-violence and compassion but are doubtful about its universal success as a strategy in the face of determined and autocratic opponents, I am sure that the Dalai Lama would point to many good contemporary examples. Who, for example, would have thought that the Berlin Wall and the autocracies that hid behind it would have fallen so completely, in so short a time – and not to a blast of guns but to the will of the people? Who would have thought that the Israelis and Palestinians would have embarked upon the tentative steps that may one day bring them to peace? Who would have predicted that those ancient enemies in Ireland would now be on a path to eventual respect for each other's dignity and rights? We must not only remain non-violent and compassionate. As human beings, we should remain optimistic. Education and profoundly enlarged sources of information and insight will ensure the ultimate triumph of justice. But we must all work to bring justice about.

Building International Institutions

It has been my privilege to participate in a number of international and regional bodies which are concerned to translate the principles of non-violence and compassion into practical institutions which will help build a better world in the twenty-first century.

In the International Labour Organisation (ILO) I took part in a Commission which visited South Africa just before the transition to democracy – to assist in measuring that country's labour laws against universal standards established by the ILO. In the Organisation for Economic Cooperation and Development (OECD), I participated in a Committee which drafted basic rules for protecting the privacy of the massive flows of data which now cross the planet. For the Commonwealth Secretariat, in London, I have worked with jurists of many lands to promote the implementation of universal human rights standards in domestic lawmaking.[7] In the World Health Organisation (WHO), I have participated in the Global Commission on AIDS. AIDS is a challenge to humanity that calls forth our instincts of compassion. But WHO must also mobilise our intelligence and resolve so that we may prevent the spread of the virus, halt the second epidemic of discrimination and provide assistance to the sick and their families. Most recently, I had the privilege of working as the Special Representative of the Secretary-General of the United Nations for Human Rights in Cambodia.

These institutional appointments, and my work in the International Commission of Jurists, have helped me to see at first hand the way in which a new world order is gradually being put together. The new order has many weaknesses and failings. Its history parallels, in a sense, the struggles of our own countries and their long quest for peace and security, economic development and respect for human rights.

The Tibetan communities are, naturally enough, impatient with some of the activities of the United Nations.[8] For every success which is achieved, there are apparent failures.[9] But at least the United Nations and its international agencies provide a forum in which the cries of the oppressed can be heard. We must be insistent upon progress but we must also be aware of the obstacles. While the highly charged political debates of the Security Council and the General Assembly tend to capture most of the media's attention, behind the political institutions lies a most worthy family of United Nations agencies. They practise non-violent help. They exercise compassion in many realistic ways. There are inefficiencies and failings, it is true. But it is important also to give credit to the achievements.

At the end of May 1995, I participated in a meeting in Geneva with the Special Rapporteurs/Representatives of the United Nations who, like me, were working on projects assigned to them by the Secretary-General

---

7 The way in which judges of the common law can do this was explained in the *Bangalore Principles*, adopted in 1988. See MD Kirby, 'The Bangalore Principles on "the Domestic Application of International Human Rights Norms"' (1988) 14 *Commonwealth Law Bulletin* 1196; MD Kirby, 'The Role of the Judge in Advancing Human Rights by Reference to International Human Rights Norms' (1988) 62 *Australian Law Journal* 514 at 531-532 and JG Starke, 'International Legal Notes' (1989) 63 *Australian Law Journal* 497.

8 See 'UN Visit A Farce' in *Australia Tibet Council News*, February/March 1995, p 3; 'United Nations Backs Predominantly Chinese Industries in Tibet' (1995) 6(5) *Tibet Press Watch* 12.

9 See 'China Fails to Block a UN Human Rights Vote' (1995) 6(1) *Tibet Press Watch* 1.

and the General Assembly. Some worked in particular countries, including Afghanistan, Cuba, Iraq, Sudan and, in my case, Cambodia. Others were assigned mandates on particular themes – the independence of the judiciary, the rights of women, prevention of extrajudicial torture and execution, protection against child prostitution and pornography and defence against religious intolerance. The Special Rapporteur on Religious Intolerance visited China and Tibet and testified to the United Nations Commission on Human Rights about his findings.[10] This network of Special Rapporteurs and Special Representatives has no soldiers to enforce its findings where there are derogations from United Nations standards. But at least this is a means to bring to the attention of the international community serious derogations from fundamental human rights principles. It is a new means of translating the aspirations of United Nations treaties into practical action. When we hear so much talk about the failures of the United Nations, we should take heart from the extremely useful work done by its many agencies and officers. We should give support to the network of human rights guardians who report, ultimately, to the conscience of the universal family of humanity.

The Role of the United Nations in the Twenty-First Century

Approaching the change of the centuries, an element of millennial madness captures the imagination of some people. Certainly, it is no bad thing to reflect upon the momentous symbolic change as we move into the next millennium. It provides an opportunity for reflection, not least upon the institutions of the United Nations itself. It is appropriate that those who have put so much faith in United Nations institutions should consider how the United Nations is working and how we can make it work better for the benefit of all humankind.

From the outset, the United Nations Charter was founded upon three fundamental objectives: the objective of ensuring peace with the consequent need for security of the member states; the objective of procuring development to meet the economic needs of the people of the world and to ensure economic justice; and the objective of protecting human rights and justice for individuals and peoples. This last objective is designed to meet the need for individuals and groups to live in dignity and liberty. The Charter thus recognises that the foundation-stone for any new world international order would rest upon respect for individual

10 Ibid, p 15. See also 'UN Rapporteur on Religion Visits Tibet' (1995) 6(5) *Tibet Press Watch* 10.

human rights and the rights of peoples, including the peoples' right to self-determination.

In the first 50 years of the United Nations, during the Cold War, most of the attention of the public face of the organisation was upon peace and security. To a large extent the debates were sterile. However, a major nuclear catastrophe which so many feared was averted, some credit for which must go to the United Nations. Now, we are entering a new era in which there are new risks to international and regional security. Some of those risks, it must be said, derive from the unrequited demands for self-determination and the failure of some states and peoples to accord appropriate respect to the rights of minorities.

The former Secretary-General of the United Nations, Dr Boutros Boutros-Ghali, released the Agenda for Development, which recognises the relationship between peace and development. It acknowledged the fact that equitable development and economic opportunity are essential to eradicating many of the most pressing socio-political conditions in which dangers for peace can arise. Dr Boutros-Ghali emphasised the need for practical international co-operation for security in areas such as emergency humanitarian assistance, effective governance, social equity and multicultural diversity. Gareth Evans, when Australian Foreign Minister, echoed this need:

> It is imperative that we improve the system's ability to develop and implement social and economic development programmes in a more coordinated and coherent manner, including by finding ways to allow the Bretton Woods institutions and UN bodies to work in closer harmony. An example of a more systematic approach to the UN system ... is the recent package of reforms undertaken by the Economic and Social Council. The new approach to operational activities and the joint programme ... to tackle the health and development impacts of the HIV/AIDS pandemic, demonstrates the achievements that are possible through such reform. But more will be required than this, including changes in the senior decision-making structure of the UN Secretariat.[11]

Clearly, there have been positive developments in the capacity of the United Nations to respond to the challenges of our era:

- the establishment of a network of human rights instruments which are gaining influence throughout the world;
- the re-affirmation of the universality of human rights in the *Vienna Declaration of Human Rights* 1993;

---

11 Statement to the 49th General Assembly of the United Nations, 3 October 1994. GJ Evans, 'Reintegrating the United Nations', *Peace and Disarmament News*, November 1994, Australian Government Publishing Services, p 9.

- the appointment of the United Nations High Commissioner for Human Rights to coordinate and give a new impetus to United Nations activities in the human rights sphere; and
- the creation of an International Criminal Tribunal for the former Yugoslavia[12] and for Rwanda, and the adoption of a statute to create an International Criminal Court to deal with gross violations of international criminal law wherever they occur.[13]

Yet a great deal remains to be done in building the institutions of the new world order. There is an urgent need to improve the United Nations peacekeeping capacity so that the ability of the organisation to respond to emergencies does not outrun the will and the financial and military support of member states. The United Nations learned a hard lesson in Somalia. It is still at risk in the Balkans, in Rwanda and in many other lands. Yet for these inadequacies we should not blame the United Nations. We should look to ourselves for the failure of resolve and of support.[14]

There is also a need for comprehensive security to replace the idea of collective security. This idea is in harmony with the teachings of the Dalai Lama about the positive character of compassion. Security should no longer be confined to political and diplomatic issues. It is now increasingly realised that true security depends upon economic equity, the just resolution of trade disputes, vigilant attention to human rights abuses and respect for the rights of peoples.

Peace-building activities must be encouraged with attention to the urgent issues of birth spacing, population over-crowding, economic refugees and despoliation of the environment. The pressure on inter-

---

12 See H Corell *et al* (Rapporteurs) (1993) *Proposal for an International War Crimes Tribunal for the Former Yugoslavia*, Council for Security and Cooperation in Europe. For the establishment of the Tribunal, see J O'Brien, 'The International Tribunal for Violations of International Humanitarian Law in the Former Yugoslavia' (1993) 87 *American Journal of International Law* 639.

13 International Law Commission, Report on Second Session, 1950; 5 UNGAOR Supp (No 12) para 145, UN Doc A/1316. See also UNGA Res 48/31 of 9 December 1993 requesting the International Law Commission to give priority to the elaboration of a draft. See also Amnesty International, *Establishing a Just, Fair and Effective International Criminal Court*, Amnesty International, Amnesty International Index IOR 40/05/94. The statute of the proposed Court was adopted in Rome on 16 July 1998. See United Nations Diplomatic Conference of Plenipotentiaries on the Establishment of an International Criminal Court, *Draft Statute for the International Criminal Court*, UN Document: A/Conf. 183/C.1/L.76/Add. 1-12 (16 July 1998), Rome.

14 B Boutros-Ghali (1995) Address to International Peace Academy Conference on Peace-keeping, Vienna, Austria.

national peace and security caused by massive flows of populations in search of economic opportunity requires a concerted global response.[15]

The special peril of the proliferation of nuclear weapons and the unwelcome detonation of nuclear devices by India and Pakistan in 1998 will require the extension of the *Treaty of Non-Proliferation of Nuclear Weapons.* As I was constantly reminded in Cambodia, there also remains an urgent need to strengthen international law in response to the grievous proliferation of anti-personnel landmines which cause such individual suffering and economic dislocation.

There is a need for new institutional responses which will settle, in a peaceful way, unfulfilled demands of peoples to the right of self-determination. At the moment, there are no such institutional means. The United Nations, which is effectively controlled (politically and financially) by member states, tends to respond ineffectively, or even antagonistically, to the demands of peoples to enjoy their right to self-determination. The international community did not respond effectively to the call of the Baltic States during their occupation by the Soviet Union. Generally, it is only when separation is achieved as a matter of practical reality that it is recognised by states and by international institutions.[16]

I do not suggest that the recognition of the people's right to self-determination, in a world where such claims can sometimes endanger peace and security, presents a problem which is simple of resolution. Somehow that right must be secured in harmony with the other interests which international law safeguards. Sometimes, as has been pointed out, demands for self-determination can be selfish and destructive.[17] The Dalai Lama has himself acknowledged that self-determination does not necessarily involve complete political independence. Thus, the Dalai Lama has said:

> I have often conveyed to the Chinese Government that theoretically the 6 million Tibetans may get greater benefit if we remain with the Peoples Republic of China, without Big Brother. After all, Tibet is a landlocked

15 See RD Kaplan, 'The Coming Anarchy' (1994) 273 (2) *Atlantic Monthly* 44; and Report of the Commission on Global Governance (1995) *Our Global Neighbourhood*, Oxford University Press, p 206.

16 Thus, Biafra was resisted when it attempted to break away from Nigeria. Bangladesh was only recognised when it became an established reality. See H Hannum, 'Rethinking Self-Determination' (1993) 34 *Virginia Journal of International Law* 1 at 5; and M Koskemmiemi, 'National Self-Determination Today: Problems of Legal Theory and Practice' (1994) 43 *International and Comparative Law Quarterly* 241 at 245.

17 A Etzioni, 'The Evils of Self-Determination' (1992-3) 89 *Foreign Policy* 21. Cf RS White, 'Self-Determination, Time for a Reassessment?' (1981) 28 *Netherlands International Law Review* 147.

> country. We need a lot of work for material development. In these fields, if the Chinese treat us as an equal and sincerely respect our culture and our way of life, then I personally feel that it may be wise to remain with the Chinese.[18]

In this, and in many other ways, the Dalai Lama has been refreshingly candid. He acknowledges mistakes. He even accepts that there has been some improvement in the human rights situation in Tibet. He called Deng Xiaoping his 'old friend' and a 'great person'. Of some aspects of the Chinese Revolution he has expressed profound admiration.[19] But he insists on the right of the people of Tibet – a distinct and unique people for the purpose of international law – to determine their own fate in terms of their political governance.

Such claims may be asserted easily enough. But at the present there is no effective machinery in the international community to test opinions and to conduct referenda in a way which contemplates the peaceful dismemberment of a state if that be the will of a people living within it.[20] If the right of self-determination is to be achieved by non-violent means, as distinct from force of arms and brutal struggle, an institutional response is required. Yet to achieve such a means will require all the eloquence of leaders such as the Dalai Lama. It runs headlong into the opposition of powerful states with their entrenched attitudes and anxious fears of separatism and instability.

Of Prophets and Paradoxes

Peering into the next century and striving to foresee some of the changes that will occur presents each prophet with the limitations and perspectives of his or her own experience. Mine make me optimistic; both in my daily life in a court of justice which carries on a tradition of eight centuries and in the many agencies of the United Nations where it has been my privilege to witness institution building and improvement of the lot of humanity by practical good works.

Many problems remain. But more will be achieved by the path of non-violence than by the ruinous methods of armed conflict. A few years after any war there remains little of the heroism – simply gravestones beside busy highways. Fortunately, the modern media make it harder to fight wars today. The horror and suffering in Bosnia, Rwanda and Algeria is brought into our living rooms.

---

18 HH The Dalai Lama, 'I Prefer Change in China without Total Collapse', *Tibetan Bulletin*, January/February 1995, p 11.

19 Ibid.

20 See 'Prominent Chinese Dissidents Support Negotiations with Dalai Lama and Plebiscite in Tibet' (1995) 7(5) *Tibet Press Watch* 3.

There has to be a 'middle way' between acceptance of injustice and force of arms. That middle way is the path of non-violence and compassion. This is not a passive idea. Nor does it involve blind acceptance of the unacceptable. It commits the holder of this view to working for peace, equitable development and true human rights as the three foundations of global governance. Those who believe in these goals will strive to strengthen new institutions and to reinforce old ones.

There is an urgent need for enlightened leadership in the world today. There is a need for fresh ideas which adapt old ways of thinking to the realities of a world radically changed by economic and social movements and by global technology. New thinking will involve us in apparent paradoxes. To be a friend of the Tibetan people is not to be an enemy of the great Chinese people. Wisdom often lies in paradoxes. Progress is not always apparent when it challenges orthodox ways of thinking.

To the many insistent calls for changes in global governance, respect for the environment, and protection of human rights, we must add the calm, insistent voice of the Dalai Lama. In a world of materialism and anger his is a message of spirituality and of compassion. Because the message is so different many do not hear its call. But the lesson of the 20th century is that, after great suffering and unprecedented violence, a new path is needed. That path leads to peace, but with justice. It leads to development, but with equity. It leads to respect for the rights of peoples and of individuals.[21]

As the new millennium beckons, I believe that we can be optimistic. We are on the high path towards human progress and enlightenment. Our journey cannot be reversed. We are guided by the wellsprings of our human nature. It is our human nature which compels us toward peace. Our human nature urges us on to economic progress, in balanced harmony with our environment. And it is our human nature that insists upon respect for the essential dignity of other human beings, sharing with others the privilege of self-determination. The international community and its many peoples are taking this journey. So are the states and nations of the world. But each one of us has an individual responsibility. This responsibility should cause us to lift our voices and not to remain silent. Silence is complicity. To be human is to feel the pain of brothers and sisters everywhere. Feeling that pain we must each do whatever we can to build a better world. Some will call this misty-eyed dreaming. The Dalai Lama declares that it is our privilege as free spiritual beings. He is right.

21 See HH The Dalai Lama (1990) *Freedom in Exile*, John Curtis, p 273.

Chapter 2

Refugees: Their Need Has Never Been Greater

The following speech, given just before his appointment to the High Court of Australia, was made at the launch of Australia's National Refugee Week, 14 June 1995. Michael Kirby draws upon his own experience of being deported from Spain, in addition to his first-hand knowledge of the refugee problem at the international level, to criticise the 1995 amendments to the *Migration Act* 1958 (Cth). These and later amendments have made it more difficult for migrants to enter Australia, to receive social security and other benefits and to seek judicial review of decisions affecting their status. He highlights the many myths that seem to have influenced legislators in framing Australia's migration laws, whilst acknowledging that national and international laws can only provide band-aid solutions. His message is that the refugee question is a global problem and beyond the control of any one country, although this is not to deny each country's responsibility to accept refugees. It is Michael Kirby's belief that the underlying causes of unchecked population growth, lack of self-determination and inequities in wealth and resources must be tackled at their source. Otherwise, the efforts of the United Nations, other agencies and individual countries such as Australia will only scratch the surface of the problem.

Personal Insights and Arresting Experiences

I have a strong empathy with refugees. I once had a very small taste of what they go through. On my 40th birthday I was in Paris, chairing a committee of the OECD. I was invited to celebrate in Madrid with a friend who had remigrated from Australia. I arrived at the barrier at Madrid's airport without a visa to enter Spain. I was told 'no visa, no entrada'. I was arrested and detained as an illegal immigrant. Nobody had told me that visas had been reintroduced by Spain for Australian citizens.

I naturally insisted on appeal. There were no great delays in Spain. I was marched upstairs to an official. He was reading the afternoon newspaper with his shoes on the desk. But he was sitting on an elevated platform. So I knew he was important. I gave my excuses. I was also important. I had an official passport. I even had an American Express gold card! The appellate judgment was swift. 'No visa. No entrada'. I was deported on the next plane. I walked the streets of London for hours getting over my humiliation. But at least, with my gold card, I could sink my sorrows in a clean hotel far from Port Hedland.[1]

The experience made me sensitive to the reform of migration law. In the Australian Administrative Review Council, where I served for a decade, whenever migration legislation came up, the federal officials would slap their foreheads in despair at my insistence on due process: 'Here comes Kirby with that Madrid story again!'

More recently, I have seen some of the international problems of refugees at close hand. It is estimated that there are 26 million refugees worldwide.[2] In my work in Cambodia as Special Representative of the Secretary-General for Human Rights, I was closely involved in the attempts of the United Nations to resettle a colony of displaced Vietnamese boat people at Chrey Thom. Five thousand of them went there, under the protection of the United Nations flag. They had fled to Chrey Thom to avoid violence during the elections sponsored by the United Nations Transitional Authority in Cambodia (UNTAC). Most of them remain there to this day in their little boats: without proper food, sanitation, medication and education for their children. Many have produced to me documents that show that they have lived for several generations in Cambodia. But the Khmer Rouge ruthlessly played on ethnic hatreds in Cambodia. The return from Chrey Thom to the villages and fishing grounds of Cambodia is as protracted as the refugee review process is in Australia.

In 1995 I diverted from a visit to Geneva for the United Nations to address an Inter-Parliamentary Conference held in the chamber of the Parliament of Portugal in Lisbon. Vivid accounts were told of the shocking sufferings of refugees from East Timor, many of whom have sought asylum in Australia. In that same year I also travelled to Delhi for an international symposium to mark the 60th birthday of the Dalai Lama, leader of another major international refugee community, the Tibetans.[3] Everywhere there are refugees.

---

1 Port Headland Detention Centre for illegal immigrants lies about 1500 kilometres northwest of Perth, Western Australia. Detainees are isolated because of the vast distances between support services and the detention centre. The United Nations Human Rights Committee has ruled that the compulsory detention of asylum seekers breaches Australia's human rights obligations under the *International Covenant on Civil and Political Rights*. See N Poynder, ' "A" v Australia' (1997) 22 *Alternative Law Journal* 149 and N Poynder, 'The Incommunicado Detention of Boat People: A Recent Development in Australia's Refugee Policy' (1997) 3 *Australian Journal of Human Rights* 53.

2 United Nations High Commissioner for Refugees (1998) *UNHCR by Numbers*, UNHCR <http://www.unhcr.ch/un&ref/numbers/numbers.htm>.

3 See Kirby, Chapter 1.

When the office of the United Nations High Commissioner for Refugees (UNHCR) was established in 1951 it was assumed that, once the post-war refugees were integrated, UNHCR would be wound up. How wildly optimistic that prediction now seems. Instead, the pressures for refugee assistance have grown enormously. In 1978 there were fewer than 5 million known refugees looking to the international community for assistance and protection. While the end of the Cold War has led to many benefits for freedom, it has also produced a reconfiguring of many of the world's social and economic problems. It is as if a spring, held under tight check, has been released, producing enormous populations of refugees and internally displaced persons (IDPs) from Haiti to Rwanda; from Palestine to Bosnia; from Chechnya to Southern China; and from the Middle East to Australia.

Great international achievements have been secured by UNHCR, led by the High Commissioner, Mrs Sadako Ogata. I pay tribute to the work of UNHCR in Cambodia that resulted in the resettlement of a million people. The dark green tents are still used in some border areas. They still house dislocated villagers who were caught up in the fighting. But a mighty achievement has been accomplished. Credit must be given to UNHCR and to the Cambodian Government for that achievement.

Whenever I visit Amsterdam, I always make a pilgrimage to the Anne Frank Huis. With typical Netherlands honesty, the photographs of the Jewish and other refugees in and after the Second World War bear a warning. It reads: 'Do not blame only the Germans, the foreigners, for what is portrayed here. These wrongs were done by Netherlands policemen, shopkeepers and farmers. We must look into ourselves to find the explanation for such events'. On the wall as you leave the Huis is a map of the world with the destinations of the Jewish and other refugees from Hitler's Europe. Australia, at that time, took precious few.

Now, through Austcare and other organisations, Australians are taking an admirable part in the worldwide effort to help refugees and other displaced people. I especially applaud the projects in Cambodia, Mozambique and Afghanistan to support mine clearance and to promote education about landmines. Other priority programmes of Austcare include training in literacy and empowerment, particularly for women refugees from Afghanistan and orphaned children from the Sudan. What we can do to cope with crises overseas is clear enough. We can:

- support immunisation programmes in Ethiopia;
- help provide emergency medical aid in Rwanda;

- train people in rehabilitation for Afghan refugees, victims of landmines;
- assist United Nations relief work in Gaza;
- help in the care and education of Vietnamese children in the remaining detention camps in Hong Kong;
- provide health services for women victims of war in Kosovo; and
- assist with HIV/AIDS training on the Thai/Burma border.

Closer to Home

Most Australians, to the extent that they have thought about it, would probably support all of the foregoing activities. They would applaud the efforts of UNHCR to sustain refugees and IDPs in emergencies and to help them return to their homes when the emergencies have died down. However, sometimes emergencies last for decades. Sometimes the danger of political retaliation, racial hatred or religious intolerance is enduring. Then the crunch comes. Do we, in our relatively peaceful and prosperous country, open our doors to refugees, as humanity and international law require? Or do we slam the door or make it difficult for the 'reffos' to come here – just as we did in the 1930s for those who sought to escape the Nazi Holocaust. It is at moments like these that Australia's commitment to humanity and human rights is really tested.

In my lifetime I have seen a truly remarkable passage of Australia from a fortress, resolutely adhering to 'White Australia', to a multicultural nation of diversity and a high measure of tolerance. I hope that this will endure. We should give ourselves two cheers for the fact that our Constitution and laws, as well as the moral sense of our people, have moved in a way that, at least on paper, presents a kind of model for ethnic tolerance for the twenty-first century. In a world where, in so many other places, ethnic conflict is causing such suffering and producing many refugees, we in Australia have generally done well. The *Racial Hatred Act* 1995 (Cth) is but the latest example of our attempt to strike at the causes of ethnic stereotyping and to promote harmony.[4]

Yet this law contrasts with various amendments of the *Migration Act* 1958 (Cth) made in 1995 and 1996.[5] Those amendments have made the

4 See L McNamara and T Solomon, 'The Commonwealth *Racial Hatred Act* 1995: Achievement or Disappointment?' (1996) 18 *Adelaide Law Review* 259.

5 See C Sidoti, 'Boat People and Human Rights' (1996) 31 *Australian Lawyer* 5 and N Diesel, 'Refugee Week Shame' (1996) 5(3) *Human Rights Defender* (<http://www.austlii.edu.au/au/other/ahric/Secondary/hrd/hrdindex.html>).

lives of refugees more difficult. For example, there is now reduced scope for judicial review of migration decisions in the Federal Court when natural justice and reasonable decision-making are said to have been offended.[6] In addition, the introduction of conclusive Ministerial certificates has excluded the Refugee Review Tribunal from certain decisions where the Minister states that it would be contrary to the public interest, on grounds of security, defence or international relations, for a decision in a particular case to be reviewed.

The *Migration Legislation Amendment Act* of 1995 was designed to reverse the decision of the Refugee Review Tribunal and of the Federal Court in *Minister for Immigration and Ethnic Affairs v Respondent A*.[7] It was there held that a married couple were refugees within the meaning of the *Convention Relating to the Status of Refugees*,[8] incorporated in the *Migration Act* 1958 (Cth), because they feared possible forced sterilisation of the woman under the one-child policy if they were to return to China. That decision was subsequently overturned by the High Court of Australia.[9] Commentators have remarked upon the conflict involved in forbidding racial hatred at home and singling out Chinese couples for a unilateral modification of an international treaty definition laid down by international law ratified by Australia.[10] The majority decision of the High Court obviated the necessity to rely upon that discriminatory statutory provision.

It is probably true to say that the decision and the federal stand under successive governments have the support of many Australians. Forgetting that all Australians (other than indigenous peoples) are 'boat people' of one kind or another, most citizens of this country are probably fearful of a potential pool of millions of Chinese couples arriving on their doorstep and asserting a right to stay in the country because of a fear of forced sterilisation at home. Despite the obvious emotional appeal of this 'floodgates' argument, it is noteworthy that no similar legislation has been enacted by the United States or Canada, which are preferred destinations for refugees. Australia is one of the most difficult countries in the world for refugees to enter. We have nearly universal visa requirements, carrier sanctions on airlines and others that bring people without valid visas, and no common land

---

6 *Abebe v Commonwealth* (1999) 73 ALJR 584.

7 (1994) 127 ALR 383.

8 28 July 1951.

9 *'Applicant A' v Minister for Immigration and Ethnic Affairs* (1997) 190 CLR 225.

10 S Kneebone, 'Refugee Test and the "One Child Policy" ' (1997) 4 *Australian Journal of Administrative Law* 173; S Marsic, 'Membership of a Particular Social Group' (1997) 22 *Alternative Law Journal* 97.

borders with our neighbours. But the spectre of hordes of people arriving from Asia remains deep in the Australian psyche, long after the White Australia policy has been formally abandoned.

Refugee Mythology

The debate about this topic has demonstrated the many myths that still exist amongst the Australian population in respect of refugees:

Myth 1: That Australia does not have enough resources to support more people

In fact Australia has a very low natural population growth, approaching zero population growth. We have emigration of about 35,000 people each year. Some migration is needed simply to sustain our population as it is and to support economic growth. The admission of refugees and those needing humanitarian acceptance is part of the legal obligations of a country such as ours. But it is also in our self-interest.

Myth 2: Charity begins at home, with Aboriginals and other disadvantaged groups

Charity should not be considered in such a divisive, rationed way. The Aboriginal population of Australia is now increasing. Like other people who have suffered, Australia's Aboriginals understand, more than most, the duties of humanity.

Myth 3: Refugees take our jobs or go on unemployment benefits

It is true that newly arrived refugees have higher unemployment rates than the community average. But many arrive with little more than the clothes on their backs. Most have been traumatised by their experience. They receive 500 hours of free English language instruction that must be taken in the first two years. Experience in Australia, and in other times and places, shows that refugees and their children have enormous motivation to succeed. To restore their damaged sense of self-esteem and to repay a debt of gratitude to this country they ordinarily embrace the target programme and usually become model citizens.

Myth 4: They have no right to come here and expect us to help

One's place of birth is an accident to which none of us contributed. Being born in Australia is like winning in the lucky dip of life. Australians are better placed than most countries to offer refuge. International law defends the right to seek freedom from persecution and Australia has ratified the treaty that recognises legal obligations to refugees. Through its democratic national Parliament, Australia has enacted legislation that incorporates the requirements of international law in domestic law.

Myth 5: If we let one in, they will come in floods

Apart from its geographical barriers, Australia does not make it easy to secure refugee admission. The great delays in processing and the review system produce grave uncertainty as to the outcome. Detention in some of the most remote places on the face of the earth is the 'welcome' which many refugees receive when they first arrive.[11] Few are offered roses.

Myth 6: Refugees cannot possibly contribute to Australia

Then it is said that most refugees are illiterate peasants with little to contribute to Australia. But this is not so. Many are educated middle-class people, such as the Afghan former judge whom I have befriended and who, but for the grace of God, might be myself. Their education, professional and political backgrounds have drawn them to the attention of authorities. Typically, it is these features of their backgrounds that have resulted in the persecution that is the foundation of their refugee status. By definition, refugees are survivors. In their memories are the messages of determination and struggle that will make Australia and other countries places of achievement and compassion. In their suffering are the lessons of respect for others and the need to build a tolerant society that upholds diversity and human values throughout this continent.

It is the obligation of every civilised and informed person to dispel the myths about refugees. Falsehoods are easily sold to good citizens fearful of strangers. Those who know the facts have an obligation to make them known.

Tackling the Basic Causes

I cannot pretend that the global challenge of refugees is easily solved. The figures continue to mount – a couple of million in 1946, 11 million in 1986, 26 million in 1997.[12] Heroic efforts are made. And still the tide continues to grow.

11 See N Poynder, 'Marooned in Port Hedland' (1993) 18 *Alternative Law Journal* 272.

12 UNHCR (1998), <http://www.unhcr.ch/un&ref/ numbers /numbers.htm>.

There is a tendency in life, which I see constantly in the law, to tackle symptoms, affixing band-aids whilst the underlying problems continue to grow unattended. The underlying issues that give rise to the global tide of refugees should be recognised and tackled. Half a century after the establishment of the United Nations we should remember its three foundation objectives: to defend peace and security; to uphold human rights, including the right to self-determination; and to promote economic development. Although great progress has been made with each of these objectives, in some parts of the world things are actually going backwards.

The unrequited right to self-determination is a source of tremendous unrest, cruelty and exodus – as Bosnia, Rwanda, Tibet, Chechnya and East Timor illustrate. The burgeoning global population puts enormous pressures upon political government. The shattering of expectations of newly liberated masses has led to a resort, in desperation, to religious and political fundamentalism. It has also led to violence and the dislocation of populations which put unbearable pressure on the capacity of the world to respond.

It sometimes becomes difficult to distinguish the economic migrants seeking a better future from true refugees fleeing from violence, dislocation and persecution. The growth of gigantic shantytowns in many developing countries has led to a worldwide demographic pressure that we, in Western countries at least, should try to understand. After all, the Americas and Australia were themselves populated in past centuries by an earlier exodus of economic migrants from Europe. If our forebears had the right to come to settler colonies (often displacing the indigenous people) by what right do we exclude the next wave – except by our power?

Robert Kaplan has described the enormous dislocation caused by the rapid expansion of the human population: gobbling up resources and mortgaging the water, cropland, forests and fish of the next generation.[13] Over the next 50 years the earth's population will probably soar from the present 5.5 billion to more than 9 billion. The impact of this growth upon the earth's resources and environment, unless checked, will be devastating. Tad Homer-Dixon conjures up the following image:

> Think of a stretch limo in the potholed streets of New York city, where homeless beggars live. Inside the limo are the air-conditioned post-industrial regions of North America, Europe, the emerging Pacific Rim,

---

13 RD Kaplan, 'The Coming Anarchy' (1994) 273(2) *Atlantic Monthly* 44.

> and a few other isolated places, with their trade summitry and computer-information highways. Outside is the rest of mankind, going in a completely different direction.[14]

According to this view of the future, the battle is yet to come. Unless the virus of human population can be controlled, the conflicts of the future will be over water and other vital resources:

> Future wars will be those of communal survival, aggravated or, in many cases, caused by environmental scarcity. Those wars will be subnational, meaning that it will be hard for states and local governments to protect their own citizens physically. This is how many states will ultimately die. As state power fades ... peoples and cultures around the world will be thrown back upon their own strengths and weaknesses.[15]

One does not have to accept this gloomy picture in its entirety to appreciate that there is a germ of truth which world leaders must address now, urgently.

The fact that there are even greater challenges looming is not, however, a reason to pull up the drawbridge and throw compassion into the moat that marks us off. The humanitarian mission which UNHCR leads must be continued with renewed energy. Many Australians work selflessly for refugees. They do so with loving kindness. There will be fewer – not more – refugees like Anne Frank. But if we look dispassionately into the future, it seems likely that, without radical action now to address the basic causes of huge global population movements, our current expedients (however well meaning) will prove feeble and ineffective. If compassion is not enough to make us see this reality, practical self-interest, defence of our species and of our environment, as well as the control of conflict in an increasingly inter-dependent world, should motivate us. There is only so much that can be done through refugee camps and refugee acceptance in a country such as Australia. The fundamental problems need to be tackled in the shantytowns of the developing world and in the countryside laid waste by deforestation, land mines and erosion. The basic challenges that existed at the establishment of the United Nations remain to be solved, 50 years on. The building of human rights. The defence of the peoples' right to self-determination. The real achievement of the right to development for all. Defence of the environment. Urgent steps for birth spacing.

Australians share one continent. But we do not only share it among ourselves, selfishly and nationalistically. Australia is part of a wider

---

14 Cited in Kaplan, ibid, p 60.

15 Ibid, p 74.

region and a larger world. We must therefore consider how, in the future, we can do better. Doing better means more help to refugees here and abroad. But it also means urgent attention to the underlying causes of their terrible plight. And the journey to these truths will be helped by seeing refugees as we see ourselves – as people aspiring to life, dignity and hope.

Go to the Anne Frank Huis in Amsterdam. Look at the map. Read her diary. Dispel the myths.

Chapter 3

Cambodia: The Struggle for Human Rights[1]

Michael Kirby served as the Special Representative of the Secretary-General of the United Nations for Human Rights in Cambodia from 1994 to 1996. The following text is partly based on his Heindorff Memorial Lecture 'Human Rights and Cambodia', given on 12 September 1995 to the Queensland Branch of the Australian Institute of International Affairs. The text has been updated by including sections of Michael Kirby's last report as Special Representative, entitled 'Cambodia: A Departing Assessment', which was presented to the United Nations Commission on Human Rights at Geneva on 1 April 1996. In these papers, he outlined many of the achievements in Cambodia that had been brought about with United Nations assistance. However, he also expresses concern about media independence, the lack of democratic checks and balances on the exercise of power and the persecution of opposition members. The June 1997 coup by Prime Minister Hun Sen was to prove many of his fears well founded, with many serious human rights violations occurring, including political executions, in the lead up to the 1998 general election and thereafter.

Until 1 May 1996, for two and a half years, I served as the Special Representative of the Secretary-General for Human Rights in Cambodia. My resignation from that office arose following my appointment to the High Court of Australia. My period of service gave me the rare opportunity to see the implementation of programmes for human rights protection in a country sorely afflicted in the past by human rights derogations amongst the most grave that a century of horrors had witnessed. It may be of interest to consider my experience and to observe the way in which the United Nations contributes in practical ways to human rights protection.

There are about 30 Special Rapporteurs and Special Representatives of the United Nations reporting to the Commission on Human Rights. Some have thematic responsibilities (summary executions, independence of the judiciary, rights of women). However, most are dedicated to

1 An earlier version of this paper was published as 'Human Rights, the United Nations and Cambodia' (1995) 67(4) *Australian Quarterly* 26.

scrutinising and reporting upon human rights in particular countries. My own responsibilities fell under that item of the agenda of the Commission on Human Rights dealing with 'Technical Assistance'. It derived from a provision in the 1991 Paris Peace Agreements by which peace was brought to Cambodia after decades of war, revolution, genocide, invasion and resistance.

My work in Cambodia could not be confined to luxury hotels in the capital, Phnom Penh. It took me, and those who worked with me, into the country regions. In 1995, I travelled to Sihanoukville shortly before the capture and murder nearby of three foreign tourists, including the Australian David Wilson. They had been on a peaceful, youthful journey on a train in pursuit of knowledge about Cambodia and about life. So this was a task not without some risk. But it was a mission of importance for the building of human rights in Cambodia.

Entering upon my responsibilities in Cambodia, I was very conscious of the suggestion that there are different priorities for human rights in countries in the Asian region. Some commentators have even suggested that there is an Asian exception to the universality of human rights, reflective of the traditional emphasis placed by at least some of the philosophies of Asian societies upon duties, not rights; upon the community, not the individual; and upon the rule of powerful men of virtue, not the rule of law.[2] One observer describes the emerging debate in these terms:

> The ideological debate between East and West then, and between North and South now, has … affected the realisation of [human] rights. In the past, socioeconomic rights were seen as requiring a strong state and forceful state action. They were thus championed strongly by the former Soviet Union and Eastern European countries. The countries of the West, on the other hand, sometimes did not even recognise them as rights. This was one reason why the General Assembly adopted two Covenants and not one.
>
> A similar ideological clash is taking place now. Countries of the South, led by China, India, Indonesia and Malaysia, argue that socio-economic rights are equally important as, if not more important than, civil and political rights. Very few of these countries have recognised socio-economic rights as human rights, though they have spoken strongly in favour of these issues at several international fora. Their views, however, have been given increasing prominence because some of these countries are in the forefront of the economic boom that is now taking place in the Asia-Pacific region.[3]

---

2 R Little and W Reed (1989) *The Confucian Renaissance*, Federation Press.

3 M Gomez, 'Social Economic Rights and Human Rights Commissions' (1995) 17(1) *Human Rights Quarterly* 155 at 161-162.

When proponents from the West speak of the universality of human rights, perceptive commentators from the East point to the imperfect protection, in earlier decades in Western countries, of rights now claimed to be universal and fundamental. Women did not secure the vote in England until this century. African Americans did not have an effective right to vote in some parts of the United States until 1965. In many countries homosexual citizens were criminalised and punished until even more recently. These points are made to emphasise that perception of what are fundamental human rights takes time. Accordingly, so it is said, Western countries and their citizens should not be insensitive to the different stages at which Asian countries find themselves in the process of 'enlightenment'.[4]

Within the resolutions and declarations of the United Nations, the notion of an Asian cultural exception, or of the division of human rights into different priorities, has been rejected. The *Vienna Declaration* of June 1993 affirms:

> All human rights are universal, indivisible and inter-dependent and inter-related ... While the significance of national and regional particularities and various historical, cultural and religious backgrounds must be borne in mind, it is the duty of States, regardless of their political, economic and cultural systems, to promote and protect all human rights and fundamental freedoms.[5]

By definition, universal human rights are just that: a common heritage of all humanity. Human rights provide one of the three pillars upon which the United Nations has been established – securing peace and disarmament; pursuing economic and social development; and building the new world order upon the foundation of individual human rights and the rights of peoples.

The human rights with which the United Nations is concerned include those stated in the *Universal Declaration of Human Rights*, the *International Covenant on Civil and Political Rights* and the *International Covenant on Economic, Social and Cultural Rights.* There are now many other international instruments that express the dedication of the United Nations to fundamental human rights and peoples' rights. But if you look at these documents, whilst civil and political rights find their place amongst them, the priorities reflected in their language are, typically, those which were expressed to me in Cambodia. As well as

---

4 Statement to the Vienna Conference by the Singapore Minister for Foreign Affairs, 23 June 1993.

5 World Conference on Human Rights, *Vienna Declaration and Programme of Action*, United Nations Document A/Conf/157/23 para 1/10, n 18.

consideration of the issue of civil rights come assertions of rights to equal dignity, conscience and freedom from discrimination of any kind. The United Nations statements of human rights include rights to free choice of employment; to adequate rest and leisure; to a proper standard of living with adequate protection for health and well being; and to food, clothing, housing and medical care. The right to education is part of the fabric of fundamental human rights. So is the right to participate freely in cultural life and the entitlement to a social and international order where the rights and freedoms affirmed by the United Nations may be fully realised.

In addition to these, there are the familiar civil rights: not to be held in slavery or servitude; not to be subjected to torture or cruel, inhuman or degrading treatment or punishment; to be equal before the law; to have effective remedies for legal rights; to be free from arbitrary arrest, detention or exile; to have fair access to the courts; to have particular rights when charged with criminal offences; and to enjoy rights to privacy, to freedom of movement and to freedom from persecution.

In my work as Special Representative of the Secretary-General I did not follow my own idiosyncratic opinions on human rights. My function was to examine the laws and practices of Cambodia measured against the criteria of the United Nations' principles of human rights. It was then to report on any departures from these standards, first to the government of Cambodia itself and then to the Secretary-General and the United Nations. From the beginning, I reported not only upon progress and problems in the area of civil and political rights but also in the fields of economic, social and cultural rights. Thus, every report contained some scrutiny of issues such as the right to health; the protection of cultural rights; the furtherance of rights to education; and protection of the right to a healthy environment and to sustainable development.[6]

Economic Development

In my reports, I called to notice the progress that had been made in the Cambodian economy. Predictably enough, following the end of war and the confinement of rebellion to a small area of the country, economic activity began to flourish once again. With it came employment opportunities, educational demands and a gradual improvement (at least in the cities) of general standards of living. Derelict buildings were

---

6 See Report of the Special Representative of the Secretary-General for Human Rights in Cambodia. UN Doc E/CN.4/1996/93 (26 February 1996).

repaired to provide office and housing space. Long abandoned canals were restored. A ready measure of economic progress could be seen in the increased number of motor cars and motorised bicycles visible upon every new visit to Cambodia. Although economic development is not a necessary assurance of improvement of human rights, it is difficult to provide the environment for respect for the whole range of human rights referred to in United Nations' instruments without the basic necessities that a modern economy can provide. Credit must be given to the government of Cambodia for promoting at least some of the improvements in the infrastructure necessary for modern economic development. Amongst other things, such developments raise the aspirations of those people who are its beneficiaries. Such people begin to demand reading matter and access to informative, non-propagandist radio and television. They travel, both within their own country and overseas. They become aware of derogations from basic human rights. They organise themselves and call for improvements.

These are the positive sides of economic development in Cambodia relevant to human rights. But there are also negative consequences with respect to the environment, as I observed in my last mission in January 1996.[7] The protection of Cambodia's environment is particularly important because of the vulnerable ecosystem and the damage already done by the large-scale destruction of forest timber and the substitution of large-scale agri-business. Apart from the obvious danger of causing damage to the environment for short-term, and relatively modest, economic returns, such developments threaten fundamental human rights through their long-term effect on living standards.[8]

To its credit, Cambodia signed the *Convention on Biological Diversity*.[9] When I departed, it was planning enactment of a law on environmental protection and natural resource management. The government facilitated a review of its forest resources by the World Bank, the Food and Agriculture Organisation (FAO) and the United Nations Development Programme (UNDP). A National Environment Steering Committee was established. It will need to be vigilant because of the highly vulnerable position of Cambodia's forests and water ecosystems.

---

7 Ibid.

8 During the last mission to Cambodia in 1996, I visited the province of Rattanakiri in the remote north-east of Cambodia. I received many complaints of the intrusion of foreign-backed developers who, reportedly, for a relatively small fee, gained exclusive concessions over land. These entitled them to clear forest areas, sell the removed timber and substitute palm oil and other agri-businesses to the destruction of the environment of the indigenous people who have lived there since time immemorial.

9 United Nations Environment Programme No 92-7807, 5 June 1992.

Women

In one of my recommendations to the United Nations I called attention to the particular vulnerability of women in minority communities:

> Women, especially those in indigenous communities, may often be in the disadvantageous position of traditional subservience and subject to onerous work and child-rearing obligations. ... The Government of Cambodia [should] introduce sensitively into minority communities the awareness that women in such communities have human rights which will be upheld. In particular, they have freedom of personal relationships and reproductive rights which must be respected. Such women must be fully consulted and involved in decisions affecting the future of their communities and their economic, cultural and other interests. Such issues should not be disposed of by male members of such communities with the excuse of traditional practices. ... The appropriate NGOs, in consultation ... [should] continue their study of the particular vulnerability of women and girls in traditional indigenous communities.[10]

Women form more than 60% of the population of Cambodia – one of the legacies of prolonged war. They perform an enormous amount of unpaid and lowly paid work. In practice, they do not enjoy educational opportunities. With the advent of economic development, they are particularly susceptible to new and additional disadvantage and exploitation. It is essential that the differential impact of economic development on males and females be considered both by the United Nations and by the governments of member states. Often it is women who bear the greatest burdens. The male members of the village escape to the towns. The women and children are left behind to farm in reduced conditions because of the often irreversible environmental and social damage caused by multi-national and local investors questing for immediate returns.

Cambodia is not more neglectful than other countries of the region in respect of the human rights of women. However, one function of the United Nations Commission on Human Rights, and its Special Rapporteurs and Special Representatives, is to bring the jurisprudence of the international covenants down to the grass-roots, offering advice on local practices when these are measured against the international standards and found wanting. The aim is to assist governments to translate the fine language of the international instruments into practical reality.

---

10 Report of the Special Representative of the Secretary-General for Human Rights in Cambodia, para 90.

Amongst my recommendations were some directed to the need to provide school education for women concerning their rights; to provide education to judicial officers about the particular vulnerability of women; and to support the establishment of shelters (some of which I inspected) that afford temporary and long-term sanctuary to women subjected to physical, sexual or mental violence. I called attention to the imbalance in female participation in education in Cambodia. I drew to notice the need to provide basic school education in mathematics and sciences in day classes rather than night classes, which female students often find difficult to attend. I recommended a review of all laws and practices for compliance with the non-discrimination provisions of the international treaties that Cambodia had signed. I addressed the special needs of women in Cambodia's dilapidated prison system and the special vulnerability of women in squatter communities and in communities of present and former sex workers.

In 1996, for the first time in Cambodia, a woman was appointed to ministerial responsibility for women's affairs. Previously, the office was held by a man. As well, a very active Committee on the *Convention on the Elimination of All Forms of Discrimination Against Women*[11] has co-operated with non-government organisations (NGOs) in the preparation of a report on Cambodia's compliance with that Convention. Even more than in developed societies such as Australia, securing more women in governmental positions and in political office is a problem that needs to be addressed in Cambodia.

The United Nations treaty and human rights mechanisms may not be perfect. But at least they provide standards to measure basic human rights and institutions to scrutinise compliance. They create international venues in which people can express their grievances. It is easy to condemn the weaknesses of the treaty system, the human rights institutions and their office-holders. But many of the recommendations I made secured the concurrence of the government of Cambodia. Relevant to women, the only item in the response of the government that was negative concerned my suggestion that the criminal law should be changed in order to introduce an offence of rape within marriage. It was suggested that such an offence would not be appropriate at this stage of Cambodia's development. Some of my proposals will doubtless be overlooked or ignored. But others, I feel sure, will influence policy and legal development in Cambodia to the improvement of human rights generally and specifically those of women and other vulnerable groups. With some notable and noisy exceptions, I found most Cambodian

11 United Nations GA Res 34/180, 18 December 1979.

politicians and officials keen to learn about global human rights and to secure the advice of the United Nations on how they could modernise their country and secure its compliance with international norms. In part, their horrific experiences, still fresh in memory, prepared them for the message I brought.

Other Issues

I wish to review some of the other good and bad news that I experienced in Cambodia in my visits as Special Representative. Of the bad news, there is generally enough in the international media. It is the good news that is frequently untold. Necessarily, it must be stated in summary form. I will organise the following information along the lines of items of good news followed by some troubling developments that I must disclose to provide an accurate balance.

Good News

National Assembly: The Cambodian National Assembly continues to function. The work of the Human Rights Commission of the Assembly has been enhanced by the establishment of the Centre for Research and Documentation. Legislation continues to receive scrutiny in the Assembly. Sometimes it is changed. Clearly, a properly working democratic parliament is the fulcrum of the rule of law and of respect for human rights. On schedule, in July 1998, national elections were held and the government submitted to the judgment of the people at the ballot box. Although the election was accompanied by violence and complaints of rigging and interference, no party questioned the obligation of the government to be answerable to the people.

Active NGOs: The non-governmental organisations which flourished after the United Nations Transitional Authority in Cambodia (UNTAC) continue to work energetically for human rights. The government ultimately accepted recommendations that I made to the effect that the phasing out of court defenders, who represent poor people in criminal trials, should be delayed. Court defenders may not be legally qualified. However, their work is essential to the just disposition of court business, pending development of a qualified legal profession. I have urged that the NGOs should be regularly consulted by the ministries on matters of mutual concern. Cambodia still awaits an effective law on civil associations. It is essential that this be liberal and supportive of bodies that reflect and strengthen the diversity of a modern civil society.

Centre for Human Rights: The United Nations Centre for Human Rights is still busily at work in Phnom Penh and in provincial centres. The Centre provides technical help and assistance. Its existence encourages the work of NGOs concerned with human rights. A proposal of the government, early in 1995, that the work of the Centre be phased out during the year was eventually withdrawn after a visit to Cambodia of the Special Envoy of the Secretary-General. The Cambodian government emphasised that it had no objection to the continuance of my mission. On my retirement I was succeeded as Special Representative on Human Rights by a distinguished Swedish diplomat, Mr Thomas Hammerberg. On the United Nations side, we have honoured not only the letter but also the spirit of the promise of closer consultation with the Cambodian government as worked out with the Special Envoy. There have also been some improvements in consultation on the Cambodian side.

Land mines: The problem of anti-personnel and anti-tank land mines continues to bedevil Cambodia. The government states that it is committed to the eradication of these mines. Good work was done by the Cambodian Mine Action Group which in my hope was led by the Minister, Mr Ieng Mouly, and many NGOs assisted by overseas military advisors. The Minister supported my proposal for strong legislation to prohibit the further deployment of land mines in Cambodia. He promised to look into the possibility of compensation for their many victims.

Repatriation of Khmer Rouge: Good progress was also made in securing the defection of elements of the armed forces of the Khmer Rogue (KR). Under amnesties offered by the Cambodian government, large numbers of former KR soldiers and their families returned to the constitutional side. In Chamkar Bei, I saw such a settlement with houses, a school and hospital built to welcome to the fold of the Cambodian nation those who had long lived in exile from the law. These are very positive developments. They need the sustaining support of the international community. For instance, simple well-digging equipment is needed in such settlements as a means to translate aspirations into reality.

Rights of the child: A major focus of my sixth mission in 1995 was a study of the rights of the child. The office of the UN Centre for Human Rights in Phnom Penh is assisting the Cambodian government in the preparation of its first report of Cambodia's compliance with the *Convention on the Rights of the Child.*[12] I examined the work being done by NGOs for street children, orphans and the disabled. Special attention has been given by my successor to the problem of child trafficking and the prostitution and abuse of minors. A Youth Rehabilitation Centre for juvenile offenders has been established by the government to separate

---

12 United Nations GA Res 44/25, 20 November 1989.

them from hardened criminals. There is a huge post-war increase in the number of children in Cambodia. Almost half the population of the country is under the age of 15 years. This presents both an opportunity for the future and a great challenge to the present.

Media: The news-stands in Cambodia remain full. There are nearly 40 regular journals in the Khmer language and in foreign languages. A second journalists' association has been established. It has promised to be vigilant for its independence. Diversity of opinion is less evident in the Cambodian electronic media, which tends to be controlled by the government and the armed forces. But, in comparison to many countries of the region, Cambodia continues to enjoy a relatively high number of press outlets.[13]

Migration: The *Migration Law* was enacted by the National Assembly. It contained a number of provisions that were contrary to my advice. In particular, the problem of the ethnic Vietnamese boat people held at Chrey Thom on the border with Vietnam remained unresolved to the end of my mission and after, despite the efforts of the United Nations High Commissioner for Refugees (UNHCR), the International Committee of the Red Cross and others. In Hanoi, in January 1995, the governments of Cambodia and Vietnam agreed to solve their differences by negotiation. Thirteen ethnic Vietnamese families have been allowed to return to their villages from Chrey Thom and more may follow. I hope that gestures such as this signal a commitment to respecting the rights of all minorities in Cambodia.

The KR in its death throes played ceaselessly upon ethnic tensions and hatreds. It is important that the United Nations continues to be a voice for tolerance and principle. In this regard, the organisation had the sterling support of the King of Cambodia, who has insisted upon respect for the human rights of the ethnic Vietnamese and other minorities in Cambodia. A worrying element in the 1998 general election was the way in which some politicians played upon ethnic prejudices. However, in this regard, Cambodia is by no means alone. In recent times, the same has occurred in developed countries, including Australia.

United Nations agencies: The agencies of the United Nations press on with their vital work. These include the efforts of the World Health Organisation in the struggle against malaria and HIV; the FAO in promoting the planting of higher yield rice grain; the International Labour Organisation in supporting work generation schemes; the World

---

13 Not always matched by the levels of professionalism, accuracy and fairness in press reporting.

Food Programme in providing food for work; the United Nations Educational, Scientific and Cultural Organisation in training journalists and restoring the Ankor Wat; UNHCR in helping refugees and displaced persons; and UNDP in supporting many crucial development projects. Over and above the particular issues of human rights, the work of the office of the Centre for Human Rights in Phnom Penh, and the many other UN agencies in the field in Cambodia, bring great credit on the United Nations and much tangible assistance to the people of Cambodia. In March 1996, the High Commissioner for Human Rights signed a memorandum of understanding with the government of Cambodia to enhance co-operation and assistance, including to the Human Rights Commission of the National Assembly. With support from the Centre for Human Rights, members of the Cambodian administration visited Geneva to watch the Human Rights Commission in action. I hope that this pattern will continue. Isolation and ignorance reinforce attitudes that are inimical to human rights observance.

Troublesome Areas

Constitutional arrangements: The Constitutional Council, envisaged by the Constitution, had not been established by the end of my mission. This is the body that will provide constitutional review to ensure that the government and legislature remain within the Constitution and observe fundamental human rights there enshrined. The King had named his three nominees to the Council. However, the nominees of the National Assembly and of the Supreme Council of Judicature were still awaited. In the absence of the Constitutional Council, it was not possible to secure an authoritative national determination of the question, which arose during 1996, of the disputed power of the National Assembly to expel a member.

Opposition parties: Despite the commitment in the Paris Peace Agreements to multi-party democracy, reinforced in the Cambodian Constitution and endorsed in UN human rights treaties, various obstacles were initially put in the way of the registration of opposition political parties. There can be no democratic freedom without the privilege to organise parties and to express dissenting views. The way that the government and the National Assembly of Cambodia respect the rights of opposition parties, including the Khmer Nation Party of Mr Sam Rainsy and the Son San faction of the Buddhist Liberal Democratic Party (BLDP), provided a litmus test for the true commitment of the Cambodian government and legislature to multi-party democratic elections. It would be a tragedy if Cambodia were to return to a system of government where only one point of view could be given an effective voice. After the genocide and their great sufferings, the Cambodian people deserve better. The United Nations must continue to defend the rights of opponents of the government against those who would put the clock back because they cannot tolerate criticism or the expression of a contrary point of view. It is the duty of the United Nations' Special Representative to call to attention any evidence of a reversion to autocracy.

Expulsions from the National Assembly: In 1995, a member expelled from the National Assembly claimed that this happened because he was a vocal critic of government policy. He was first removed from his political party. It was then claimed that this required, and authorised, his removal from the National Assembly despite the fact that he had been voted there by the people of his constituency. As Special Representative, I cautioned that the expulsion appeared contrary both to the member's right of free expression and to his political rights and also contrary to Cambodia's Constitution and laws. My concern was not so much the member, as such. It was to protect the rule of law and the Assembly, and a nation that accepts dissent and free expression. After his expulsion the member's bodyguards were allegedly arrested and harassed by people, apparently in military uniform.

This and later expulsions, intimidation and trials of opponents of the government were the subject of representations by me as they have been by my successors in the United Nations. Allegations do not prove the facts. But such serious allegations must be energetically investigated and publicly reported upon. Criminal wrongs, once found, must be redressed. Unlawful acts, once proved, must be corrected. I urged the Chairman of the National Assembly, and all who would listen, to avoid expulsions of elected members lest this damage the democratic legitimacy and reputation of the National Assembly. Building a parliamentary democracy requires vigilance for the privileges of elected parliamentarians. In part as a response to my efforts the Inter-Parliamentary Union investigated these events. Although I was rebuffed by the Cambodian government on this issue, I hope that the intervention of this respected international body will discourage further such expulsions. The Special Representative of the Secretary-General cannot enforce his recommendations. But he can make a lot of fuss when they are ignored.

Judicial independence: Another essential pillar for the rule of law and human rights in any country is judicial independence. Yet Cambodia's judges were paid, at the time of my period of service, the equivalent of only $US20 per month. Clearly, this was completely inadequate. Whereas other professionals can often supplement their earnings, judges cannot easily do so with propriety. There is an urgent need to pay judges the minimum that will ensure that they can live with complete financial independence of government and other litigants. I raised this problem with the World Bank. If effective protections for human rights are to be provided, special arrangements must be made to put the judiciary of Cambodia beyond financial temptation, or the appearance of temptation. In 1998 the Minister of Justice proposed to the National Assembly a significant increase in the salary of judges. Clearly, this is to be welcomed. Improvements in the scheduling of cases and rigorous training of the judiciary are also needed to enhance the reputation of judges and the respect in which they are held by the community. The members of the Supreme Council of Magistracy and of the Constitutional Council envisaged by the Constitution should be appointed so that these guardians of the rule of law can be set up. Those who challenge the constitutionality of present laws have no effective legal redress in Cambodia. This must be provided, without further delay, to assure that the rule of law is upheld where it matters most.[14]

Military immunity: A major problem, seen on every visit to Cambodia during my mission, was that of too many firearms. There is a need to collect these weapons and to instil strict discipline in those who are entitled, by law, to carry arms. There have been some serious instances of oppression by military commanders drawn to the notice of the authorities but not effectively brought to justice, including at least one alleged case of cold-blooded murder. Difficulties have arisen in the co-operation between judicial and police forces in different provinces. These structural problems must be met resolutely so that, in reality as well as theory, everyone in Cambodia is brought under the discipline of law.

Civil service immunity: One legislative provision that came to notice during my last mission in 1996 was a provision that gave a form of immunity to senior civil servants. They could not be prosecuted without approval of their superiors. This provision, doubtless well intended, made it difficult or impossible in some cases for judges and prosecutors to bring powerful accused persons before the courts. Provisions of this kind should be repealed or radically amended.

Freedom of expression: Although press publications remain plentiful in Cambodia, the *Press Law*, finally enacted in 1995, permits imprisonment of journalists to an extent that I believe conflicts with international human rights principles. It is essential to monitor the operation of that law with close attention. The administrative power to close media outlets needs revision. At least, there should be a right to effective court

14 B Fernando (1998) *Problems Facing the Cambodian Legal System*, Asian Human Rights Commission, p 89.

supervision and review. As a result of proceedings against journalists, which pose the threat of imprisonment and closures of outlets, I received many representations complaining about a perceived turning away from the principles of freedom of expression enshrined in the Cambodian Constitution and in the international instruments which Cambodia had ratified. A small group of students (the 'balloon six') was arrested on the very eve of my sixth mission to Cambodia in 1995. I have seen the English language version of the pamphlet that they were handing out and which apparently occasioned their arrest. It dealt with political issues; but in a respectful way. In fact, it called for the assignment of more constitutional power to the King. This view may be misguided. But it is a political opinion which Cambodian citizens should be free to express, just as Australians can peacefully advocate a peaceful change in their Constitution. Despite representations on behalf of these persons they were held in custody without trial for an unconscionable period.

Similarly, true freedom of expression requires that opposition viewpoints should have access to the media, including the electronic media. At the moment such access is effectively denied to opposition opinion, especially in radio and television (save for brief statements during the July 1998 general election). There cannot be free and fair choice in elections without such access being assured on a regular and impartial basis. Without it, elections become a charade. Control of the airwaves by government and government parties presents a risk, unless firmly restrained, of a return to autocracy. Law must uphold, and not only at election time, the right to the expression of political views critical of the government. It is essential that, without delay, a fair electoral law should be enacted conforming fully to the United Nations standards for the conduct of free and fair elections.

Prisons: In all of my visits to the Provinces of Cambodia, I made it my business to visit the prisons. The prisons in Kampot and Kampong Cham were of a very poor standard. The latter was not really a prison at all, but a former school. Its prisoners suffered from tuberculosis, scabies and malnutrition. They were locked in their cells for 23 hours a day. There was a lack of proper exercise and recreational facilities. In one prison, I saw a cell with little light and even manacles and leg irons that appeared to still be in use. It is essential that the condition of prisons be improved. I applaud the support given by the Australian government to this rather thankless task, vital for respecting the human rights of an unpopular minority who are otherwise out of sight, out of mind.

HIV/AIDS: Until the elections sponsored by the United Nations, Cambodia was largely isolated from the world. Cambodia's terrible suffering, revolution, genocide, invasion and civil wars to some extent cut it off from HIV/AIDS. But now cases are spreading rapidly. The first testing of the blood supply in 1991 found less than 1 per cent HIV positive. In every successive year there has been an increase of a further 1 per cent. The government has established an inter-ministerial committee. But total funding for health care and education is extremely low, only $1 per head per annum. Monitoring of the national blood supply was, until recently, inadequate. A particular phenomenon of non-formal medicines, including the administration of glucose and like injections with unsterile equipment, presents grave risks of the rapid spread of the virus. In several hospitals, and even amongst private medical practitioners, reports were received of the multiple use of unsterile needles by untrained workers.

In a well-meaning response to the sudden increase in the spread of the epidemic, the Cambodian government ordered police to close brothels on the perimeter of Phnom Penh. Obviously, this did not stamp out prostitution. It merely helped to drive it temporarily underground. It made sex workers vulnerable to official oppression and bribery, distancing them from educational messages and the provision of condoms. In the name of sexual modesty, the government also censored media advertisements calling attention graphically to HIV/AIDS, its causes and means of prevention. Such messages continued to come into Cambodia in foreign language broadcasts and journals. But not in the Khmer language. The efforts of the combined United Nations agencies to tackle HIV/AIDS and to assist the government and Cambodian society in prevention were often frustrated by a general lack of willingness to discuss the issue openly and candidly and to take the effective action that was urgently needed.

Land law: The problem of land law remains substantially unattended to. As a result of the emptying of the cities in Pol Pot's time there are many dispossessed people and countless land disputes between well-placed occupiers and returnees. I spent much time during my last mission in 1996 with squatters and their organisations. They are the by-products of homelessness. Their needs demand sensitive treatment, rehousing, and the provision of facilities and education for children. Dispossession is a major source of deprivation of human rights and of flashpoints for conflict, violence and disaffection.

Co-operation: Although, during my sixth mission, I was received in audience by the King of Cambodia and met the Ministers for Foreign Affairs, Justice, Information and Children's Affairs, the two Prime Ministers declined to meet me. This was the first time following my appointment in 1993 that such a difficulty had arisen. It came in the face of the statement, before the visit of the UN Special Envoy in 1995, that the government of Cambodia would continue to welcome my visits to Cambodia. The Second Prime Minister (Hun Sen) was reported to have said that if I wished to continue in my post I would have to change my attitude. He also declined to receive my successor and made veiled threats to him, as he had to me. The provision of advice and assistance to the Cambodian government in the promotion and protection of human rights requires dialogue, including at the highest level. Refusal of dialogue, because occasionally the advice is unwelcome, is not an appropriate or effective way of clarifying differing perspectives and of isolating areas in which co-operation can be fruitful.

Backing away from legitimate and honest criticism of the Cambodian government and institutions where I saw departures from fundamental human rights would have been a betrayal of my duty to the Secretary-General and the United Nations, to the Paris Agreements and of the hopes of the international community that post-UNTAC Cambodia would be rebuilt on the foundations of human rights and constitutionalism. It would have been a betrayal of the Cambodian people and of the principles which, I believe, the overwhelming majority of them support. They still have faith in the United Nations. The United Nations must prove itself worthy of that faith.

It was not only Hun Sen who gave me a hard time. The clandestine radio of the KR warned that if I continued my work in Cambodia, particularly in expressing support for the rights of the ethnic Vietnamese minority, they would 'smash my head in'. There were other threats. This was the environment in which I performed my work in Cambodia. Against the background of Cambodia's recent history, such threats could not be treated as idle boasting. Notionally, human rights workers of the United Nations also wear blue helmets.

Professionalism and Idealism

I remain hopeful about Cambodia. On balance, during my time, the good news was more important than the bad. Progress continues to be made.

I carry with me many vivid memories of the three years during which I served as the UN Special Representative:

- Of the mother, grieving in a village house near Kampot for the senseless death of her son, killed by the reckless use of one of the flood of guns in Cambodia, apparently used in senseless anger. 'He would have been a general', she moaned. She appealed to me to do what I could to help stop the lawlessness.

- Of the villagers re-settled under the shadow of Vine Mountain: once a stronghold of the KR who there murdered my fellow countryman, David Wilson, and his British and French companions. Such lawlessness is gradually being replaced by re-settlement. Banditry is gradually giving way to constitutionalism.
- Of the eyes of the young judge in training at Kampong Cham, to whom I spoke candidly about corruption and its insidious effect on the reputation of the judiciary and the rule of law. We must find a solution to this problem. Otherwise, it will eat at the fabric of Cambodia's newly established institutions.
- Of the prisoners peering at me as my eyes adjusted to the gloom of the cell in which they spent 23 hours of every day of their lives. They are humans too. Their dignity and self-respect must be defended. If the United Nations Special Representative does not speak for them, who will?

I pay tribute to the many officers of the United Nations who devote their lives to the improvement of human rights in Cambodia and to helping the government in its enormous task of reconstruction. I hope that the historical elements of intolerance of diversity will be kept in check. It is essential that Cambodia persist with the multi-party democracy, founded on political pluralism, that it committed itself to in the Paris Peace Agreements. There is no other effective way to make Cambodia a modern society which cherishes all of its people.

I pay tribute to my colleagues in the office of the Centre for Human Rights, both in Geneva and in Cambodia. And to the High Commissioner for Human Rights who retains a vigilant interest in the success of the Cambodian operation. Finally, I offer my respects to the Cambodian human rights workers who retain their faith in the United Nations and whom we must not let down.

Chapter 4

The Human Genome[1]

As a member of the UNESCO International Bioethics Committee and the Ethics Committee of the Human Genome Organisation, Michael Kirby addressed the Bioethics Advisory Panel at the Australian Catholic Bishops Conference on 15 September 1997. His speech, originally entitled 'Meeting Our Friend, The Genome', highlights the ethical and legal implications of human genomic research and genetic engineering. He discusses privacy and confidentiality, intellectual property and human rights issues and questions whether it is possible to limit genetic research to the testing, preventing and treating of genetic disorders. His insight is that technological advances with the potential to transform human evolution tend to run ahead of ethical responses and legal regulation and that if lawmakers and religious leaders do not take action they risk allowing 'science and technology to take our species where they will'.

Encounter with the Genome

My qualifications to address the ethical problems of the human genome arise out of my work on the International Bioethics Committee of the United Nations Educational, Scientific and Cultural Organisation (UNESCO) in Paris and the Ethics Committee of the Human Genome Organisation (HUGO) in London. Each of these bodies is considering a number of the ethical, social and legal questions that arise out of genomic research and the genetic engineering to which it will give rise. The UNESCO Committee in 1996 adopted a draft Universal Declaration on the Human Genome and Human Rights. This was, with some modifications, approved by the General Conference of UNESCO in Paris in November 1997.[2] We stand at the brink of remarkable scientific and technological developments concerning our genes. Belatedly, governments and the international community are beginning to respond. But what path should they take?

---

1 This paper contains extracts from 'Challenges of the Genome' (1997) 20(3) *University of New South Wales Law Journal* 537.

2 UNESCO (1997) *Universal Declaration on the Human Genome and Human Rights.*

Difficulties in the Path

In the business of the genome, we are talking about nothing less than the future of the human species. It is, therefore, a topic appropriate to international consideration and, eventually, international law. However, the difficulties of securing a consensus about such a topic are only too obvious. They include the different religious, cultural and legal traditions that must be brought into harmony and the different economic interests of different countries involved in the development of therapies. There are disparities in attitudes to intellectual property protection and in sheer investment in, and the potential to make profits from, these scientific developments. The inclination of local lawmakers is generally to put such matters in the 'too hard' drawer, preferring instead to address more manageable local controversies that have greater political attraction.

There is also a feeling of resignation in some quarters arising out of the belief that the tide of science and technology cannot be held back by any law and that any attempt to prevent scientists from experimenting is bound to fail and so should not be attempted. Finally, there is a feeling on the part of some that such scientific progress is bound, in the long run, to be for the betterment of humanity and is, in any case, a product of the inherent skills and abilities of the human species and thus an extension of human beings, not something alien to them.

What are we talking about? The Human Genome Project is the largest co-operative scientific activity in history. It is larger by far than the Manhattan Project that resulted in the development of the atomic bomb. Yet its implications are in some ways similar. It is important that the Project should advance with a full understanding of the ethical, social and legal consequences that come in its train. This is recognised by HUGO itself. It gives an impetus to the work of the HUGO Ethics Committee and also to that of the International Bioethics Committee of UNESCO. Yet the reality is that the funds devoted to the ethical, social and legal consequences of genomic research are but a tiny fraction of those devoted to the scientific research itself.

Legal and Ethical Implications

There are many practical implications which the unlocking of the mysteries of the genome will have for humanity. They include implications for medical therapies, criminal law, privacy and confidentiality, third party interests, intellectual property and human rights.

Medical Therapies

Scientists are now discovering the genes which 'trigger' various genetic diseases which, in turn, constitute a large part of the inherited causes of the suffering of humanity. Take Huntington's Disease. The genes which express that serious affliction have been identified on the genome. This discovery permits the conduct of extremely accurate tests that can now identify those people who carry and may transmit this genetic condition. That knowledge would, theoretically, in combination with amniocentesis and abortion, permit the future elimination of carriers of Huntington's. But is this desirable? Can it be distinguished from the abortion of a foetus with Down Syndrome? Where does this process of medical elimination of 'defective' genes begin and end? Is there a less life-destructive means of using the genetic information to delay the onset or diminish the symptoms of Huntington's Disease whilst respecting the life of a person born with those genes or others like it?

Criminal Law

For the lawyer, the discovery of genetic causes of disorders relevant to some antisocial conduct may have implications for the future. The criminal law is built upon the hypothesis of free will. For the crime to be established it is normally necessary to prove both the act of the accused and the will (*mens rea*) occasioning that act. But what are the implications for the law of discovering that, in some cases at least, for some people, the act is practically no more than the product of a genetic characteristic? Can we persist with the unquestioned hypothesis of free will in the face of scientific knowledge that casts doubt upon it?

Privacy and Confidentiality

The basic rule of the healthcare professions has long been respect for the confidences of the patient. This rule goes back to the Hippocratic Oath. It existed in ancient civilisations. But when a disorder is of a genetic characteristic, is the 'patient' the individual or the entire family? Does a family in such circumstances have a right to override the wishes of the patient and to secure data about the patient's genes relevant to genetic features important for them all? Does a patient have a right *not* to know the determinants of his or her future medical conditions?

Third Party Interests

This last question leads to the rights of third parties. Should an employer have a right to require an employee to submit to genetic testing to show, with greater perfection, the likely future health status of the employee?

Should an insurer be entitled to secure a detailed genetic profile of the insured? Until now, insurance has generally involved the sharing, within the community, of the risks attached to medical conditions that are largely unpredictable. If such conditions can be predicted with perfect or near perfect accuracy, would that not shift the scales unfairly to the advantage of insurers? Yet, where insurers can require those seeking insurance to submit to old-fashioned medical tests, will it be sensible, in the future, to close off knowledge of the best medical information that may be available from genetic tests?

Intellectual Property

One of the key issues of genetic research concerns the desirability of permitting the patenting of human genes or their sequences as the basis for therapeutic applications. Of course, in every country, the patentability of such matter depends upon the terms of the local law on intellectual property protection (patents, copyright etc). That law is itself normally the product of national legislation and is generally influenced by international law. At conferences on the genome, strong views are frequently expressed by participants from developing countries and elsewhere about this topic. Opponents urge that the human genome is the common heritage of humanity. They argue that it belongs to the human species as a whole – some say to God – and not to private corporations engaged in research, however potentially beneficial such research may prove to be. They point to the fact that the great scientists, James Watson and Francis Crick, who first described DNA, and began humanity's journey to a full understanding of the genome, never attempted to secure the slightest commercial advantage for themselves from their discoveries. I shall return to this topic later.

Human Rights

An important element in the UNESCO Declaration is the attempt to reconcile the development of genetic technology and research on the human genome with fundamental human rights and human dignity. The UNESCO Declaration states in Article 6:

> No one shall be subjected to discrimination based on genetic characteristics that is intended to infringe or has the effect of infringing human rights, fundamental freedoms and human dignity.[3]

The eugenics movement earlier in the twentieth century was a doubtless well-intentioned effort to eliminate, in effect, genetic

---

3 UNESCO (1997) *Universal Declaration on the Human Genome and Human Rights.*

characteristics deemed undesirable to society. For the most part, the movement was targeted at so-called 'mental defectives' but it affected (as we now know) large numbers of persons who manifested quite modest mental impairment or none at all. Unsurprisingly perhaps, the eugenics movement had strong supporters in the Nazi effort to 'cleanse' the German population of so-called 'undesirables'. That effort notoriously attacked people for their genetic identity: specifically their Jewish or gypsy ethnicity. But it also imposed its uniform conception of the human species upon others who presented genetic or other conditions deemed undesirable to the Nazis: homosexuals, the physically disabled and the mentally impaired. The terrible experience of the Holocaust stands as a dire warning to humanity of what can happen when people with a stereotyped view of human existence gain totalitarian political power. We should not consider that this is a problem of ancient history. It endures into our own time. We have recently seen it in one form in the 'ethnic cleansing' in Serbia, Bosnia and Rwanda. At the outset of the genomic revolution in medicine, therefore, it is timely to insist that developments should occur in a context of respect for fundamental human rights and human dignity. I would expect that religious faiths would lend their support throughout the world to the effort of the United Nations to insist upon such preconditions.

Patenting Genes

One advantage of my appointments to the UNESCO and HUGO Committees is that I have the opportunity and obligation to read scientific literature. Not for me is it a single diet of the *Commonwealth Law Reports*. In a recent issue of the journal *Science*, the heat of the debate concerning intellectual property law protection of genes and gene sequences was illustrated.[4] The journal records that in June 1997 the National Academy of Sciences in the United States asked its President, Dr Bruce Alberts, to write to the Director of the United States Patent and Trademarks Office about this problem. The Academy expressed particular concern about the apparent willingness of the Office to grant patents on mere fragments of human genes, particularly those known as Expressed Sequence Tags (ESTs). These can be used to identify the presence of full-length genes. ESTs are relatively easy to capture. But they reveal little about the biology that they control. The fear is that patenting ESTs – a few have been patented so far and thousands of applications are pending – could create a tangled maze of intellectual property rights that would actually impede research. 'It would be sad

4 'Academy Joins Debate Over DNA Patents', *Science*, vol 277, 4 July 1997, p 41.

indeed if patent policies diminished the pace of discoveries or wealth of practical applications'.[5] The Academy appealed to the Patent Office to consider granting DNA patents only where 'real world' applications are described in the patent application or detailed information about the gene is already known or supplied by the applicant.

The appeal by Dr Alberts parallels one made in March 1997 by the Director of the National Institutes of Health in the United States, Dr Harold Varmus. Dr Varmus wrote to the United States Patent Office after an official of that office gave a speech favouring patents on ESTs as diagnostic or research probes.[6] His concern was that such patent policies might block research and development on more important discoveries such as complete genes and thus stifle beneficial gene-based therapies.

The response of the Patent Office to pressure of this kind is predictable. It simply says that it will apply the law. If the Congress of the United States wishes to restrict or forbid the patenting of life forms, that is for the Congress to say. Naturally, there are many in the United States and elsewhere who assert that patenting of genomic discoveries – and even more so gene sequences whose effects are not fully known – should be no part of intellectual property law. That this information belongs to all humanity. That no individual or corporation should make a private profit from living matter. However, there are difficulties in such assertions. 'Man-made' micro-organisms have been patentable in the United States at least since 1980.[7] The potential for medical therapies of developments arising out of exploration of genes is enormous. The profits riding on such discoveries run into billions of dollars. The investment in research said to warrant intellectual property protection is likewise substantial. In these circumstances, striking the right balance between respect for the common genomic heritage of humanity, protection of people in developing and other countries so that they gain some of the benefits, and assurance of a fair economic return to scientific investors is not an easy dilemma to solve.[8]

---

5 Ibid.

6 'Renewed Fight Over Gene Patent Policy', *Science*, vol 276, 11 April 1997, p 187.

7 *Diamond v Chakrabarthy* 447 US 303 (1980). Cf *Ex parte Latimer* 46 AG 1638 at 1640 (1889); and *Funk Brothers, Seed Co v Calo Inoculant Co* 333 US 127 (1948).

8 JC Venter, 'The Patentability of Genetic Discoveries' in BBV Foundation (Spain) *The Human Genome Project: Legal Aspects*, vol 2, p 123; and C Byk, 'Patenting Human Genes', in BBV Foundation (Spain) *The Human Genome Project: Legal Aspects*, vol 2, p 127.

The Genome and Evolution

In another article in *Science*, the authors appealed for the development of a new view of evolution arising from the contemporary study of genes.[9] It was in the late 1970s that scientists at Harvard University began to focus on genes in order to better understand evolution, including human evolution. But it was not until the mid-1980s that the new tools for studying developmental genes began to generate the data which could explain how, in the comparatively short period of the Earth's existence, such a remarkable myriad of living creatures found on earth – vertebrate and invertebrate – could have developed, presumably from the basic living cells present at the beginning.

Recent research has shown a number of genes to be common across a very wide range of animals. Such genes have similar or related functions across completely disparate species. For example, a gene which stimulates the development of eyes may cause no more than a photosensitive area in a very primitive animal, but may stimulate the development of a compound eye in an insect or the highly developed eye of a mammal, such as a human being. The same or a very closely similar gene can operate in a related fashion across vast periods of evolutionary history. This discovery has obvious relevance to the patenting of human genes. If the same, or a closely similar, gene in an animal has the same, or closely related, functions across a very wide range of living species, and it is suggested that the patenting of human genes is somehow repugnant or socially undesirable, would a distinction between the human and non-human gene be a way out of this dilemma? Or would the recent discoveries indicate that if human genes are not to be patentable then no genes of living matter (human or animal) may be patented?

The exploration of the genome has also offered a possible answer to a dilemma about evolution that has puzzled biologists for some time. If evolution proceeded by a process of substitution in DNA chains of particular species, then our current knowledge of mutation rates makes it absolutely clear that four billion years (the Earth's estimated existence) is simply not long enough to arrive at the richness and variety of the species now existing. If, however, species can use a modular genetic approach to building new genes and gene functions, this would help explain the occasional rapid speeding up of the process of genetic change. A comparison has been drawn between one team of computer programmers, starting from scratch to design a whole series of

9 E Pennisi and W Roush, 'Developing a New View of Evolution', *Science*, vol 277, 4 July 1997, p 34.

programmes to carry out a variety of widely different functions, while another team starts with a number of already developed programme parts with known functions whose task is merely to put the modules together in new ways.[10]

An Adjunct to Medicine or A New World?

The fundamental question that is presented by genomic research is this. Should such research be seen as no more than an adjunct of improving the health of the current human species? Should it be limited by law, and otherwise, to removing this or that disease from human beings but keeping them, in every other way, basically as they are? In short, should genomic research and genetic engineering be viewed as nothing more than an assistant to established medical science? To provide tests for genetic maladies? To provide the foundation for treatment of genetic disorders? According to moral conviction and law, to provide a basis for eliminating foetuses which demonstrate grave genetic disabilities or potentialities?

These questions are hard enough. But the lessons of science and technology are that to foresee developments of the future we must engage in controlled leaps of the imagination. It seems unlikely to me that genomic research will stop at being a mere adjunct to current medicine. If it becomes possible to alter the human species in particular potentialities, are we really talking about an aid to the human species? Or are we on the brink of considering something which may actually change the human species itself? A kind of scientific speeding up of evolution?

If you alter a large number of features of the human species – eliminating Huntington's Disease, expelling the potential to Alzheimer's, excluding Parkinson's, removing Down Syndrome – where does this path lead? Certainly it leads to the reduction of much human pain and misery which presently affect patients and their loved ones. But taken to the extreme, might it not also lead to a change of what it is to be a human being? Add to the exclusion of serious genetic disorders – the elimination of baldness, the removal of a potentiality to obesity, the exclusion of undue height or undue shortness – and you are well on the way to redesigning the human species. The experiments of Dr I Wilmut and his colleagues demonstrate that embryonic sheep eggs can reproduce the nuclei of differentiated cells, enabling the cells to develop into any type.[11] This showed that it may now be possible to envisage reproductive

10 Letter to the author from Dr JR Coulter, Adelaide, 29 August 1997.

11 'Clone mammals … clone man?', *Nature*, vol 380, 13 March 1997, p 119.

cloning of adult humans in a completely asexual fashion. If it can be done with sheep, given time, it can undoubtedly be done with humans. And what or who will stop it?[12]

Forbidden Territory or The Next Step for Humanity?

With catchy phrases, writers in the scientific literature talk of our era as one where human beings will pass from 'Genesis to genetics'.[13] Obviously, developments in scientific knowledge have significant implications for religious faiths that accept as doctrine the teachings of a Holy Book. As scientists and technologists report their discoveries, religious teachers and theologians must explain and justify the revealed scientific truths, reconciling them with the previous understanding of Scripture and religious teachings which was expressed in an earlier time when the scientific truth was completely unknown.

In the summer of 1993, a team of researchers at the United States National Cancer Institute announced that they had evidence linking male homosexuality to a gene in the region of the X chromosome.[14] It looks increasingly likely that sexual orientation is, in part at least, a genetic phenomenon and thus beyond the 'wicked' choosing of a 'wilful' individual. If this is the case, then prima facie to discriminate upon that basis would be as morally impermissible, and even repugnant, as to discriminate upon any other genetic basis such as gender, race, skin colour or a pre-programmed disease or characteristic over which the individual has no control.

It might be said that, exceptionally, sexuality is one genetic condition that the individual should just try to struggle against and to deny. It might even be said that this is one genetic condition that should be eliminated in whatever way possible. The Chief Rabbi of the Commonwealth of Nations, controversially, suggested that this should be done to get rid of homosexuals, thereby provoking cries of outrage from Holocaust survivors and other Jewish intellectuals. But if sexual orientation is, indeed, part of the genome of our species, a serious moral question is plainly presented. By what right can we say that it is not part of Nature's – or God's – great purpose? That purpose, as the Church has taught, is not always clear to us, mere mortals. We see through a glass darkly. But will it be the Human Genome Project as it develops

12 GP Smith, 'Judicial Decisionmaking in the Age of Biotechnology' (1999) 13 *Notre Dame Journal of Law Ethics and Public Policy* 63 at 112-116.

13 Ted Peters, 'From Genesis to Genetics', *New Scientist*, 15 March 1997, p 42.

14 Ibid.

that helps us to see '[f]ace to face: now I know in part, but then shall I know even as also I am known'. [15]

An even more fundamental question than this is presented. For all those (including in the Church and the United Nations and its agencies) who urge that we should keep genetic alteration as an adjunct of human existence *as it now is*, others dispute. For the disputants, genetic discoveries arise out of the intelligence of human beings. That intelligence is given by Nature – or God – to discover reality as it exists. The genome and DNA existed for millennia before they were discovered, in our generation, through the intelligence of Watson and Crick.

If the genome is discovered, that discovery is, arguably, the outgrowth of a human development that was ordained for us in this era or, at least, that was likely to occur somewhere at this time in human evolution. That development will itself not stand still. It will take us further down a path that might indeed be called 'evolutionary'. It is itself the product of our human intelligence. It may be a path that involves leaps of evolutionary history – a type of fast forward of the kind that seems somehow to have occurred without human intervention in the past. It may even be a path that involves a reconsideration of what it is to be a human being and what, if any, are those characteristics of the human species that are to be regarded by scientists as absolutely forbidden territory. In any case, no law can stop science and technology completely. There will always be a small corner of the world that will give sanctuary to the free spirit of the enquiring scientist and the technologist at work in the laboratory. Especially will this be so if profits dangle tantalisingly at the end of the endeavour.

If the Christian churches or other religious teachers take a different view, they must explain that view and argue for it. It seems unlikely that dogmatic assertion or even scriptural texts will win the argument today. Reason and a return to fundamental wisdom may help in the persuasion as may an appeal to universal notions about the things that all human beings share in common. But if we do not join this debate it will surely pass by default.

Informed Decisions

This is why I consider the work of the UNESCO International Bioethics Committee and the Ethics Committee of HUGO as amongst the most important that I have been involved in. For a lawyer, like a theologian, it

15 1 Corinthians 13 xii.

is somewhat intimidating to stand staring at a new era of genetics. The scientist and the technologist rush ahead. The lawyer, the ethicist and the theologian amble slowly along, their heads full of puzzlement at the problems which seem so insoluble. Yet to do nothing is to make a decision. It is to permit science and technology to take our species where they will. We know enough now to realise that there are quandaries here for human beings to answer. The ultimate question is whether we will have the will and the means and the wisdom to devise the answers.

Chapter 5

Privacy in Cyberspace[1]

The following text is based on a paper published by UNESCO in *International Dimensions of Cyberspace Law.* Michael Kirby discusses the many developments that have taken place since the OECD first established guidelines on the protection of privacy in the context of trans-border data flows, 20 years ago. In this period, the Internet has come onto the scene, giving rise to many new challenges to human rights and to the institutions of law and governance. It is Michael Kirby's belief that what is lacking is an understanding of the relevance of scientific developments for the *concept* of human rights. Instead of developing new approaches, human rights instruments developed for earlier times are scrutinised in an effort to solve the dilemmas presented by entirely new technology. He makes several suggestions for tackling the challenges posed by the new technology, maintaining that the overarching goal must be the building of a compatible legal order based on a foundation of respect for human rights and fundamental freedoms.

A New Dynamic

Twenty years ago, in the Organisation for Economic Co-operation and Development (OECD), work was beginning towards guidelines on the protection of privacy in the context of trans-border data flows.[2] Ten years ago work towards the subsequent OECD guidelines on security of information systems was commenced.[3] I chaired the two groups which prepared those guidelines.[4] This work opened my eyes to the enormous implications of modern technology for law and human rights, and to the capacity of international institutions occasionally to help domestic law-makers respond to global problems. The work of the OECD on the social and legal issues presented by informatics illustrates the way in which the international community is slowly (and unsurely) constructing

---

1 An earlier version of this paper was published in the Thematic Edition of the University of New South Wales Law Journal on Electronic Commerce and the Law: (1998) 21(2) *University of New South Wales Law Journal* 323.

2 OECD, *Guidelines on the Protection of Privacy and Transborder Flows of Personal Data*, Paris, 1980.

3 OECD, *Guidelines on Security of Information Systems*, Paris, 1992.

4 OECD Expert Groups on Privacy (1978-80) and Data Security (1991-92).

a mutually compatible legal order on the foundation of 'respect for human rights and fundamental freedoms'.[5]

Ten years ago, I suggested that what was lacking at both the domestic and the international level was a perception of the relevance of scientific developments for the *concept* of human rights.[6] This was due to a fragmentation of priorities, the dominance of lawyers (often ignorant of science) in the debates on human rights, the limited perspective of specialised institutions and the highly controversial nature of many of the moral dilemmas posed. It is useful, I think, to repeat my conclusion:

> [T]here has been little endeavour to reflect the major scientific and technological developments of the last fifty years, and their impact on human rights, in a conceptual way. Instead, old human rights instruments developed for earlier times are scrutinised for their possible utility in solving the controversies presented by the new technology. Piece-meal legislation is enacted. No Luther of jurisprudence has emerged to pull together the implications of nuclear physics, informatics and biotechnology for 21st century man and woman.[7]

In the decade since those words were written, the fundamental problem remains unresolved while the urgency of finding solutions has increased. In informatics, there has been a rapid convergence of technologies. Telecommunications has merged with computerisation linked with other systems of communication.[8] Connections have been forged between nuclear physics, informatics and biotechnology. The Star Wars system proposed by President Ronald Reagan had a worrying potential to link nuclear weaponry and informatics. The Human Genome Project would not be possible but for the linkages of information technology and biological research.[9] It is important to realise the interconnections of scientific advances and to study their impact on human rights. For example, the privacy of genetic information is as much an issue for human rights in the context of informatics as it is in the context of biotechnology. Principled responses, defensive of the rule of law,

---

5 Preamble to the Charter of the United Nations. See LM Goodrich and E Hambro (1949) *Charter of the United Nations: Commentary and Documents*, 2nd ed, Stevens, p 87.

6 MD Kirby, 'Human Rights and Technology: A New Dilemma' (1988) 22 *University of British Columbia Law Review* 123 at 127.

7 Ibid, pp 130-131. Cf AES Tay (1981) *Teaching Human Rights*, Australian Government Publishing Service, p 2.

8 J Bond, 'Telecommunications is Dead, Long Live Networking', *I-Ways*, Third Quarter 1997, p 26.

9 See Chapter 4. See also R Cook-Deegan (1994) *The Gene Wars*, Norton, p 283ff; MD Kirby, 'The Human Genome Project – Promise and Problems' (1994) 11 *Journal of Contemporary Health Law and Policy* 1. See now UNESCO (1997) *Universal Declaration on the Human Genome and Human Rights*, especially Articles 7, 8 and 9.

human rights and fundamental freedoms, will necessarily have common themes.

In the 20 years since the OECD guidelines on privacy were formulated, the Internet has been launched. The reach of the Internet expands at an astonishing rate, with the number of users doubling every 12 months.[10] William Gibson's vision of cyberspace is fast becoming a reality.[11] Starting with 8.5 million users in 1995, the Internet is expected to reach over 142 million users by the year 2000.[12]

Imagine the way in which, in the future, the lives of human beings will be altered as the global network of inter-connected users of information technology becomes bigger and even more powerful. Already, informed writers are offering their predictions. Edward Cornish, for example, has sketched 92 ways in which, he claims, the lives of ordinary people will change over the next 30 years as a result of the Internet.[13] Global culture, education, employment, production and even crime will be affected. Local cultures and languages may decline. Drug use and the risks of cyber-crime and terrorism will be large problems. Privacy will be harder to maintain. Inter-personal relationships will be increasingly unstable. Governments will have limited control over cyberspace and the pace at which globalisation of the inter-connected human consciousness is occurring. Cornish's conclusion is that the unprecedented power to choose will often result in less sensible action and greater conflict.

Endangered Privacy

Many of the privacy issues identified in the 1980s have been enlarged or altered by the development of the Internet. The speed, power, accessibility and storage capacity of the technology are now greatly increased.[14] In the past, some of the chief protections for individual

---

10 R Miller, 'The Internet in Twenty Years: Cyberspace, the Next Frontier?' (1997) OECD Future Studies Information Base Highlight, No 14, May, p 1.

11 W Gibson *Neuromancer*, cited in MS Borella, 'Computer Privacy vs. First and Fourth Amendment Rights', <http://www.eff.org/pub/Privacy/comp_privacy_4th_amend.paper>. As Miller (1997) notes, cyberspace will eventually come to life on the Internet infrastructure as a range of information and services spanning, at least for a few analysts, almost all aspects of human experience. Cf E France, 'Can Data Protection Survive in Cyberspace?' (1997) 8(2) *Computers and Law* 20.

12 Miller (1997) p 1.

13 E Cornish, 'The Cyber Future: 92 Ways Our Lives Will Change by the Year 2025' (1996) 30(1) *The Futurist*, pp 27-42, abstracted in OECD (1997) p 12.

14 A Cavoukian and D Tapscott (1996) *Who Knows – Safeguarding your Privacy in a Networked World*, Vintage; SD Balz and O Hance, 'Privacy and the Internet: Intrusion, Surveillance and Personal Data' (1996) 10(2) *International Review of Law, Computers and Technology* 219.

privacy arose from the sheer costs of retrieving personal information; the impermanence of the forms in which that information was stored; and the inconvenience experienced in procuring access. Other protections arose from the incompatibility of collections with available indexes and the effective undiscoverability of most personal data.

These practical safeguards have largely disappeared in the digital age.[15] The determined investigator can now collate a vast amount of data, identified to a particular individual. The individual then takes on a digital persona made up of a collection of otherwise unconnected and previously unconnectable data. Private sector corporations now want to centralise these collections.

The quantity of personal information about individuals is likely to increase rather than decrease.[16] Access to this information is what occasions the contemporary fragility of privacy – a right that has been steadily eroded over the past century.[17] To the extent that the individual has no control over, and perhaps no knowledge about, the mass of identifiable data which may be accumulated concerning him or her, and to the extent that national lawmakers have only limited power to protect the individual, individual privacy is undermined.[18]

It is not always appreciated by web users that, unless they take specific initiatives, visits to particular web sites can usually be resurrected and used to present a profile of the user. These visits may illustrate the subjects in which they are interested and their inclinations, political, social, sexual and otherwise.[19] An early indication of the potential of this form of surveillance occurred during the confirmation hearings in the United States Senate considering the nomination of Judge Robert Bork to the United States Supreme Court. A reporter retrieved the record of Judge Bork's video rentals as itemised by computer.[20] In another case, Senior Petty Officer Timothy McVeigh, a naval officer stationed in Hawaii, was discharged from the United States Navy after he came under investigation following a search of his America OnLine (AOL) profile, which included the word 'gay'. An acquaintance turned the

15 G Greenleaf, 'Privacy and Cyberspace – An Ambiguous Relationship' (1996) 3(5) *Privacy Law and Policy Reporter* 88.

16 Ibid.

17 R Wacks (1997) 'Privacy in Cyberspace: Personal Information, Free Speech and the Internet' in P Birks (ed) *Privacy and Loyalty*, Oxford, p 93.

18 Ibid, p 110; Balz and Hance (1996) p 220.

19 Balz and Hance (1996) p 222. Most Internet users do not seem to appreciate that an image of a site they may have visited many weeks earlier could be stored in their personal computer and easily viewed by another person having access to the computer.

20 Ibid, p 228.

profile over to Mr McVeigh's command. The latter treated it as a breach of the United States government's 'Don't ask; don't tell' policy regarding the sexual orientation of service personnel. Mr McVeigh did not tell, but AOL did.[21]

One of the particular dangers of data profiling is the human tendency to assume that because information comes out of an automated system it must be accurate. Data profiles have a potential to magnify and endlessly reproduce human error.[22] There are many examples of the mistakes which can occur: the brother who paid a defaulting sibling's rent and found himself black-listed as an unreliable tenant; the network user whose facilities were used by someone else to visit a child pornography web site or to download child pornography whilst the user was away; and many others.

The damage that can be done through defamation on the Internet is illustrated by a case in Western Australia.[23] A message from an anthropologist appeared on the World Wide Computer Network Bulletin Board defending a university decision not to grant academic tenure to the plaintiff. The message mentioned an accusation of sexual misconduct which thereupon became available to approximately 23,000 academics and students, within the relevant specialty, having regular access to the bulletin board. Defamation was found and damages were awarded.

Additional problems have arisen because of the growing use of information systems by business and government. Because these systems are connected to the Internet, many transactions by individuals are now potentially inter-connected and examinable. Data about the individual may be distributed to remote places and to persons or organisations with which the individual may have no other connection.

The advent of search engines, robots, wanderers and Internet indexes presents a new dimension to personally identifiable data profiles. The extensive indexes and search engines of Internet sites such as Yahoo and Altavista (with the subsequent proliferation of e-mail, telephone,

---

21 Human Rights Campaign, 'Human Rights Campaign Learns Pentagon Postponing Expulsion of Sailor with "Gay" in His America OnLine Profile', <http://www.hrc.org/feature1/mcveigh.html>.

22 T Miller, 'Law, Privacy and Cyberspace' (1996) 1(4) *Communications Law* 143 at 145; H Wright, 'Law, Convergence and Communicative Values on the Net' (1996) 7 *Journal of Law and Information Science* 54 at 65.

23 *Rhindos v Hardwick* (unreported, WA Sup Ct, 31 March 1994), noted in G Hughes, 'Nowhere to Hide? Privacy and the Internet' (1996) 29 *Computers and the Law* 21 at 22; B Todd, 'From Village Pump to Superhighway: Internet and the Modern Law of Defamation' (1996) 1 *Media and Arts Law Review* 34; P Bartlett, 'Internet & the Legal Tangle' (1995) 1(4) *Computer Law and Practice* 110.

address and Usenet directories) have changed forever the personal profile potential of the individual.[24] In his essay 'Private Lies' John Hilvert writes (referring to Altavista):

> [It] gobbles and disgorges in a very accessible way the entire catalogue of some 22 million web pages (12 billion words) and about two months of the content of 15,000 news groups. It handles 5 million search requests a day. ... The subject tried *Altavista* on the news groups and was sickened. 'What I found ... using my name or e-mail address as search parameters, was a copy of almost every post I've made to Newsnet news groups since the first week in January. ... That includes my posts to these two news groups, and all rejoinders from anyone here who included my name in his or her reply. Make out of that what you wish. My reaction to it is somewhere between disgust and fury. What I do not expect is that the news group clubhouse is bugged and that what is said there, by any of us, will be recorded and made available to any person on the Internet, for whatever reason persons might have'. [25]

It is not accurate to say that the Internet is a law-free zone. Much local law applies to the activities occurring there. But it is true to say that there is no global authority which controls the Internet. There is no uniform global regime to regulate and enforce standards.[26] To some extent the absence of a controlling and enforceable law facilitates free expression, the communication of ideas and individual opinions, which are themselves important human rights. However, such values are not the only human rights. There are other fundamental human rights which sometimes compete, or conflict, with the right of free expression. The right to privacy, to reputation and honour, and to the confidentiality of communications must also be protected.[27] In the world of the Internet, technological capacity tends to favour the spread of information. The protection of competing values is decidedly weak.

Users commonly think that, because they do not enter their names or other details to gain access to web pages, this means that there is a high degree of privacy in their use of the Internet, ie, that it is virtually anonymous. However, with most web browsing software, any request to a web site discloses the network identity of the machine used to access the web, the web page immediately previously accessed, and related

24 Greenleaf, 'Privacy and Cyberspace' (1996) p 88. A catalogue of Internet privacy issues may be found at <http://www. anu.edu.au/people/Roger.Clarke/DV/Internet.html>.

25 Cited in Greenleaf, 'Privacy and Cyberspace' (1996) pp 89-90.

26 Miller (1997) p 145.

27 *Universal Declaration of Human Rights*, Article 12; *International Covenant on Civil and Political Rights*, Article 17.1. See generally HH Perritt and CJ Lhulier, 'Information Access Rights Based on International Human Rights Law' (1997) 45 *Buffalo Law Review* 899 at 906ff.

'cookies', such as information stored by the web server on the computers of users who have accessed it, the list of previously accessed web pages or transactional information generated while accessing those web pages.[28] If this does not cause anxiety about the potential loss of privacy of Internet users, nothing will.

Of course, this is not a reason, Canute like, to hold up the hand against progress. We can scarcely prevent the rapid continuing growth in Internet users. Nor would one wish to do so. But it does present a challenge to those who would defend fundamental human rights (including privacy) and those who realise that false, distorted, damaging, hurtful and intrusive information can be compiled about an individual based upon data received from a multitude of digital sources and given an apparent authenticity by digital delivery. Web crawlers, spiders, robots and trawlers introduce a new dimension to the info-privacy debate. They also challenge the applicability, in today's technology, of some of the OECD Guidelines prepared in the context of the technology of earlier decades, when such intense 'dataveillance' was not foreseen.[29]

Challenges to Law

In addition to the foregoing concerns an even deeper malaise must be addressed. It relates to the capacity of presently existing lawmaking institutions to respond adequately to the problems which the new technology presents. Privacy is only one area in which the Internet poses new challenges. Organised crime, terrorism, infringement of intellectual property rights, and unconsensual or under-age pornography are some of the other problems examined in the literature.[30] There are also concerns about the implications of the Internet for the integrity of financial markets, for tax avoidance and as a potential tax haven.[31]

---

28 Greenleaf, 'Privacy and Cyberspace' (1996) pp 91-92. Without spiders and robots it would be very difficult to find information on the web. These 'devices' continually travel the millions of Internet servers on the web and index every significant word or phrase on each one. Web masters can prevent their sites from being so indexed. The awareness of the danger and the ways of meeting it have heightened in recent times. In 1994, an attempt was made to draft a *Robot Exclusion Standard.* See <http://web.nexor.co.uk/mak/doc/ robots/norobots.html>.

29 R Clarke, 'Profiling and its Privacy Implications' (1994) 1 *Privacy Law and Policy Reporter* 128; Wacks (1997) pp 93-97.

30 C Downey, 'The High Price of a Cashless Society: Exchanging Privacy Rights for Digital Cash?' (1996) 14(2) *John Marshall Journal of Computer and Information Law* 303.

31 Wacks (1997) p 111.

Equally controversial is the impact of the Internet upon cultural sovereignty and diversity, issues of serious concern to societies struggling to preserve and defend their language, religious or spiritual values, moral norms and distinct social diversity.[32] In striking down the censorship provisions of the *Communications Decency Act*,[33] the Supreme Court of the United States recognised that the practical consequence of its decision would reach far beyond American borders:[34]

> Once the provider posted its content on the Internet it could not prevent that content from entering any community. Thus, when the UCR / California Museum of Photography posts to its website nudes by Edward Weston and Robert Mapplethorpe to announce that its new exhibit would travel to Baltimore and New York City those images are available not only in Los Angeles, Baltimore and New York City but also in Cincinnati, Mobile or Beijing – wherever Internet users live. Similarly, the safe sex instructions that 'Critical Path' posts to its Web site written in street language so that the teenager receiver can understand them, are available not just in Philadelphia, but also in Provo and Prague.[35]

People in every country are, in a sense, beneficiaries or victims (depending on your point of view) of decisions made regarding the First Amendment to the United States Constitution. Not all societies, and certainly not all governments, share the social values reflected in United States court decisions.

In a number of countries attempts have already been made by law to control the Internet.[36] A draft law in Thailand purports to prohibit dissemination through the Internet of information that is against 'public peace and order and may lead to disunity of the nation or deterioration of international relationships'; information that is 'immoral', that disparages religion or 'highly respected persons' and 'inappropriate information' concerning the King of Thailand, the Thai Royal Family and also 'Heads of State of friendly foreign countries'.[37] This law was roundly criticised when it was published in January 1998, on the ground that the last-mentioned provision would create criminal offences for

---

32 S Davies, 'Strategies for Protecting Privacy in the New Information Structure' (1995) 2(2) *Privacy Law and Policy Reporter* 23; cf *I-Ways*, Fourth Quarter 1997, p 9.

33 Embedded within the *Telecommunications Act* 1996 (US).

34 *Reno v American Civil Liberties Union* 138 L Ed 2d 574 (1997), noted in (1997) 13(5) *Computer Law and Security Report* 371.

35 Ibid, p 372.

36 China, Singapore and Germany have introduced laws. See Wacks (1997) p 99.

37 Internet Promotion Bill 1998 (Thailand) (Draft 4), noted in *Bangkok Post*, 12 January 1998, p 1.

disseminating sexual information concerning President Clinton. The subsequent publicity given to allegations against the President, and its dominance of much of the global news media, demonstrated once again the difficulty (and possibly the undesirability) of censoring the international flow of data of this kind.

Another illustration lies in the efforts of the British government to prohibit publication of information and commentary which had the potential to endanger the fair trial of Rosemary West. Mrs West was accused of involvement in notorious serial killings. Such efforts of control might have been effective in the traditional news media. But they were wholly ineffective with respect to the Internet.[38]

Governments and legislatures are not entirely powerless in the face of the Internet and global media. But the force of the technology (and the vast audiences which it gathers up) suggests that common global standards will tend, in time, to swamp local values and customs. There will be little which most countries can do to influence the information flow except to enact laws enforceable in their courts in the rare instances where they can catch the offenders within their jurisdiction.

The contribution of the Internet to free expression, democratic practice and individual liberty cannot be denied. But in the gap created by the receding power of national law and the lack of effective international law, there are certain dangers. Threats to those human rights which compete with the free flow of data. Threats to stable social regulation in societies which object to the values which multimedia and the Internet promote.

An Agenda for Action

The extraordinary development of informatics continues to present puzzles and challenges both to the international community and to the lawmaking institutions of the nation states that make it up. A number of things can be done to begin to address these challenges:

1. Every jurisdiction needs to review its applicable laws and policies in an effort to adapt them to the new technology. In the United States a constitutional amendment has even been proposed to update some of the present legal guarantees and to permit courts to fashion new principles in harmony with the new technology and values.[39] In Australia, in the space of a few years, three discussion papers have

38 T Miller (1996) p 145.

39 Wacks (1997) p 99.

been produced by official bodies.[40] Currently, there is a Senate inquiry on self-regulation in the information and communications industries.[41] It is highly desirable that in every jurisdiction legislators, governments, academics and the general community debate the social implications of the new technology. Such debates need to be supplemented by international initiatives which seek to devise principles as global as the technology itself. Otherwise, we will persist with a legal patchwork of dubious effectiveness and more and more communication will take place in extra- and supra-jurisdictional space.[42]

2. The development of 'cyber manners' and of Internet standards generally, the initiatives of bodies such as the Global Internet Liberty Campaign,[43] as well as domestic initiatives to advocate endangered values such as privacy,[44] deserve support.

3. There is an urgent need, in the light of technological change and the enhanced capacity of the Internet, for a review to be conducted of the information privacy principles developed by the OECD 20 years ago. There are serious gaps in those principles. New privacy principles are already being suggested, such as:

    - a right not to be indexed – if a 'rogue' robot indexer ignores existing or new contemporary standards which exclude indexing;

---

40 The three initiatives of the Australian government are explained in T Hughes, 'Regulation of the "Net"' in Australian Law Reform Commission (1997) *Reform*, Issue 71, 23 at 24. They concern privacy protection, copyright reform and the regulatory framework of online services. The Australian government then withdrew an electoral commitment to enact privacy legislation governing the private sector. See S Davies, 'The Australian federal government has abandoned its election promise to enact privacy legislation for business' (1997) 13(6) *Computer Law and Security Report* 429. However, at the end of 1999 new legislation was again foreshadowed by the Federal Attorney General. See note 51 and accompanying text.

41 The Australian Senate Select Committee on Information Technology.

42 G Greenleaf, 'Privacy Principles – Irrelevant to Cyberspace?' (1996) 3(6) *Privacy Law and Policy Reporter* 114 at 118-119. The European Union has proposed a process that could lead to an International Communications Charter. See *I-Ways*, First Quarter 1998.

43 Greenleaf 'Privacy Principles' (1996) p 119.

44 The Australian Privacy Charter Council is a non-governmental organisation established to promote the protection of privacy. It has issued a Privacy Charter. See (1995) 2 *Privacy Law and Policy Reporter* 44. See also the European Union's *Data Directive* (Directive 95/46/EC). Cf G Greenleaf, 'European Commission tests adequacy of our privacy laws' (1998) 4(8) *Privacy Law and Policy Reporter* 140 and S Lau, 'Observance of the OECD Guidelines and the EU Directive in Asia' (1998) 4(8) *Privacy Law and Policy Reporter* 145.

- a right to encrypt personal communications effectively;[45]
- a right to fair treatment in key public infrastructures, so that no person is unfairly excluded in a way that would prejudice that person's ability to protect their privacy;
- a right to human checking of adverse automated decisions and a right to understand such decisions;[46]
- a right, going beyond the mere aspiration of the OECD openness principle, of disclosure of the collections to which others will have access and which might affect the projection of the data profile of the individual concerned.[47]

4. A common theme of many of the proposed revisions of the OECD privacy guidelines is the need to render 'data collection practices ... fully visible to the individual ... Any feature which results in the collection of personally identifiable information should be made known prior to operation and ... the individual should retain the ability to disengage the feature if he or she so chooses'.[48] Whilst some observers would contest such an absolute statement of the right of disengagement (and others might question the marginal utility of notification of all identifiable information about an individual without any initiative on the part of that individual) clearly the openness principle of the OECD guidelines is one of the weakest in the collection. The advent and potential of the Internet requires that there be new attention given to it.[49]

---

45 See OECD (1997) *Guidelines for Cryptography Policy*, which include eight principles relevant to this discussion. Principle 2 relates to users' rights to choose cryptographic methods. Principle 5 relates to the individual's rights to privacy including secrecy of communications and protection of personal data. OECD Doc:C(97) 62/FINAL. Cf J Adams, 'Encryption – The Next Big Thing?' (1998) *Computers and Law*, February, 39-40.

46 Greenleaf 'Privacy Principles' (1996) p 118.

47 Clarke (1994) p 129. See also R Clarke, 'Beyond "Fair Information Practices": A New Paradigm for 21st Century Privacy Protection', <http://www.anu.edu.au/people/Roger.Clarke/DV/BeyondFIP.html>.

48 Perritt and Lhulier (1997) p 899. See also Greenleaf 'Privacy and Cyberspace' (1996) p 92. Cf M Rotenberg, 'Privacy Protection – A US Perspective: Data Protection in the United States – A Rising Tide?' in (1998) 14(1) *Computer Law and Security Report* 38.

49 Davies (1995) p 38. The openness principle in the OECD guidelines states: 'There should be a general policy of openness about developments, practice and policies with respect to personal data. Means should be readily available of establishing the existence and nature of personal data, and the main purposes of their use as well as the identity and usual residence of the data controller'. The Australian Privacy Commissioner has issued National Principles for the Fair Handling of Personal Information which include an anonymity principle.

5. The role of national governments as the defenders of privacy and fundamental rights also needs careful consideration, given the past record of many governments as intruders into such fundamental rights.
6. One feature of Internet reporting is the intensification of the competition for getting the 'news' first. This puts great pressure upon modern journalistic standards. The kind of reporting which has intruded into the private lives of public personalities such as Diana, Princess of Wales, and President Clinton is, in part, a product of the new technology. No public figure is entitled to protection in relation to aspects of private life which may have relevance to public duties. But unless public figures can enjoy a private zone where their lawful family, sexual, relationship, health and other data belongs to *them* and is respected by others, the result is likely to be serious erosion of the quality of persons offering to serve.

A second generation of information privacy principles, in harmony with the development of the Internet, must be drawn up without delay. The Internet should develop in a way that is respectful of fundamental human rights and democratic governance. Its expansion should reflect global values and human diversity. This is a mighty challenge. Yet the Internet itself was conceived in the minds of human beings. It should be possible for humanity to devise and apply just rules for its operation.[50] As a step along the way, and after several false starts, the Australian government late in 1999 promised to introduce new federal privacy legislation to extend privacy principles to the private sector.[51] It remains to be seen whether the new laws attempt to update the old principles. And whether, by the time they are enacted, it will already be too late – the legislators finding, as *The Economist* has predicted, that privacy is already dead.[52]

50 B Phillips (Canadian Federal Privacy Commissioner) cited in France (1997) p 24.

51 See Attorney-General's Office, Press Release, 'Further Consultation on National Privacy Legislation', 30 November 1999.

52 *The Economist*, 1 May 1999, p 12. See also Wacks (1997) p 93.

Chapter 6

Same-Sex Relationships: Some Australian Legal Developments[1]

This speech was written for a conference on the legal recognition of same-sex partnerships held on 3 July 1999 at King's College School of Law of the University of London. In it, Michael Kirby reflects on the progress of homosexual law reform in Australia, both at the federal level and at the State level in New South Wales. He outlines some of the positive developments that are taking place in the areas of property relations, migration law, superannuation and employment benefits generally. However, he cautions that much remains to be done, and calls attention to the many legislative provisions that continue to discriminate on the basis of a person's sexuality. His simple but compelling argument is that there are no excuses for blind prejudice and unreasonable conduct towards homosexual citizens, and that it can only be in the interests of society to protect and promote stable and supportive relationships and mutual economic commitment.[2]

A Changing Legal Environment

A conference on legal recognition of same-sex partnerships could not, and would not, have happened even a few years ago. The attendance at such a conference of senior judges from a number of countries would have been unthinkable. Same-sex relationships were considered to be the outward manifestation of impermissible love. Such love, or at least the physical acts that gave it expression, were criminal in many countries. If caught, those involved would be heavily punished, even though their acts were those of consenting adults, performed in private. Needless to say,

---

1 This paper was first published in (1999) 19(1) *Australian Bar Review* 4 (Butterworths Australia).

2 In 1998 Michael Kirby included in his entry in *Who's Who in Australia* details of his relationship with his partner of 30 years, Johan van Vloten. Such information had not been previously published by *Who's Who*. This fact was noted by sections of the media in Australia in April-May 1999 with mixed reviews. See for example, P Akerman, '"P" Marks a Spot in History', *Daily Telegraph* (Sydney), 22 April 1999, p 11; 'Australia: A Non-Secret is Out', *The Canberra Times*, 22 April 1999, p 8; B Lane and L Slattery, 'Australia: Without Prejudice', *The Australian*, 20 April 1999, p 15.

such laws, whether enforced or not, led to the profound alienation of otherwise good citizens, to serious psychological disturbance when people struggled to alter their natural sexual orientation, to suicide, blackmail, police entrapment, hypocrisy and other horrors.

It is fitting that, as the modern criminalisation of homosexual conduct largely derived from the laws of England, and was copied faithfully throughout the British Empire, leadership in the direction of reform should eventually have come from the United Kingdom. The Wolfenden Report[3] in 1957, and the reform of the law that followed,[4] became a model for the nations of the Commonwealth.[5]

The Wolfenden reforms and their progeny responded to changes in community opinion about homosexual conduct. These changes, in turn, have influenced social attitudes towards people who are homosexual, bisexual or trans-gender in their sexual orientation. Once the lid of criminal punishment and social repression was lifted, people began to know their gay and lesbian fellow citizens. The realisation dawned that homosexual citizens have all the same human needs as the heterosexual majority. The need for human love, affection and companionship; for family relationships and friendships; for protection against irrational and unjustifiable discrimination; and for equality in all matters where distinctions cannot be morally and legally justified.

A measure of the continuing erosion of public opposition to legal change in this area, and of strong generational differences in attitudes to homosexuality, can be seen in a recent survey conducted in the United States.[6] Accepting that country as probably the most conservative on this subject amongst the Western democracies, what is notable in the comparison with the results of a similar survey conducted 30 years ago is the strong shift towards acceptance of the legalisation of homosexual relations (then 55 per cent; now 82 per cent) and the strong support amongst younger people for legalising homosexual relations. Similar surveys in other Western countries, including Australia, indicate identical and even stronger shifts in public opinion.

Significantly, the principal reason given in the American survey by those personally opposed to homosexuality was 'religious objections' (52 per cent). Yet even amongst the major religions in many Western

---

3 *Homosexual Offences and Prostitution*, Command paper 247, HMSO, 1957.

4 *Sexual Offences Act* 1967 (UK).

5 Unfortunately, some of the more autocratic societies within the Commonwealth have recently rediscovered the sodomy offences and utilised them against political critics.

6 'Opinions on Homosexuality', *Washington Post*, 26 December 1998, p A12. The survey was conducted by the *Washington Post*/Kayser Family Foundation/Harvard University.

countries, there has been a cautious shift to recognition of the need for change.[7] In Australia some thoughtful commentators within the Catholic Church (now the largest religious denomination in the country) have begun to talk about sexuality beyond the absurd proposition that would accept the fact of homosexuality but prohibit all of its physical and emotional manifestations. Thus Bishop Patrick Power in Canberra, Australia, has called for 'solidarity with the poor, the marginalised, the oppressed'.[8] He has said: '[There] is a very real difficulty for the Church in terms of its credibility in the wider community. Some members of the Church community and hierarchy appear to act quite cruelly towards people such as single parents, homosexuals, divorced and remarried couples, former priests and religious'.[9]

The advent of the Human Genome Project and the likelihood that, in many cases at least, sexual orientation is genetically determined, means that no longer does any informed person have an excuse for blind prejudice and unreasonable conduct towards gay men and lesbians. Sexual orientation is part of one's nature. What is unnatural are demands that people deny their sexuality or try to change it. An increasing number of citizens in virtually every Western democracy are coming inexorably to this realisation. Once people recognise the overwhelming commonalities of human experience, the alienation of homosexual citizens crumbles. Once they reflect upon the utter unreasonableness of insisting that homosexuals change their sexual orientation, or suppress and hide their emotions (something they could and would not demand of themselves), the irrational demand for legal sanctions tends to fade away. Once they know friends and family members who are gay, the hatred tends to melt.

In the wake of changing social attitudes inevitably come changes in laws; both statutes made by Parliaments and the common law made by judges. Virtually every jurisdiction of the common law is now facing diverse demands for the reconsideration of legal rules as they are invoked by homosexual litigants and other citizens who object to

---

7 Commentators on the Pope's visit to the United States in January 1999 remarked on the 'sharp generational polarisation' in the Church on issues such as homosexuality, premarital sex and the ordination of women priests. See G Niebuhr, 'In US Pontiff to look to the new generation', *International Herald Tribune*, 26 January 1999, p 2. For parallels between discrimination against women and against homosexuals, see MC Nussbaum (1998) *Sex and Social Justice*, Oxford University Press.

8 Citing *Instrumentum Laboris* #3. Bishop P Power (1998) 'Marginalised People: In Society and in the Church', address to the Oceania Synod of Bishops.

9 Ibid.

discrimination.[10] To some extent the standards of change have been set by regional bodies such as the European Court of Human Rights[11] and international bodies such as the United Nations Human Rights Committee.[12] In the past, litigants could not be found to prosecute these issues because of various inhibitions: the risk of criminal prosecution; the fear of social or professional stigmatisation; the desire to avoid shame to oneself or one's family. With the lifting of these inhibitions, courts and legislatures will face increasing demands that legal discriminations be removed and quickly. The game of shame is over. Reality and truth rule. Rationality and science chart the way of the future. The same thing happened earlier to laws and practices which discriminated on the grounds of race and gender. The same opposition was mooted in the name of religion, of nature and of reason. No one of value believes the myths of racial or gender inferiority anymore. There is no reason to believe that it will be different in respect of discrimination on the ground of sexuality.

The Australian Constitutional Setting

In order to understand Australian legal developments it is necessary to appreciate the nature of the Australian federation. The Constitution divides the law-making power between the Commonwealth (the federal polity) and the States. Generally speaking, as in the United States of America, if a legislative power is not expressly granted by the Constitution to the Federal Parliament, it remains with the States. The result of this arrangement, again speaking very generally, is that large areas of private law – and especially of criminal law – are left to State law-making. The Federal Parliament, outside the Territories where it enjoys plenary constitutional powers,[13] has tended to be concerned in

---

10 Sometimes litigants will be able to invoke a national charter of rights, as in Canada: *Egan v Canada* [1995] 2 SCR 513; *M v H* [1999] SCJ 23. See generally R Wintemute, 'Discrimination Against Same-Sex Couples: Sections 15(1) and 1 of the Charter, *Egan v Canada*' (1995) 74 *Canadian Bar Review* 682; R Wintemute, 'Sexual Orientation Discrimination As Sex Discrimination: Same-Sex Couples and the *Charter* in *Mossett*, *Egan* and *Layland*' (1994) 39 *McGill Law Journal* 427. Sometimes these cases will involve very large questions as in a case in New Zealand: *Quilter v Attorney-General* [1998] 1 NZLR 523. At other times they will involve technical legal issues such as the English case involving the construction of the *Rent Act*: *Fitzpatrick v Sterling Housing Association Ltd* [1999] 3 WLR 1113.

11 *Dudgeon v United Kingdom* (1981) 4 EHRR 149; *Norris v Republic of Ireland* (1988) 13 EHRR 186; *Modinos v Cyprus* (1993) 16 EHRR 485; *Lustig-Prean v United Kingdom* (unreported, European Court of Human Rights, 27 September 1999) (gays in the military).

12 *Toonen v Australia* (1994) 1 Int Hum Rts Reports 97 (No 3); reproduced in HJ Steiner and P Alston (1996) *International Human Rights in Context*, Clarendon, pp 545-548.

13 Australian Constitution, s 122.

matters of law-making with subjects of national application and in federally specified areas.

This general description must be modified by appreciation of three important developments which have gathered pace in recent decades. First, the Federal Parliament, encouraged by expansive decisions on the grants of federal constitutional power, has extended its legislation into areas which almost certainly were not expected to be regulated federally when the Constitution came into force in 1901. Thus, by the use of tax incentives, a large framework of federal legislation has recently been enacted governing the law of superannuation in Australia.[14]

Secondly, although Australia has neither a comprehensive constitutional charter of rights nor a statute-based guarantee of fundamental civil entitlements, much anti-discrimination legislation has been enacted, including at the federal level. Some of this has been supported by the federal power to make laws with respect to external affairs. International treaties to which Australia has subscribed have sometimes provided a means of supporting the constitutional validity of federal legislation outside traditional federal fields. It was in this way, in reliance upon Australia's obligations under the *International Covenant on Civil and Political Rights*, that the Federal Parliament enacted the *Human Rights (Sexual Conduct) Act* 1994 (Cth).[15]

Thirdly, over the past 20 years, there has been a rapid growth in the number and importance of federal courts and of federal jurisdiction in Australia. This has been, in part, a response to the general enlargement of federal law, the growth of the federal bureaucracy, the expansion of federal administrative law rights[16] and the need for effective judicial supervision to bring the rule of law into every corner of federal administration in Australia.

As well as the six Australian States, the two mainland Territories (the Northern Territory and the Australian Capital Territory) have been granted substantial self-government. Accordingly, outside the areas

14 *Attorney-General of the Commonwealth v Breckler* (1999) 73 ALJR 981.

15 That Act was adopted in response to the decision of the United Nations Human Rights Committee in *Toonen v Australia* (1994) 1 Int Hum Rts Reports 97 (No 3). That decision found that the sodomy laws of Tasmania, the sole Australian State then to retain such laws, imposed an arbitrary interference with Mr Toonen's privacy in respect of his adult, consensual, private sexual relationship with his partner. Following a decision of the High Court of Australia in favour of Mr Toonen and his partner (*Croome v Tasmania* (1997) 191 CLR 119), the Tasmanian Parliament repealed the offending provisions. It has since enacted non-discriminatory offences which make no distinction on the basis of sexuality.

16 *Administrative Appeals Tribunal Act* 1975 (Cth); *Administrative Decisions (Judicial Review) Act* 1977 (Cth).

regulated directly by federal law, there are eight significant legal jurisdictions. All have their own separate statutory regimes dealing with the vast array of private law matters, local administrative law and most matters of criminal law. It is beyond the scope of this essay to review the legislation in each of the eight sub-national Australian jurisdictions. This chapter therefore concentrates on New South Wales, which is the most populous State in Australia and on this subject, so far, the most progressive.

New South Wales Legislation

As in most jurisdictions which inherit statutes going back to much earlier colonial times, a large number of enactments of the New South Wales Parliament (some of them not so old) reflect discrimination against homosexual citizens. This has been called to notice by the Anti-Discrimination Board.[17] The examples are many and are found in every corner of the law – even unexpected corners. The *Stamp Duties Act* 1920 (NSW), for example, provides that, if a share of a jointly owned property is sold by one party in a heterosexual relationship following the end of that relationship and if so ordered by a court, the remaining partner may be exempted from paying stamp duty. There is no such entitlement to exemption for a same-sex partner. Similarly, the *Superannuation Act* 1916 (NSW) contains a definition of 'spouse' in relation to a death benefit which has the consequence that, where a contributor to a superannuation scheme or a pensioner dies leaving a partner who is not a legally recognised spouse, that person's estate will receive only a refund of contributions without interest. This leads to less favourable treatment for individuals in same-sex relationships and others who do not have a lawful 'spouse'.

The *Adoption of Children Act* 1965 (NSW) provides that a court may make an adoption order in favour of a married couple or, in certain circumstances, to a man and a woman in a de facto relationship. Such an order cannot be made in favour of persons in a same-sex relationship, whatever its duration and whatever the exceptional circumstances of the case. The *Evidence Act* 1995 (NSW) contains certain legal privileges in respect of opposite-sex couples which are not extended to same-sex partners.

The New South Wales Anti-Discrimination Board has repeatedly submitted to the State Parliament and government that State legislation needs to be changed to afford wider recognition to same-sex

---

17 *Equal Time*, February 1999, New South Wales Anti-Discrimination Board Newsletter.

relationships and to other persons in non-traditional and/or extended family relationships. Because of the growing numbers of persons in a variety of human relationships that fall outside the protection of the present law, reform of the law is urgently needed.[18]

Legislative Changes

As a background to what now follows, it is appropriate to say that such studies as have been conducted in Australia to sample the opinion of same-sex partners seems to indicate that the majority surveyed (80 per cent) do not consider that marriage or marriage equivalence, as such, is a priority.[19] However, those surveyed do want discriminatory laws removed and the provision of legal protections against discrimination. At least in New South Wales, the legislators are responding.

In 1998 the Same-Sex Relationships (Compassionate Circumstances) Bill was introduced into the New South Wales Parliament to meet what were described as 'urgent areas of need which relate to wills, family provision and hospital access' for same-sex partners.[20] The purpose of the Bill, a private member's measure, was to pick up on a commitment given by the State Premier to the President of the AIDS Council of New South Wales before the election in which his party was elected to government in 1995. That commitment was stated as follows:

> Labor is committed to reform of legislation around same-sex relationships so that same-sex partners have the same rights and responsibilities as heterosexual de factos when their partner is hospitalised or incapacitated. We will also ensure that same-sex partners are not discriminated against in the operation of the will and probate and family provisions.[21]

This measure was not enacted when the government cancelled the allocation of time to private members for the remainder of the parliamentary session. Several other private members' Bills on related

18 The Equal Opportunity Tribunal established by the *Anti-Discrimination Act* 1977 (NSW) is empowered to hear complaints in certain circumstances where a person claims to have suffered discrimination on the grounds of homosexuality.

19 S Sarantakos, 'Legal recognition of same-sex relationships' (1998) 23 *Alternative Law Journal* 222; S Sarantakos, 'Same-Sex Marriage: Which Way to Go?' (1994) 24 *Alternative Law Journal* 79. The basic ground of objection is usually that it attempts to impose, without modification, an imperfect heterosexual paradigm on a homosexual relationship.

20 C Moore MP (NSW), Media Release, 20 October 1998.

21 Letter from the Hon R Carr MP to the President, AIDS Council of NSW, 22 February 1995. See statement by C Moore MP in New South Wales Parliamentary Debates (Legislative Assembly) 22 October 1998, p 59.

topics also lapsed when the New South Wales Parliament was dissolved for a State election held in March 1999.

The new State Parliament which convened after the re-election of the government moved quickly to enact the *Property (Relationships) Legislation Amendment Act* 1999 (NSW). The debates over the Bill were notable for the enlightened views expressed by members of both Houses and both sides of politics. State Attorney-General JW Shaw stated:

> In an open and liberal society, there is no excuse for discrimination against individuals in our community based on their sexual preference. To deny couples in intimate and ongoing relationships within the gay and lesbian community the same rights as heterosexual de facto couples is clearly anomalous.[22]

A speech by a National Party member, representing a country electorate and a party sometimes described as conservative, was specially striking:

> Generally, they [people in same-sex relationships] have faced life, they have been through agonies and they, in a lot of instances, are probably far better adjusted than many married couples who are living in a state of acceptance by the community, the church, and the laws of this country.[23]

The legislation broadly assimilates same-sex partners within the *De Facto Relationships Act* 1984 (NSW) (which is renamed the *Property Relationships Act* – itself a sign of how common de facto relations of all kinds are in Australia today). The legislation also amends a multitude of State statutes to impose on same-sex couples the same obligations to disclose interests as would exist in the case of spouses. The thrust of the *Property Relationships Act*, as amended and renamed, is to allow for court orders adjusting property relations on the termination of a domestic relationship without discrimination on the basis of the sex of the partners. The rights affected include real and personal property rights, such as rights to succession on intestacy, taxes in relation to property transfers between partners, insurance contracts, protected estates, family provision (following inadequate testamentary provision) and, to a minor degree, State judges' pensions. Non-property rights are conferred in relation to human tissue and medical treatment decisions, participation in coronial inquests, decisions about bail for arrested persons, guardianship and mental health decisions, rights in retirement villages and accident compensation.

---

22 New South Wales Parliamentary Debates (Legislative Council) 13 May 1999, p 228; 26 May 1999, p 36.

23 See New South Wales Parliamentary Debates (Legislative Assembly), Mr R Turner MP, 1 June 1999, p 741. Subsequently the leader of the National Party was reported as predicting that there would be 'no more watering down of our opposition to indulgent and selfish gay rights laws': *Sydney Morning Herald*, 19 June 1999, p 11.

Areas acknowledged as still requiring attention include adoption, foster parenting and superannuation for State government employees. The New South Wales Legislative Council's Standing Committee on Social Issues has a reference from the New South Wales Parliament on relationships law reform. The Chair has called for submissions on the ways in which the *Property (Relationships) Legislation Amendment Act* does not sufficiently address concerns regarding residual discrimination against same-sex domestic partners under State law. Another matter on the list for the future may be the age of consent laws which, as in England,[24] discriminate between males (18 years) and females (16 years).[25]

With the exception of Queensland, no other Australian State government has so far followed the lead of New South Wales.[26] On a national level in Australia, the importance of the New South Wales developments should not be exaggerated. But self-evidently, they are welcome and symbolic. In a federation, reforms enacted in one jurisdiction tend, in time, to influence developments in others. Once it was South Australia that led the way in such matters (including anti-discrimination legislation). This time it is New South Wales.[27]

Changes in Federal Legislation

Migration Law

Under the Australian Constitution, one matter upon which the Federal Parliament enjoys legislative power is 'immigration and emigration'.[28] Since 1984, in part because of lobbying by the Gay and Lesbian

---

24 In April 1999, the House of Lords, for the second time, succeeded in postponing consideration of the Sexual Offences (Amendment) Bill 1999 (UK). This Bill was designed to remove discrimination from the age of consent in sexual offences.

25 A Bill to establish an equal age of consent for males and females in New South Wales was denied a second reading on 18 November 1999. See *Hansard*, NSW Legislative Council, pp 28-29.

26 In December 1999 the *Property Law Amendment Act* 1999 was passed by the Queensland Parliament. The Act gives those in de facto relationships the same rights as married couples regarding property and financial matters arising when the relationship breaks down. The law does not discriminate between heterosexual and same-sex de factos.

27 Even before the foregoing reforms were adopted legislation was enacted in New South Wales which provided an interesting model to afford protection to people in same-sex relationships. See the new definition of 'de facto relationship' added by Schedule 6 to the *Workers Compensation Legislation Amendment (Dust Diseases and Other Matters) Act* 1998 (NSW).

28 Australian Constitution, s 51(xxvii). The Federal Parliament enjoys legislative powers with respect to naturalisation and aliens (s 51(xix)) and external affairs (s 51(xxix)).

Immigration Task Force (GLITF), changes have been introduced into Australian migration law and practice which have expanded the rights of entry into Australia of persons in same-sex relationships.

The main breakthrough occurred in 1985 when regulations and practices were adopted which, to a very large extent, removed discrimination and provided for the consideration of applications for migration to Australia from same-sex partners largely (but not entirely) on an equal footing with those from opposite-sex couples.

Entry into Australia of non-residents is regulated by the *Migration Act* 1958 (Cth) and the regulations made under that Act. The regulations now provide for visa subclasses to permit the entry into Australia of people in 'inter-dependent' relationships.[29] The relevant visa classes permit migration to Australia of a person sponsored by his or her partner. The categories mirror those applying to persons seeking entry to Australia on the basis of a de facto heterosexual relationship.

The annual migration programme for Australia contains an allocated number of places available to persons in the 'inter-dependent' categories. By comparison to the total size of Australia's migration programme, the numbers are very small. For the financial year 1996-97, only 400 places were reserved for interdependency visas.

Some discrimination remains in migration law and practice. For both heterosexual de facto relationships and 'interdependent relationships', the partners must be able to prove a relationship of 12 months duration before being eligible to proceed with the application. In the case of heterosexual relationships, this precondition can be overcome, quite simply, by marriage. In those countries which still criminalise, prosecute or stigmatise persons who establish a same-sex household, proof of 12 months cohabitation might be difficult or even impossible.[30]

A second important omission from current immigration law is that of persons seeking either to migrate or enter Australia temporarily who cannot include in their application as members of their family unit (and thus bring with them) persons with whom they reside in their country of origin in a same-sex relationship. GLITF has made representations for the amendment of the law in this regard. However, the Minister has indicated that a same-sex partner of an applicant for immigration must apply for a visa in their own right if they wish to join their partner in Australia. A person in a same-sex relationship with an Australian citizen, permanent resident or eligible New Zealand citizen is able to apply for

---

29 This is the adjectival clause which has been adopted to describe same-sex partners.

30 Provision is made for waiver of this requirement in compelling circumstances.

an interdependency visa for migration to Australia, sponsored by the eligible partner.[31]

Notwithstanding these defects, it is clear that Australian migration law is comparatively enlightened on this subject. As yet, only a small handful of countries (the Netherlands, the Scandinavian nations, Australia, New Zealand and Canada) recognise same-sex relationships in any way for immigration purposes. Not until October 1997 did the United Kingdom Minister announce a 'concession' whereby at least some categories of unmarried relationships would be recognised for immigration purposes, including same-sex partners, a category formerly rejected.[32]

In the field of refugee law, Australia is a party to the *Convention Relating to the Status of Refugees*, which is incorporated into domestic law.[33] One of the categories of persons entitled to refugee status includes a person who 'owing to well-founded fear of being persecuted for reasons of … membership of a particular social group … is outside the country of his nationality and is unable or, owing to such fear, is unwilling to avail himself of the protection of that country'.[34] The possibility that in some countries homosexuals and others in same-sex relationships would be so categorised has been recognised in a number of decisions in Australia and the United Kingdom.[35] In Australia, for at least five years, both the Department of Immigration at the primary level and the Refugee Review Tribunal have granted refugee status to both male and female homosexuals who could establish a well-founded fear of persecution in their country of nationality.[36] Various difficulties can arise in such a case, however, because of views sometimes taken in the

31 GLITF (NSW) (1997) *Same-Sex Couple Discrimination for Independent and Business Visa Applications*, submission to the Australian Human Rights and Equal Opportunity Commission.

32 R Wintemute (1995) *Sexual Orientation and Human Rights*, Clarendon, pp 103-105; W Gryk (1998) 'The Recognition of Unmarried Relationships Under British Immigration Law – An Evolving Process?', presented at the International Bar Association Conference, September.

33 *Migration Act* 1958 (Cth), s 4(1).

34 As defined in the United Nations Convention, Art 1A(2).

35 Cf *Applicant A v Minister for Immigration and Multicultural Affairs* (1997) 190 CLR 225 at 304 (fn 296). See also *R v Immigration Appeal Tribunal; Ex parte Shah* [1999] 2 WLR 1015 at 1044 per Lord Millett: '[g]iven the hostility encountered by all homosexuals in such a society and the obvious problems the applicant would have in satisfying his tormenters of his own sexual abstinence, I doubt that the difficulty [of establishing that a fear of persecution was well founded] would be a real one'.

36 D Bitel (1998) 'Recognition of Same-sex Relationships in Australian Immigration Law', presented at the International Bar Association Conference, September, p 4 5.

Tribunal concerning the need for applicants to prove their sexual orientation and because of a paucity of information about the persecution of homosexuals in some countries.

Superannuation

As stated earlier, superannuation in Australia is now largely regulated by federal laws. In September 1997, the Senate Select Committee on Superannuation reported on the Parliamentary Contributory Superannuation Scheme and the Judges' Pension Scheme.[37] The Committee put forward 'as a general proposition' that persons without defined dependants (such as a spouse or eligible children) should have an entitlement under federal law to nominate a beneficiary so that they do not lose entirely the benefit of entitlements which would otherwise accrue to them were they in a recognised relationship. The Committee recognised that the present provisions were a 'discrimination against those ... not in a recognised relationship'.[38] The Committee held back from making a recommendation that provision should be made for the nomination of a dependant because of reconsideration of the current structure of the scheme established by the Act.[39] However, the Committee recommended that the rules under which the benefits were paid 'should be reviewed to ensure that they are in accordance with community standards'.[40]

A Bill designed to remove discrimination against same-sex couples in relation to superannuation has recently been introduced into the Federal Parliament by an opposition member.[41] In 1995, a similar measure was introduced into the Australian Senate by a Senator of the Australian Democrats party. It was referred to the Senate Legal and Constitutional References Committee. In December 1997, that Committee tabled a

---

37 Australian Parliament, Senate Select Committee on Superannuation (1997) *Parliamentary Contributory Superannuation Scheme and the Judges' Pensions Scheme*, 25th Report, Canberra.

38 Ibid, par 4.6.

39 Ibid, par 4.7.

40 Ibid, recommendation 4.1.

41 Superannuation (Entitlements of Same-Sex Couples) Bill 1998 (Cth). The member introducing the Bill gave the Second Reading Speech for the Bill on 7 June 1999. This means that the Bill will not lapse. But debate is adjourned until the government allows it to be brought forward for further debate and a vote. The speech followed shortly after a report of the Australian Human Rights and Equal Opportunity Commission *Superannuation Entitlements of Same Sex Couples* (June 1999) was tabled in the Federal Parliament by the Attorney-General. The Commission found that present Australian superannuation law was in breach of two international conventions to which Australia is a party, the *International Covenant on Civil and Political Rights* and the *ILO Discrimination (Employment and Occupation) Convention.*

report recommending that couples or partners should be protected by superannuation entitlements regardless of their sexuality or gender. Neither of these Bills has yet attracted the support of the Australian government.

However, the government has introduced the Superannuation Legislation (Commonwealth Employment) Repeal and Amendment (Consequential Provisions) Bill 1998 (Cth). The Bill proposes amendments to superannuation and like legislation to deal with a number of situations including that where an 'eligible person' who was party to a superannuation scheme dies without leaving a spouse or child to whom pension payments can be made. According to the Bill, in such a situation, there will be payable to the legal personal representative of the deceased person an amount equal to the total of the minimum amounts which the federal authorities would have had to contribute to a complying superannuation fund for the benefit of an 'eligible person'.

Other Employment Benefits

Discrimination in the field of superannuation and like benefits has become more noticeable as other federal legislation, and legislatively encouraged moves in Australia, have come to recognise and protect the employment benefits of persons whose employment is governed by federal law. Nowadays, it is much more common to consider a person's total employment 'package' rather than just their base salary. Where there is a significant difference between employees with respect to superannuation and other employment benefits, unconnected with professional performance and concerned only with an employee's private domestic arrangements, unjust discrimination can be seen in sharp relief.[42] Fortunately, politicians of most political alignments in Australia have begun to perceive the injustice which is caused by current superannuation and like laws in the case of persons living in stable same-sex relationships.[43]

Recently, an Australian Ambassador, presenting his credentials to the monarch of the country to which he was accredited by Australia, was

---

42 See D McCarthy, 'Superannuated', *Brother-Sister*, Issue 182, 15 April 1999, p 7.

43 C Pearson, 'Saving not such a super idea for same-sex couples', *Australian Financial Review*, 3 May 1999, p 19. Ms Leane Burke MP, for Prahran in the Victorian Parliament, proposed a motion which was adopted by the Victorian State conference of the Liberal Party of Australia. It urged the federal government to 'ensure same-sex partners are given equality of treatment with respect to superannuation payments as those given to opposite sex de facto partners'. See J McKenzie, 'Super Boost for Equality Campaign', *Brother-Sister*, Issue 182, 15 April 1999, p 3.

accompanied by his same-sex partner. Such relationships are legally recognised in that country where the action of the Ambassador would have been unremarkable. Yet the diplomat and his partner had to suffer the indignity of an Australian tabloid headline reducing his serious professional career to the insult: 'Three Queens in One Palace'.[44] It took more courage and honesty for the Ambassador to do as he did than to continue with pretence. It certainly took more courage and integrity than that exhibited by the anonymous by-line writer in the newspaper concerned.

It must be acknowledged that the Australian Department of Foreign Affairs and Trade has, in this respect, observed a non-discriminatory policy. The certified agreement adopted by the Department under the *Workplace Relations Act* 1996 (Cth) states:

> The conditions regarding the official recognition of de facto relationships for the purpose of the conditions of service apply regardless of sexual preferences.[45]

Similar statutory certified agreements have been adopted by other federal departments and agencies in Australia. In practice, this means that for most benefits of office (but not yet superannuation) same-sex partners enjoy similar employment benefits in the federal service in Australia. Thus, in the Australian foreign service, such benefits include airfares to and from a posting, the payment of supplementary living allowances as a couple whilst overseas, the payment of other incidental allowances on the same basis where an entitlement arises (eg clothing allowances) and the payment of health cover by the federal government for both partners during the posting.[46] These and other benefits are closely assimilated to those enjoyed by any other non-married de facto partner. The achievement of such entitlements and practices evidences a commitment by those responsible to the principle of non-discrimination in the matter of sexuality and federal public employment.

The Federal Parliament in respect of its own members and in some areas of its legislative responsibility, has begun to act. The executive government has quite properly moved, in respect of its officers, to abolish discrimination in employment benefits and to exercise its powers under delegated legislation in a non-discriminatory way. Even the federal

---

44 *Daily Telegraph* (Sydney), 26 February 1999, p 7.

45 Australia, Department of Foreign Affairs and Trade, Certified Agreement, 1998-2000.

46 It is necessary to have the relationship officially recognised by the relevant department before the partners proceed to the posting, by the provision of a statutory declaration with accompanying evidence.

judicature of Australia has begun to change its rules in respect of its affected members.[47] Further change is needed. In time, it will surely come.

The Journey of Enlightenment

There are other changes that are occurring in the statutory regimes governing the benefits of same-sex partners in Australia. The changes are occurring bit by bit and piece by piece. While the end of unfair discrimination has not yet been achieved, Australia, like other countries, is on a journey of enlightenment. It has taken important steps; but many more remain to be taken. It seems likely that progress towards the removal of discrimination will continue. Australians are a people committed to equal justice for all under the law and I have confidence that those who make the laws in Australia, will, in due course, eradicate unfair discrimination on the basis of sexuality. Injustice and irrational prejudice cannot survive the scrutiny of just men and women.

It can only be in the interests of society to protect stable and mutually supportive relationships and mutual economic commitment. It is against society's interests to penalise, disadvantage and discourage such relationships. Australia is coming to recognise this truth.

47 In September 1999 the Federal Attorney-General agreed that the same rules for domestic travel as apply to a judge's spouse should also apply to a nominated permanent partner of a judge. The *Judges Pension Act* 1968 (Cth) remains unreformed.

Chapter 7

HIV/AIDS: Anger, Hope and Love

On 19 May 1996 Michael Kirby spoke at the Candlelight Aids Memorial in Sydney in remembrance of those men, women and children who have been lost to the AIDS epidemic. His speech is a moving account of the various emotions experienced by those who are living with HIV/AIDS, their carers and their loved ones. Above all, he offers a message of hope and solidarity. He calls for action in the face of AIDS to remove discrimination against homosexuals and those who are HIV positive. He celebrates the determination of doctors, carers and educators fighting to uphold human dignity. Finally, he pleads for a lifting of the worldwide conspiracy of silence that has surrounded the epidemic for so long, especially in developing countries.

Light and Life

During my childhood, Australians celebrated Empire Day in late May. As the weather became cold and miserable, children would try to fend off the winter with a single night of fire and light. Bonfires were lit and not a few of them burned down neighbouring homes. Rockets were fired, to the great danger of all about. Roman candles and Catherine wheels lit the sky. It was dangerous; but it was exciting. Thousands of lights seemed somehow to lift our spirits. On the serious side, they reminded us that we were part of a worldwide family of nations. The ceremonies planted in my mind notions of solidarity and internationalism that have never left.

Now we gather together with candles and light for a different purpose. Would I have believed it if I had been told, back in 1950, that we would be here tonight for this purpose? That lights would be lit all over the world to cause us to reflect upon a common problem? It was easier in childhood days not to think about such serious things – or to look into the future. It was easier to live for the moment, staring into the lights and taking joy from the affirmation of existence that they offered.

We come together in the second decade of a most unexpected and horrible epidemic. It has taken away mothers, fathers, brothers, sisters, friends and lovers. We join together to share emotions. By our candles of light, we remember precious friends 'hid in death's dateless night'.[1] What are the emotions that we express by this act of affirmation, by candlelight?

Puzzlement

We feel a sense of astonishment that this unpredicted and unpredictable virus should have chosen our generations and our decades of existence to manifest itself on earth. Where did it come from? Did it jump the species? Is it truly out of Africa? Why now? Do any of these questions matter?

Each of us will remember the first time the acronym AIDS crept into our consciousness. For me it was in the early 1980s. At first it seemed a minor problem. But it spread like wildfire throughout the world. Now it threatens millions. Our puzzlement continues. What is nature getting at? Why does it choose the vectors of pleasure – the moment of sexual union when two people for an instant become one? The moment when a baby suckles at its mother's breast? Why does such an insidious visitor enter the body's portals at such a time of pleasure and sharing? AIDS is still a great puzzle and a mystery. But the reality of its manifestations soon brings us down to earth and requires us to face grim truths.

Anger

We feel angry that our generations, and these decades, have been chosen by this first truly global epidemic. The older ones remember the years of the 1970s, before HIV/AIDS. We remember a world which promised liberation, enlightenment and tolerance and then appeared to dash the cup from our hands: as if to laugh at such optimistic aspirations. We feel anger at the pain of loved ones. We feel anger at the loss of lovers, friends, colleagues, brothers and sisters. We feel anger at our own inadequacy in the face of grim news and hard times. We are ashamed of our human inclination to escape, fleeing the realities of this epidemic. We are angry with ourselves and with the world. Often we are angry with the very people who suffer most because we feel so helpless and inadequate in the face of their suffering.

1 W Shakespeare, *Sonnet 30*.

Frustration

We also feel frustration and rage. Frustration at the slow progress towards the cure which twentieth-century medicine has taught us to expect. Frustration at the lack of a vaccine to protect the young against the suffering we have seen. Rage at the expenditure on armaments and the trickle of the world's capital that is diverted to the scientific endeavour to cure or arrest HIV/AIDS. We ask ourselves: if there were truly a war on AIDS would not the funds be gathered to find a cure by the concentration of the best minds of humanity? The cure is taking too long. Funding is difficult. Sometimes it is even cut. The rage and anger we feel in Australia, where there has been much understanding and support, is nothing to the fury of frustration in the African village and the despair of the Caribbean slum. Occasionally the anger and rage boil over, even in middle-class Australia. People act up to demand greater commitment from their governments and fellow citizens. Fellow citizens watch. Some understand and share the anger and the rage. These are days of frustration and anger.

Hope

But in dark times there is also hope. It is human to hope. The marvellous achievements of our time in science and technology give us cause for hope. Already the primitive early responses to HIV/AIDS have given way to complex combinations of drugs and therapies. They can give real hope of a long-term delay to the feared onset of symptoms. Scientists at conferences express hopeful words about a vaccine within a decade. Others say, in hope, that AIDS will be like diabetes – not cured but controlled: its symptoms kept under check. We hope that the therapies will improve, and quickly. Our hopes are raised when we hear word of new drugs that will arrest the condition or palliate the suffering. We hope that no more precious friends will be lost. We hope that, with support from governments and people everywhere, the struggle against this epidemic, like earlier ones, will soon be won. We live in hope. It is our nature to do so.

Determination

We have determination not to give in in the face of AIDS. We continue the efforts to educate all about its danger. At least in some classrooms in Australia, we bring the message to schoolchildren in very candid and direct terms. At least in Australia, we have had the determination to break taboos and to educate younger generations about the danger of HIV/AIDS. Many of our politicians have had the determination to respond to a great human challenge. Our response was not perfect. But it was better than most.

We have determination to sustain the messages of prevention, for it is human to lapse. Knowledge is not a suit of armour against this insidious enemy. Sometimes love and trust can weaken the armour. It can allow the virus its chance, even in those that know.

We must have the determination to turn this epidemic into an occasion for the removal of all vestiges of discrimination that linger in the consciousness of humanity – even here in (mostly) enlightened Australia. We must turn it, with determination, to a movement for the removal of discrimination in laws and policies and attitudes. We must learn, with determination, that AIDS is a paradox. Paradoxically, the best way to fight HIV, and to command the minds of those who are most at risk, is to win their trust and confidence by laws and policies that protect their rights and uphold their human dignity. This means laws that protect the rights and uphold the dignity of gay men, of mothers who have seroconverted, of migrants with the virus, of injecting drug users, of sex workers, and of other vulnerable groups who need protection and support.

It is difficult sometimes to maintain determination. It is human to let it weaken and to question its demands. But we have maintained this determination for more than 15 years. And the battle is only just beginning. When we weaken in our determination we must think of dear friends who have shown us, by their determination, the dignity and courage that our entire society must come to display.

We celebrate the determination of the carers who go out to homes to tend the sick and clean for them. We honour the determination of doctors and nurses who, without a miracle cure or simple injection, have continued the noble struggle. We are determined to support the loved ones who have travelled the journey together. We are determined to reach out to those who have lost loved ones. Many are here with us tonight to show that the pain continues. But also there continues a determination to turn that pain to something positive.

Solidarity

Why have we come out on this May night when there are no bonfires or rockets or Catherine wheels but just our candles to light the way? We have come out in solidarity. To show that as citizens, we are together. We share the burden of this epidemic. We lead other citizens to realise that such suffering buys attention and it buys rights. We are here from every segment of the Australian community: men, women and children; married and unmarried; people who are positive and people who are not; gay men and lesbians; transsexuals, heterosexuals and bisexuals; Aboriginals and Torres Strait Islanders and Australians of the old Anglo-Celtic community, the newcomers and Australians of Asian descent; citizens and non-citizens; those with high constitutional offices and those with no jobs at all. With us are strangers from overseas who are strangers no longer. We must feel solidarity with the orphaned children in sub-Saharan Africa. We must reach out and help, with the lessons we have learned, gay men in India, sex workers in Cambodia, truck drivers in Zimbabwe, mothers in Morocco and drug users in Haiti. This epidemic knows no boundaries. In the face of it, humanity is one.

Love

But basically we are here because of love. We think of the precious friends we have lost. They come marching back in our minds, full of life and laughter, with human weaknesses and with much-loved qualities. Perhaps we know one who lived with this virus. Perhaps, like a rosary, we can list their names. For a moment they are back with us. Our candles light their way. Their departure was too soon. It was undeserved. We are here to affirm to each other and to the world that we love them. And we love those who battle every day against the virus. We rededicate ourselves to turn our love to practical support. Help to those in need. Sustenance to those who grieve. Education and reinforcement to those who are spared. Support for science and research. Reform of the law and of society so that all this suffering will not have been in vain.

Resolution

Let us, therefore, here resolve to take up the battle cry voiced by Dr Peter Piot, head of the United Nations Programme on HIV/AIDS (UNAIDS), at the Commission on Human Rights in Geneva:

> A conspiracy of silence continues to surround HIV/AIDS. This conspiracy keeps couples and communities unaware that HIV is in their midst. It allows governments to close their eyes to the urgency of action. It keeps HIV off agendas on which it should be. It fuels an 'us/them' mentality in which the uninfected deny the existence, the human value and the dignity of the infected.

We must break this silence. We must raise our voices to Australia and to the world to shatter the silence. All of us must lift our voices in solidarity with the 20 million people in the world who daily live with HIV/AIDS and the countless millions of their loved ones and carers, including those here in our community. Raise our voices! Lift the candles! Shine the light!

Chapter 8

Civil Liberties: Early Days and Days Ahead[1]

This chapter is adapted from an address at a reception given in honour of Michael Kirby by the New South Wales Council for Civil Liberties on 3 May 1996, following his appointment to the High Court of Australia. He speaks of his early involvement in civil rights issues as a member of the New South Wales Council for Civil Liberties. The CCL served as a valuable training ground for many young lawyers who went on to become prominent legal figures in Australia, fostering a life-long interest in human rights and the use of law to remedy injustices. He reflects upon the evolution of human rights in Australia since the early days of the CCL and on the continuing need to be vigilant against the erosion of civil liberties and alert to new challenges.

Early Days Remembered

In celebrating the work of the New South Wales Council for Civil Liberties (CCL), my mind goes back to my early, impressionable days as a young lawyer. I had the privilege then to work with many fine leaders of the legal profession who participated in the CCL's work. When the CCL was established, on the turn of the years 1964–65, it gathered together a group of fine citizens, by no means all of them lawyers, dedicated to the ideals of the rule of law, protection of human rights and respect for minorities. I was roped in. I think that this happened because, as a superannuated student politician of Sydney University, I had taken on the task of giving free legal representation to students who came into trouble with the law. My reputation as a pro bono 'easy touch' was naturally something that soon caught the vigilant attention of the founders of the CCL, ever avid for free legal assistance for worthy causes.

The minutes of those first meetings tell of the splendid men and women who took the initiative to establish the CCL. They included Dr John Hirshman, Mr (later Professor) Ken Buckley; and Miss Berenice Grainger who later married Ken Buckley. The Buckleys became a most

---

1 This paper was first published in the *Australian Journal of Forensic Science*, Vol 28 No 1, January-June 1996, pp 3-6. It also appeared in (1996) 34(10) *Law Society Journal* 44.

formidable duo of the CCL. Other members were Dr Dick Klugman, who served for a time in Federal Parliament; the late Maurice Isaacs; Robert St John, who later took Silk and became a Judge of the Federal Court of Australia; Jack Sweeney QC, later also a Judge of that Court; Mr Neville Wran, later a Silk and Premier of New South Wales; Marcel Pile QC, a true gentleman who became a District Court Judge; Mr Maurice Byers QC, later Sir Maurice and Solicitor-General of Australia; Mr Trevor Martin, that fine spirit of the law who was to become a District Court Judge and a philosophical mentor for the CCL; and Mr Colin Marks, solicitor. I also remember Jim Staples, who was to be a Deputy President of the Arbitration Commission and who was let down by the legal profession when his appointment was effectively terminated and judicial independence was challenged; and Gordon Johnson, who did so many cases for the cause of justice. Mary McNish is still playing a vital role in the CCL. The list of distinguished people does not stop there: Professor Ted Wheelwright of Sydney University; Mr Torre Sudano, later a District Court Judge; Dr Joan Child; Jim McClelland, later a federal Senator, Minister and Judge; Hal Wootten, whose remarkable career has spanned the Bar, the judiciary and academe; Mr Jeffrey Miles, now the Chief Justice of the Australian Capital Territory; and Caroline Simpson, now a Judge of the Supreme Court of New South Wales. My brother, David Kirby, also joined me at the CCL.[2] What a team of free spirits we were.

The meetings of the CCL were never boring. The problems were incessant. The challenges were great for they were very orthodox and rather unquestioning times. The cases were too numerous. The lawyers who would act without fee were limited in number but not in dedication. It was a lively, energetic, happy group with a real commitment to the rule of law and to ensuring that our society became a better and more tolerant place. Interestingly, the CCL had a variety of political and social outlooks. When a special call went out to leaders of the Bar to help in particular cases, they usually responded. This was the environment in which I learned the craft of lawyering. I learned it from fine lawyers, dedicated optimists and committed idealists. I will never forget that time. It was crucial to my professional and spiritual development.

The Cases

I took part as a solicitor in numerous cases that marked the early days of the CCL. They included the Flock Inquest into the death of a young man

---

2 David Kirby was appointed a Judge of the Supreme Court of New South Wales in 1998.

shot by the police.[3] Acting pro bono for the deceased's family, we summoned a coroner's jury – a rare event. Only the combined talents of Kevin Holland QC and Jim Staples saved me from the perils of misprision of felony after we had met in secret a young accused who had fled from the police gunfire.[4] Mr Holland, later a judge, warned me of my obligation to notify the authorities of our clandestine meeting. Had I not done so, I might have been behind bars and my grand career cut off in its infancy.

There was *Crowe v Graham*,[5] a case of a publisher of what was deemed an indecent publication (pictures of naked women and extracts from *Fanny Hill*) but was distinctly underwhelming by today's standards.

And then there was *Corbishley's Case*.[6] That case taught me many things. Mr Corbishley, an invalid pensioner, was charged with minor offences (damage to property and assault). He had the misfortune to come before Mr Locke SM whose terrifying reputation persists even to this day. Justice Holmes, in the Court of Appeal, said that it would need 'a Fielding or a Dickens to describe in words and a Hogarth to portray pictorially ... [w]hat happened that day'.[7] Mr Locke's court was an unusual place. But Mr Locke, convicting Mr Corbishley in a most unjust procedure, at least gave him a bond. In the endeavour to correct the magistrate's serious departures from due process, the Council for Civil Liberties authorised action. I, Mr Corbishley's solicitor, lodged both an appeal to the Quarter Sessions (as the District Court was for this purpose then called) and a statutory prohibition to the Supreme Court. The statutory prohibition on its own would have succeeded. Perhaps it should have succeeded anyway. But the Court of Appeal said that, an appeal having been lodged to the District Court, the matter should proceed there to the Quarter Sessions, where doubtless Mr Corbishley would receive justice. Prohibition to quash the convictions and bond was therefore, reluctantly, refused. It was Mr Corbishley's melancholy fortune to run into a District Court judge who conducted the trial scrupulously but then confirmed the conviction and actually increased the sentence. Without warning, he sentenced Mr Corbishley to three months imprisonment.

---

3 The details of the Flock Inquest are told in R Harding (1970) *Police Killings in Australia*, Penguin.

4 Misprision of felony is the concealment of a felony when the person knowing of it is bound in law to report to a justice or (now) to the police.

5 (1968) 121 CLR 375; [1967] 2 NSWR 207.

6 See *Ex parte Corbishley; Re Locke* (1967) 67 SR (NSW) 396; [1967] 2 NSWR 547.

7 [1967] 2 NSWR 547 at 549.

As I went out to Long Bay Gaol and looked at the baleful eyes of Mr Corbishley, I reflected on the capacity of the law, sometimes, to be blind to justice. Mr Corbishley asked how it was a possible that a man who had suffered, as he had, in a way that it would take 'a Fielding or a Dickens to describe in words and a Hogarth to portray pictorially', could actually suffer an increase in his sentence for having troubled to appeal to challenge such injustice. It was not a question I could easily answer. The case taught me that even conscientious lawyers, as I hope I was, can make mistakes of a procedural character. The law should cure procedural slips whenever it can. It should address its attention, whenever possible, to the central issue of justice under the law. The case also taught me of the need to have principles that would protect appellants against this form of double jeopardy.

I lay in wait for many years. My patience was almost saintly. But then, in *Parker v Director of Public Prosecutions*,[8] the Court of Appeal of New South Wales, of which by then I was President, had the opportunity. And I struck. The principle was established that in a District Court appeal, whenever the judge is contemplating an increase in sentence, and particularly the imposition of a custodial sentence which was not imposed by the magistrate, a warning must be given. This is to permit the appellant to seek leave to withdraw an appeal. That principle, which reflects a convention usually followed until (and after) *Corbishley* and universally followed by the best judges of the District Court, is now a rule of law. I have observed how the same rule has now been accepted in several jurisdictions of Australia copying *Parker*.[9] It shows that civil libertarians must have a long memory. They must display endless patience. But also resolution.

I would not wish the reader to think that I have saved up memories of other rank injustices over my professional life that I am merely waiting the chance to cure. But I have. And I will.

The Cause of Justice

In my swearing-in speech as the 40th Justice of the High Court of Australia, I naturally referred to the great judges and spirits of the law who had gone before.[10] I am proud indeed now to be a member of that Court. The High Court of Australia is one of the great courts of the

8 (1992) 28 NSWLR 282.

9 See *Brand v Parson* (1993) 68 A Crim R 147 (Vic Sup Ct).

10 'Swearing in and welcome speech – 6 February 1996' (1996) 70 *Australian Law Journal* 274.

common law world. When it has been most severely tested, as it was in 1951 in *Australian Communist Party v Commonwealth*,[11] the Court has generally taken a strong stand protective of basic civil rights. Its decision on that occasion was the more remarkable because, at the same time, in South Africa and in the United States of America, similar challenges were presented to the highest courts. Yet they did not defend the basic right of a person to believe, and to be, what he or she wished. I have always considered that the *Communist Party* case was one of the highest points in the history of the High Court of Australia. There have been others. There will be more.

But they have not all been high points. The 'good old days' were not so good in Australia if you happened to be an Aboriginal or a Torres Strait Islander. Nor were they so good if you happened to be a woman. Or gay. Or a conscientious objector. Or the publisher of the mildly erotic. Or a migrant struggling in court with the English language. Or an Asian Australian struggling against the then White Australia policy. These were the challenges that called forth the CCL. They rallied people of a like conviction about liberty and freedom under the law. There will be more such challenges in the future. It is essential that the courts and the CCL should continue to respond to them.

As I look back to 1964 and my early days in the CCL, I marvel at the prescience and dedication of the fine citizens who served in the CCL at that time. I have not named them all. But I honour them all, their memory and their fearless work. I honour them as mentors who taught me much about the law, about liberty and about life.

Yet at that time, in all of those intense and busy committee meetings of the CCL and cases fought, never once did anyone raise the human rights and civil liberties of homosexual, bisexual or transsexual Australians. It was just not on the agenda. No one discussed the issue. No one at that time saw it as an issue of human rights. And few indeed were those who saw the issue of women's rights as a civil libertarian question. Equal opportunity was just not on the agenda. Discrimination against women was not a subject of our discussions. Just a few people in those days had the foresight to look into the future and to see

11 (1951) 83 CLR 1. See M Kirby, 'HV Evatt, the Anti-Communist Referendum and Liberty in Australia' (1991) 7 *Australian Bar Review* 93; and G Winterton, 'The Significance of the Communist Party Case' (1992) 18 *Melbourne University Law Review* 630. The High Court found that the *Communist Party Dissolution Act* 1950 (Cth), enacted during the height of the Cold War by the generally conservative Menzies Government, was constitutionally invalid. The Act had declared the Australian Communist Party to be an unlawful association, dissolved it by force of the Act and imposed sanctions on persons who became or continued to be members of the party.

the importance of such topics. I pay tribute to the late Dr Peter Wilenski. He was my companion in student politics in the early 1960s. He saw issues of the rights of Asian Australians and the rights of women much more clearly than others. He talked of those issues and thereby taught others. In every generation we need such teachers.

The central question I want to pose is this. What are the issues that we today do not see but which in 20 or 30 years will be crucial questions for basic civil rights? Is the book of civil liberties closed? It hardly seems likely. In the future we may have the same enlightenment about personal use of drugs, about the rights of sex workers, about the liberties of people living with HIV/AIDS, about transsexuals – and about great issues of modern science and technology such as the Human Genome Project. We must keep our eyes and minds open for abuses of, and dangers to, civil liberties. Their character may change with the years. But they remain the challenges for the CCL and like organisations and the continuing justification for their existence.

The CCL contained many fine legal practitioners who fought the good fight to keep our society a pluralistic, tolerant one in which the laws made by the majority are upheld and the human dignity of minorities is also respected and protected by those laws. We can revere our legal institutions, as I do, but still ever strive to improve them. We can love our country, but still seek to make it a better place for all.

I pay tribute to the CCL for the work it has done. I have no doubt that its best years lie ahead.

Part II

THE LAW AND ITS INSTITUTIONS

In Part II, Michael Kirby reflects on the law and its institutions in Australia. He explores the lessons of the past and examines the challenges facing the judiciary, the legal profession and the Australian people now and in the future.

Chapters 9 to 11 explore the role and function of the judiciary. In Chapter 9, Michael Kirby considers the issue of judicial activism. He examines the debates and recent developments regarding judicial activism in the United Kingdom, the United States, Australia and India, concluding that the challenge for the modern judge is to 'find where the line lies in a particular case'. Chapter 10 traces the 'judicial metamorphosis' of Sir Anthony Mason during his service on the High Court, from the traditional approach of his early years to the judicial creativity which marked his period as Chief Justice. In Chapter 11, Michael Kirby explores the influence of Justice Lionel Murphy's ideas upon subsequent generations of Australian lawyers and judges. He believes that Justice Murphy's most enduring legacy lies in breaking the spell of the unquestioning acceptance of outdated legal rules.

In Chapter 12, Michael Kirby considers the issue of whether the source of constitutional authority in Australia is the Australian people themselves, and examines the implications of this realisation for the rights of the people and the role of the courts in defending those rights.

Chapters 13 and 14 look at the related issues of attacks on judges by the media, politicians and members of the legal profession, and judicial stress. Michael Kirby supports his contention that political and personal attacks on the judiciary are on the rise with numerous examples from the United Kingdom, New Zealand, Australia and the United States. He acknowledges that more attention to the role of the courts is healthy, but believes that some of the recent approaches in the media threaten judicial independence and raise the potential for undermining the judicial institution. Attacks on judges are just one of the many causes of judicial stress, discussed in Chapter 14. Isolation, lack of preparation for the judicial role, an unrealistic workload, rapidly changing technology – these are some of the other factors that contribute to the stress of judicial life.

In Chapter 15, Michael Kirby considers the ideals of the legal profession. He recognises that there are signs that the profession 'is in danger of losing its soul', but he maintains an optimistic outlook, encouraging the lawyers of the future to 'take the extra step', to show compassion and, above all, to recognise that nobility lies in the pursuit of justice within a framework of law and in helping others when they are in need.

Chapter 9

Judicial Activism[1]

Michael Kirby gave the Bar Association of India Lecture on 6 January 1997 in New Delhi. His lecture is concerned with the rejection of the declaratory theory of law, the growth of so-called 'judicial activism' and the desirability of using certain guideposts in the exercise of judicial choice. He examines the judiciary's response in the United Kingdom, the United States, Australia and India to the tension between activism and restraint. He finds that the debates about judicial activism are remarkably similar in all four countries. The challenge for modern judges, when looking to legal principle and policy to help solve a problem, is to 'find where the line lies in a particular case, at a particular time and place'.

Some Guideposts

In a recent lecture in Australia, I suggested that, with the decline of the declaratory theory, an important challenge before the judiciary was to try to find the guideposts which would ensure a principled and non idiosyncratic approach to judicial choice in particular cases. Commentators generally reacted adversely to this suggestion. They said that it was well meant but futile. A visiting Justice of the Supreme Court of the United States, Justice Stephen Breyer, was reported as saying that a 'bright line' between permissible and impermissible judicial creativity did not exist.[2]

Nevertheless, I consider that there are four guiding principles that may be useful to keep in the judicial mind as we approach the vexed problem of the opportunities and limits of judicial activism. They are opportunity, need, inclination and methodology.

Opportunity

There is a crucial difference between courts and legislators. It exists at the threshold of their respective activities. Courts do not choose their controversies. They do not entirely control the matters that they decide

---

1 Earlier versions of this paper were published in 'Judicial Activism' (1997) 27 *University of Western Australia Law Review* 1; (1997) 23 *Commonwealth Law Bulletin* 1224.

2 'US Judge Puts the Case for Judicial Activism', *Australian Financial Review*, 29 October 1996, p 4.

or the issues that they tackle. Many chance considerations affect the ascent of a controversy to a nation's highest court. These include the perception of the importance of an issue by the lawyers; a foolhardy willingness of the litigant to press on with appeals; and the availability of funding to permit all this to happen.[3] This point was made well by Justice SG Pollack in 'The Art of Judging':

> Artists begin with a creative impulse. Judges do not begin at all until someone starts a lawsuit. Even the most activist judges do not create causes of action, but must wait for someone else to start the process. Once the process begins, most judges depend on the adversary system to shape the case. The process is inherently rational and controlled.[4]

This truism has limitations. The courts may signal an issue. Some judges have suggested that a point will not be ripe for development of the law until such a signal is given. Some courts, including my own, can control the issues they deal with, to some extent, by the gateway of leave to appeal. The court can afford a welcoming environment for legal innovation or one that repels every attempt at change with a rebuff. The requirement to afford procedural fairness to the parties; the limits on the admission of the submissions of strangers to the litigation; and the abiding judicial obligation to provide reasons for decisions put a brake on purely idiosyncratic judicial change. This is why the history of the common law has tended to be one of incremental or interstitial change, made on notice,[5] rather than abrupt and revolutionary alteration. It should, in my view, continue in this tradition for that is the tradition of law as distinct from pure policy.

Need

Judges know, or ought to know, the limits on their legitimacy. Such limits derive from the fact that, at least in most countries, judges are not elected. True, they are appointed by elected officials. But they are only rendered accountable to elected legislatures for their office by the most extreme and exceptional power of removal.[6] Accordingly, judges must accept that their non-democratic office and their limited function puts a check on their creativity. Justice Stephen Breyer remarked that the

---

3 R Sackville, 'Continuity and Judicial Creativity - Some Observations', unpublished paper, October 1996, p 21; and D Dawson, 'Do Judges Make Law? Too Much?' (1996) 3 *Judicial Review* 1.

4 (1996) 71 *New York University Law Review* 591 at 593.

5 Patrick Devlin (1979) *The Judge*, Oxford University Press, p 11.

6 Australian Constitution s 72(ii); Indian Constitution s 124(4). See also *Sub-Committee on Judicial Accountability v Union of India* (1991) 4 SCC 699; and *Krishnaswami v Union of India* (1992) 4 SCC 605; and *S Ramaswami v Union of India* (1992) 4 SCC 506.

recognition of the 'undemocratic' nature of the judicial function was the single most important restraint on judicial activism.[7] By that I take him to mean that bold strokes, large leaps and complex, detailed reforms ought ordinarily to be left to parliaments. This is so in most cases for the simple reason that, if the people do not like what is done, they can render those who did it accountable. They can replace them with other lawmakers more to their own liking.[8]

Yet the difficulty with this oft-repeated theory of judicial deference to the elected legislature is that parliaments today all too often appear disinclined to attend to important issues of law reform. In part, this may be the result of the interaction of the media and legislatures. Issues must be simplified, even trivialised and, if possible, politicised. Unless they are part of the 'game' of politics, the needs of reform tend to be dismissed by many politicians on the unedifying basis that there are 'no votes in it'. Judicial assertions that a particular reform is up to Parliament ring rather hollow in the ears of the judges who hear them. I suspect that this is why, in recent decades, abhorring a vacuum in lawmaking, judges of the common law tradition have been more inclined than in the past to see particular areas as suitable for judicial development and reform. This is especially true of questions involving court procedures where the judges feel comfortable, know they have expertise and see the unjust results of unreformed laws and practices.[9] But it may extend to other areas of substantive law where the original rules were judge-made and where the judges of today have no real conviction that reform, if left to Parliament, will ever be seriously addressed. This may be a presumption on the judges' part. But if so, it is one born of long experience and frequent disappointments in the face of the urgencies of reform presented by societies undergoing rapid change.

Nevertheless, even in the face of clearly established need, a point will be reached where the judge should stay his or her hand. If the permanent values of the community are relatively clear and the issue is discrete and manageable, the judges may feel willing to do what predecessors in the judiciary have done and develop the law.[10] But in multi-cultural societies the 'permanent values' of the people are often hard to find.[11] These societies are also undergoing rapid social and

---

7 Breyer (1996) p 4.

8 JJ Doyle, 'Judicial Law-Making – Is Honesty the Best Policy?' (1995) 17 *Adelaide Law Review* 161 at 207.

9 *Halabi v Westpac Banking Corporation* (1989) 17 NSWLR 26 at 35-42.

10 Cf Brennan J in *Dietrich v The Queen* (1992) 177 CLR 292 at 322-324; cf Doyle (1995) p 199. See also *Wik Peoples v Queensland* (1996) 187 CLR 1 at 167-205 per Gummow J.

11 A Mason, 'Courts and Community Values' (1996) 6(9) *Eureka Street* 32.

economic change.[12] That change creates at once the urgent need for judicial activism and the obligation to restrain its largest temptations.

Inclination

The judiciary is the last empire of governmental individualism. Every judge is aware of the importance of certainty and predictability in the law, at least in those areas where the people's liberty or their major investments of capital and wealth are involved.[13] Judges vary in their inclination to develop or change the law. Some are by nature conservative; some activist; and some selectively evidence both tendencies at different times.[14] There are judges who have a large confidence in their own abilities to foresee the direction in which the 'river' of the law is flowing. If such confidence is combined with assurance that they can perceive the 'permanent values of [their] community'[15] and if they have great technical skills, much valuable reformist work may be done which is presented as a justifiable adaptation of underlying legal principles.[16]

Every judge, especially in the higher courts, nudges the law forward a little. Even judges whose inclinations are generally rule-based and whose personal predilections are conservative will occasionally strike a topic upon which the sense of justice in the particular facts moves them to do what judges of our tradition have been doing for 800 years. Nor is it appropriate to limit judicial creativity to the highest court. Necessarily, that court can accept only a small proportion of the important issues of legal principle and policy that confront the nation at any time. In Australia, the High Court has emphasised the need for the intermediate appellate courts to play their role in the development of legal doctrine.[17] Inevitably, this extends the opportunities for judicial creativity. Even dissenting judgments can play an important part in fostering new ideas and promoting the eventual emergence of new principles.

Methodology

In terms of day-to-day judging, the methodology of the common law judge also tends to impose a measure of restraint. The adversary trial limits most proceedings to a contest between particular parties who rarely, if ever, have an esoteric interest in legal developments. They just

12 Cf Doyle (1995) p 186.

13 Ibid, p 172.

14 Ibid, p 199.

15 Brennan J quoted in Doyle, ibid, p 199.

16 R Dworkin (1986) *Law's Empire*, Belknap Press, pp 243, 255.

17 *Nguyen v Nguyen* (1990) 169 CLR 245 at 268-270.

want to win the case. The stimulus to new legal authority must often come from the judge's own reading and perceptions stimulated by a sense of grave injustice. The adversary trial tends to limit the material available to the judge, particularly on the social and economic consequences of alternative solutions to the problem in hand.[18] In an often unformulated way, the judge will be conscious of the need to avoid large changes which would have wide economic and social ramifications. This is simply because these may not be wholly predictable.[19] Appeals to judicial commonsense are increasingly seen today to be suspect, given the comparatively narrow band of persons from whom the judiciary is typically drawn.

No established protocol exists for the introduction of important new legal principles by judges. Because appellate courts are ordinarily limited to the evidence adduced at a trial, some of them resist the admission of economic and social data that would help them to make correct policy choices, if that is their wish in a particular case.[20] Reading law books on the resolution of past cases will but rarely be a suitable preparation for a large leap of judicial creativity. If the role of judges in developing legal principle is to be recognised overtly and not secretly in whispers, it behoves courts to adopt a new protocol or methodology for the judicial function. This would identify the leeways for choice, invite the provision of appropriate information and materials on the social and economic consequences of the competing choices, and expand the opportunities for selected interest groups to be heard to assist the court to come to the preferable conclusion.

Yet all of this must be achieved within the framework of judge-like activity in a court disposing of real cases for real parties in a true dispute. Otherwise, courts will run the risk of expanding their procedures to take on the appearance of a legislative committee and enlarging their function beyond the disposal of the case before them by reference to legal norms. True, the norms may need to be expanded and adapted. But the judge is not a completely free agent. A measure of creativity is allowed. But it is a limited one. Its parameters are ultimately fixed by the very nature of the judicial function.

---

18 Doyle (1995) pp 172, 204.

19 Ibid, p 197.

20 Ibid, p 208. See *Attorney-General v Breckler* (1999) 73 ALJR 981 at 1004-1006.

Comparison of Debates in the United Kingdom, the United States, Australia and India

United Kingdom

The debate concerning the role of the judiciary has not, until lately, found many parallels in the United Kingdom. Doubtless this was because of the absence of a written constitution and the general judicial deference to Parliament and to the executive government, derived from the notion that the Sovereign in Parliament is the source of all power. However, in recent years, observers of the English scene will know that the judiciary has been taking a more active course. It has been striking down ministerial decisions on judicial review.[21] So vigorous has this process become that it caused a major debate in the House of Lords in June 1996, initiated by Lord Irvine of Lairg.[22] The noble Lord, now the Lord Chancellor of Great Britain, rose 'to call attention to the relationship between the judiciary, the legislature and the executive and the judicial participation in public controversy'. He said that there was:

> [U]nprecedented antagonism between the judges and the government both over judicial review of ministerial decisions and the restrictions which the government proposed on judicial discretion in sentencing. Certainly there have been a string of decisions striking down Ministerial actions as unlawful. That has even led to some conservative politicians calling judicial review itself into question. The public must be perplexed by what they perceive as a major clash over the distinct roles of parliament, ministers and the judges.[23]

The debate that ensued makes interesting reading for lawyers from countries such as the United States, Australia and India, brought up with a written Constitution, a federal system of government and constitutional procedures for judicial review. Lord Irvine cautioned:

> In exercising their powers of judicial review, the judges should never give grounds for the public to believe that they intend to reverse government policies which they dislike. That is why I regard as unwise observations off the Bench by eminent judges that the courts have reacted to the increase in the powers claimed by government by being more active themselves, and adding for good measure that this has become all the

---

21 See *Council of Civil Service Unions v Minister for Civil Service* [1985] 1 AC 374.

22 *Hansard*, House of Lords, 5 June 1996, p 1254.

23 Ibid. Note that the debate about activism extends to civil law countries. For a comment on the position in the Netherlands see M de Werd and R de Winter (1995) 'Judicial Activism in the Netherlands: Who Cares?' in R Bakker *et al* (eds) *Judicial Control: Comparative Essays on Judicial Review*, Metro, p 8.

> more important at a time of one-party government. It suggests to ordinary people ... judicial invasion of the legislature's turf.[24]

Lord Irvine went on to condemn extra-judicial statements by 'distinguished judges' who had suggested that 'in exceptional cases the courts may be entitled to hold invalid statutes duly passed by Parliament'.[25] To the noble Lord, brought up in the tradition of AV Dicey's constitutional theories about the absolute supremacy of Parliament, such judicial assertions were heretical and an anathema. Yet to us who live in federations under the rule of law, it is a regular feature of judicial and political life. Other Lords who participated in the United Kingdom debate noted that it was the growing openness of the judiciary that had led to the comments for which they were being taken to task. They hoped that the debate would not force judges back into reticence.[26] Lord Wilberforce, for example, acknowledged that there had been a period of 'enthusiastic expansion of judicial review since 1968'. However, he suggested that there were 'now signs of a rather more cautious attitude in the higher court'.[27] This passage, from one of the great judges of the century, suggested a perception of a need to quieten the fears of Parliament and to allow the expressed anxieties about judicial activism to blow over.

There is much agonising about the 'elective dictatorship' of the British system of government[28] and the differences between the judiciary in a country such as the United Kingdom and that of, say, the United States. Thus, Lord Simon of Glaisdale remarked:

> The first quality that is required of a judge [was expressed] when the eminent American judge and jurist Felix Frankfurter was asked about the three most important judicial qualities, he said, 'First, detachment; secondly, detachment; and thirdly, detachment'. Although I would certainly put detachment first, there is also room for intuition particularly by judges of instant jurisdiction, and for logical rigour, particularly on the part of appellate judges. However, I entirely agree that detachment must come first ... We must remember that every time a judge is called to conduct ... an inquiry, he is embroiled in a controversial issue and his detachment may be compromised. Indeed, the reputation for detachment of the judiciary as a whole may be compromised.[29]

---

24 *Hansard* (1996), p 1255.

25 Ibid.

26 Lord Rodgers, ibid, p 1264.

27 Ibid, p 1268.

28 Ibid, p 1276.

29 Ibid, p 1282.

I could go on with these citations from the United Kingdom debate. It was wound up by the then Lord Chancellor (Lord Mackay of Clashfern). He supported the view that judges have developed the law over the century and in so doing contributed not only to the development of the law but also to the protection of people's rights. But he went on:

> The extent to which that is permissible for them is not easy to formulate. I have seen various attempts in recent times to define the boundary between what is proper development and what is not. ... I find it difficult to enunciate what that boundary is. That can sometimes be seen in the difference of views between my colleagues as to whether that boundary has been passed. If the boundary were clear, one would not expect such a difference of opinion.[30]

Enough has been said, I hope, to show that the issue of judicial activism is very much a matter of controversy and debate in the country from which the common law has been derived. I suspect that the impact on that country of the external scrutiny of its law by the European Court of Justice and the European Court of Human Rights has afforded a healthy corrective to the insularity and self-satisfaction which have sometimes been features of English law in the past. Every legal system is improved by the scrutiny by friendly strangers of what is done and by a comparison of its systems with what goes on elsewhere. Because we of the common law enjoy a basically similar judicial institution, with functions to apply and interpret but also to develop the law, we necessarily share similar problems. It is, therefore, useful for us to examine other jurisdictions and to learn from each other's insights.

United States

In the United States of America, the tension between judicial activism and judicial restraint has been present since the foundation of the republic and the creation of the Supreme Court.

The history of the Supreme Court of the United States teaches that judicial activism is not confined to a particular ideological or social viewpoint. It may be liberal. But it may also be quite conservative. In the early years of the twentieth century, the 'judicial activists' on the Supreme Court of the United States impeded legislation enacted by the Congress, or the legislatures of the States, dealing with social or economic affairs. Thus legislation governing child labour, workers' hours and workers' rights was consistently struck down as being in violation of the commerce clause of the US Constitution or the judicially created doctrine of 'liberty

30 Ibid, p 1309.

of contract' under the due process clause of the 14th Amendment. A well-known example of this kind of judicial activism is the decision of the Supreme Court in *Lochner v New York*.[31] In that decision, the Court invalidated legislation of the State of New York regulating the hours that bakers could work. The Court held that this was a violation of 'liberty of contract'. These doctrines extended well into the 1930s. At one point they even threatened the New Deal programme of President FD Roosevelt. The 'judicial activists' were denounced by the President. He threatened to enlarge the Court to overcome their unpopular doctrines.

In more recent times it has been judicial activists of the liberal school who have attracted the ire of Presidents Nixon, Ford and Reagan. Many a political slogan was devised in the United States to attack what was seen as the 'adventurism' of the Supreme Court under Chief Justice Earl Warren. Yet it was during that time that the Court took many bold and courageous steps in the interpretation of the Constitution in matters such as school de-segregation, reapportionment of unequal congressional electorates, prohibition of school prayer, aid to parochial schools and restraints on police invasions of individual civil liberties.[32] The critics of this form of judicial activism complained that the Warren Court had promoted equality as the central doctrine of the United States Constitution at the expense of other values embedded in the Constitution and in society. The critics found most offensive the activist Justice's belief that 'progress called history would validate their course'.[33]

The appointment of new judges and the long service of Chief Justices wedded to judicial restraint (Chief Justice Burger and Chief Justice Rehnquist) changed somewhat the debate in the United States. The advocates of judicial restraint relied heavily upon the doctrine of the separation of the judicial from the legislative and executive powers under the Constitution. This is a feature not only of the United States Constitution but also of the Constitution of Australia[34] and, to some extent at least, of the Constitution of India.[35] Advocates of judicial restraint frequently suggest that the principle is grounded, conceptually, in the idea that each branch of government will stick to its own proper function. They point to the fact that courts are limited to decision-

---

31 198 US 45 (1905).

32 See A Bickel (1986) *The Least Dangerous Branch. The Supreme Court at the Bar of Politics*, Yale University Press.

33 Ibid, pp 13-14.

34 *R v Kirby; Ex parte Boilermakers' Society of Australia* (1956) 94 CLR 254. See also *Wilson v Minister for Aboriginal and Torres Strait Islander Affairs* (1996) 189 CLR 1.

35 *Ram Jawaya v State of Punjab* AIR (1955) SC 549 at 556; cf *Chandra Mohan v State of UP* AIR (1967) SCR 1987 at 1993; and VN Shukla (1996) *Constitution of India*, Eastern, p 50.

making in concrete cases and controversies according to standards already established by law. Courts are not entirely free agents. They should not decide a dispute if there is no concrete interest in the litigant to be relieved by judicial decision (standing). They should not decide a dispute if the conflict is contingent and may not become actual (timeliness). They should not decide a dispute if the conflict is purely theoretical or the controversy has passed (mootness). They should not ordinarily give merely legal opinions (advisory opinions) for it is the argument in a concrete dispute between parties which will refine decision-making apt to the functions of the judicial branch.

Each of the foregoing instruments of judicial restraint has come under consideration in common law countries in recent years. Each of them opens up large areas for legitimate differences of opinion amongst lawyers. Thus advocates for a broader standing rule and for a more relaxed approach to ripeness and mootness and the provision of judicial advice in appropriate cases point to the need for courts to be useful in the resolution of important controversies in society.[36] They argue that the delays and costs of litigation will ordinarily afford more than enough restraint to discourage mere busybodies and pure theoreticians from knocking on the doors of the courts.[37] In India, by the expansion of the law of standing, the courts have enhanced their utility to prevent infringements of fundamental rights. The practice of the Supreme Court of India of entertaining letters and telegrams addressed to the court or its judges as writ petitions, and in acting upon them, has naturally attracted criticism from some quarters.[38] On the other hand, it has often been the way by which the Court has transformed a purely theoretical right, and a hypothetical application of the rule of law, to the actual enforcement of the law in a way that brings justice under the law to many people.

Australia

For a long period the established doctrine of the courts of Australia was that expressed by Chief Justice Dixon in a passage known to every Australian lawyer and law student of my generation. Although stated in the context of constitutional interpretation, Sir Owen Dixon's words had a wider application. He said:

---

36 See *Levy v Victoria* (1996) 189 CLR 579 at 650-652; cf *Ram Jawaya v State of Punjab* AIR (1955) SC 549 at 600-605.

37 *North Ganalanja Aboriginal Corporation v Queensland* (1996) 185 CLR 595; *Truth About Motorways Pty Ltd v Macquarie Infrastructure Investment Management Limited* [2000] HCA 11.

38 See SJ Sorabjee (1996) 'Public Interest Litigation for Protection and Promotion of Human Rights: The Indian Experience' in *New Zealand Law Conference Proceedings*, p 48

> [C]lose adherence to legal reasoning is the only way to maintain the confidence of all parties in federal conflicts. It may be that the court is thought to be excessively legalistic. I should be sorry to think that it is anything else. There is no safer guide to judicial decisions in great conflict than a strict and complete legalism.[39]

In a later address to Yale University in 1955, Chief Justice Dixon accepted that judges do develop the law. But he was at pains to emphasise that it was a very limited function:

> It is one thing for a court to seek to extend the application of accepted principles to new cases or to reason for the more fundamental to settle legal principles to new conclusions or to decide that a category is not closed against unforeseen circumstances which might be subsumed thereunder but it was wrong for a judge … 'who is discontented with the result held to flow from a long accepted legal principle, deliberately to abandon the principle in the name of justice or of social necessity or of social convenience'.[40]

This was the doctrine in which I grew up in Australia. It was the purest version of judicial restraint. One of its most vivid applications came in a comment made by one of the finest judges of the High Court of Australia (Sir Frank Kitto) in a decision of the Court in 1967.[41] In response to a comment by another experienced judge (who later himself became a Justice of the Court, Sir Kenneth Jacobs), Justice Kitto remarked:

> I think it is a mistake to suppose that the case is concerned with 'changing social needs' or with 'a proposed new field of liability in negligence', or that it is to be decided by 'designing' a rule. And if I may be pardoned for saying so, to discuss the case in terms of 'judicial policy' and 'social expediency' is to introduce deleterious foreign matter into the water of the common law – in which, after all, we have no more than riparian rights.[42]

It is against the background of these exchanges that recent developments in the High Court of Australia and other Australian courts seem the more remarkable. This is not an occasion in which to review the whole range of innovative legal principles that have been stated by the High Court of Australia in the past decade. But they include,

39 'Swearing in of Sir Owen Dixon as Chief Justice' (1952) 85 CLR xi at xiv.

40 Sir Owen Dixon, 'Concerning Judicial Method' (1956) 26 *Australian Law Journal* 468 at 469-470.

41 *Rootes v Shelton* (1967) 116 CLR 383 at 386-387.

42 The comment was addressed to a remark by Jacobs JA in *Rootes v Shelton* (1966) 86 WN (NSW Pt 1) at 101-102. This case was concerned with the law of negligence in sport. See Doyle (1995) p 203.

importantly, rulings which have led to the ensuring of legal assistance in many cases in order to avoid unfair trial,[43] the exclusion of uncorroborated and unconfirmed police testimony to counteract a judicially perceived problem of unreliable confessions,[44] the over-ruling of the ancient doctrine that marriage was of itself a defence to the complaint by a wife of rape[45] and, most important of all, the reversing of nearly 150 years of decisional law in which it had been held that Australia was *terra nullius* when, on British settlement, sovereignty was acquired by the Crown. The Court concluded that Aboriginal and other indigenous peoples in Australia retained their 'native title' to land until it had been lawfully extinguished.[46]

In addition to these (and many more) general legal developments, extremely significant decisions of a constitutional character have also been handed down in recent years. Most controversial of these has been the discovery by the High Court of Australia of a new implied constitutional right, in certain circumstances, to protected free expression about political, economic and related topics.[47] This right, or some aspects of it, was re-argued before the Court in *Lange v Australian Broadcasting Corporation* and *Levy v Victoria*.[48] One of the reasons which was given for the Australian federal government's support of a reconsideration of the implied constitutional right was that:

> The role which the Court assumed for itself in these cases involves a fundamental shift in political responsibility from the Parliament to the High Court. Politically contentious issues are best handled by the Parliament as part of the political process and not by the Court.[49]

The Federal Attorney-General in the Howard government (Mr Daryl Williams QC) stated that the government would 'seek to reverse the trend towards an interventionist High Court'. It would seek to replace constitutional decision-making by the Court with effective legislation by Parliament. The Attorney-General was critical of the failure of successive Parliaments, Federal and State, to introduce reforms of defamation law.

43 *Dietrich v The Queen* (1992) 177 CLR 292.

44 *McKinney v The Queen* (1989) 171 CLR 468.

45 *The Queen v L* (1991) 174 CLR 379.

46 *Mabo v Queensland (No 2)* (1992) 175 CLR 1. See also *Wik Peoples v Queensland* (1996) 187 CLR 1.

47 *Australian Capital Television Pty Ltd v Commonwealth* (1992) 177 CLR 106.

48 (1997) 189 CLR 520; (1997) 189 CLR 579. Note the comment by Justice PN Bhagwati that 'the judiciary and the press are institutions pedestaled in fragile loneliness in the constitutions of most democratic functions'. See (1995) 4 *Centre for the Independence of Judges and Lawyers (CIJL) Yearbook* 43. He states that 'the independence of the press depends to a large extent on the vibrant activism of the judiciary'.

49 D Williams QC AG quoted in the *Courier Mail* (Brisbane), 14 November 1996, p 1.

He suggested that it was preferable that such reforms be made by the elected representatives of the people rather than by unelected judges.[50]

The initial occasion which gave rise to the application for the re-argument of the constitutional principle before the Court – which comprises seven Justices – was the retirement of two of the Justices who were in the majority which supported the extension of the constitutional 'right to free speech'. They were the former Chief Justice, Sir Anthony Mason, and the present Governor-General of Australia, Sir William Deane. They were replaced on the Court in 1995 and 1996 by Justice Gummow and myself. I therefore found myself faced with an almost daily barrage of verbal injunctions either to hold the line on constitutional free speech (voiced by the media) or to retreat to the proper role of judicial restraint (voiced by some politicians). It is worth citing one commentary by a senior academic then at a Sydney law school. Titled 'The Rise of the Hero Judge', Mr John Gava cautioned:

> The worst result of activism is that the judges may end up losing the public's faith in their most important attribute – the perception that they are impartial referees deciding according to the rule of law. Australia is wonderfully lucky in this regard. Of course our judges are human, with all the normal failings. But they do deserve their reputation for fairness and impartiality. Losing that would be a tragedy.
>
> To argue against judicial activism is not to make the mistake of believing that the judge's role especially in appellate tribunals like the High Court is anything other than creative. Of course it is. ... This does not, however, necessarily lead to activism. There is a world of difference between an attitude to choice which recognises and limits itself to incremental changes, tries to remain faithful to earlier decisions and appreciates that caution and restraint should be foremost in the judge's mind, and one which sees judging as an opportunity to act as a surrogate or replacement legislature and government. Or, as has been said, the impossibility of a completely sterile operating environment does not mean that surgeons should operate in sewers. Judicial activism should attract criticism, not hero worship.[51]

India

I have previously had cause to suggest that judges and lawyers in India and Australia should fashion new links with each other, no longer relying upon a common attention to the pronouncements of the English courts.[52] Although the detail of Indian jurisprudence is no more known

---

50 Ibid.

51 *Australian Financial Review*, 14 November 1996, p 21.

52 MD Kirby, 'India and Australia: A Neglected Legal Relationship and a Plan of Action', Address, New Delhi, India, 24 October 1996.

in Australia than that of Australia is known in India, there is a general understanding that the Supreme Court of India, and the High Courts in India under the leadership of the Supreme Court, have been particularly creative and imaginative in the development of the constitutional and common law. Sometimes, in my own decisions, I have drawn upon the jurisprudence of the Indian courts to sustain an advance in the exposition of the common law. I did so in a case involving the right of a person, affected by an administrative decision, to have reasons stated.[53] However, my decision in that respect was reversed in the High Court.[54] In other decisions, I have reached conclusions on matters of fundamental principle which, as I have later discovered, were similar to those reached by the Indian courts.[55] This has convinced me of the need to improve the flow of information between the two legal jurisdictions.

Those who trouble to examine the law of India carefully soon come to an understanding of the way in which the Supreme Court has, by a series of landmark judgments described by some as 'judicial activism', established basic principles designed to adapt the common law to the necessities of Indian society and its particular needs. I refer, in this regard, to decisions on such matters as the right to go abroad;[56] the right to privacy;[57] the right to protection against solitary confinement;[58] the right not to be held in fetters;[59] the right of an indigent person to have legal aid;[60] the right to speedy trial;[61] the right against handcuffing;[62] the right against custodial violence;[63] the right against public hanging;[64] the right, in certain circumstances, to medical assistance;[65] and the right in some cases to the provision of physical shelter.[66]

---

53 *Osmond v Public Service Board* [1984] 3 NSWLR 447.

54 *Public Service Board (NSW) v Osmond* (1986) 159 CLR 656 at 668.

55 *Ballina Shire Council v Ringland* (1994) 33 NSWLR 640; cf R *Rajagopal v State of Tamil Nadu* (1994) 6 FCC 632.

56 *Satwant Sing Sawhney v D Ramarathnan APO New Delhi* AIR (1967) SC 1836.

57 *Govind v State of MP* AIR (1975) SC 1378; (1975) *Cri LJ* 1111. Reliance was placed upon *Griswold v Connecticut* 381 US 479 (1965).

58 *Sunil Batra v Delhi Administration* AIR (1978) SC 1675; (1978) *Cri LJ* 1741.

59 *Shobraj v Supdt Central Jail* AIR (1978) SC 1514: (1978) *Cri LJ* 1534.

60 *MH Hoaskot v State of Maharashtra* AIR (1978) SC 1548: (1978) *Cri LJ* 1678.

61 *Hussainara Khatoon v Home Secretary, State of Bihar* AIR (1979) SC 1360: (1979) *Cri LJ* 1036.

62 *T Vatheeswaran v State of TN* AIR (1983) SC 361(2): (1983) *Cri LJ* 481.

63 *Sheela Barse v State of Maharashtra* AIR (1983) SC 378: (1983) *Cri LJ* 642.

64 *Attorney General of India v Lachma Devi* AIR (1986) SC 467: (1986) *Cri LJ* 364.

65 *Paramand Katra v Union of India* AIR (1989) SC 2039: (1990) *Cri LJ* 671.

66 *Shelter Shantistar Builders v NK Totame* AIR (1990) SC 630.

Within India, as in every other country, there are different views about judicial activism. Some judges, for example, find any variation from precedent an anathema and react with revulsion to the methodology and language of the judicial activist. For example, a distinguished Indian judge once wrote that 'perorations and sermons as also theses and philosophies (political or social) whether couched in flowery language or language that needs simplification, have ordinarily no proper place in judicial pronouncements'.[67]

As against such calls to restraint and under-statement, other Indian judges have deliberately invoked vivid language in order to make their legal points and to explain the reasons for their decisions in a way that will be understood by ordinary citizens (at least those who read the Court's opinions, either in English or in translations into indigenous languages). This was the way, for example, of Justice Krishna Iyer. It was he who wrote that there was 'no iron curtain' between the prisoners of India and the Constitution of India.[68] What he wrote was later taken up by other courts, including the Privy Council.[69] Perhaps it was that distinguished judge's experience, years earlier, of himself spending a night in prison, that galvanised him into a measure of 'activism' for the disadvantaged. Anxiety about social justice and a determination to remove discrimination on all irrational grounds has caused judges like Krishna Iyer to become exemplars of a kind of judicial activism that is often in tune with the deeply felt emotions of ordinary citizens. It is concerned about the rights of children. It is concerned about torture, cruel, inhuman and degrading treatment or punishment.[70] It is concerned about the struggle of citizens with the bureaucracy;[71] about debtors in the grip of penury;[72] and the rights of trade unionists and industrial workers.

I can think of no other final court of the common law that has gone so far as the Supreme Court of India did in *SP Gupta v Union of India.*[73] It there unanimously ruled that where judicial redress is sought for legal injury to a person, or a determinate class of persons who, by reason of poverty, helplessness, social or economically disadvantaged position or

67 VD Thuljapurkar J in *Manohar Rao Nath v Marod Rao* (1979) SCC (4) 93.

68 *Sunhil Patra v Delhi Administration* AIR (1978) SC 1675(I); AIR (1980) SC 1579 (II).

69 *Riley v Attorney General of Jamaica* [1983] AC 719 at 734.

70 *Raghubu Singh v State of Harayana* (1980) SC 1087 at 1088.

71 *Maneka Gandhi v Union of India* AIR (1978) SC 597.

72 *Jolly George Varghese v Bank of Ceylon* AIR (1980) SC 470.

73 1981 (Supp) SCC 87.

disability are unable to approach the Court for relief, any member of the public, acting bona fide and not for oblique considerations, may maintain an action on their behalf. Such a person may seek judicial redress for the legal wrong or injury caused to such other person or determinate class of persons.

Perhaps the special needs of India have propelled its courts into radical refashioning of the instruments of the common law and re-conceptualisation of the role of a modern judiciary in a free society. Soli Sorabjee has pointed out that:

> [I]ndignant critics forget that it is the Executive's failure to perform its duty and the notorious tardiness of legislatures that impels judicial activism and provides its motivation and legitimacy. When gross violations of human rights are brought to its notice, the judiciary cannot procrastinate. It must respond.[74]

However, to some critics, this is an unconvincing defence of judicial activism. In India, from the highest level of the judiciary, there has been a recognition that excessive or ill-judged activism may damage the very institution which gives birth to it. Thus Chief Justice Ahmadi suggested that the phenomenon of judicial activism, evident in contemporary India, may be a temporary phenomenon, responding to the peculiar needs of the nation at the time.[75] Into a vacuum left by the failure of the other branches of government to respond to urgent legal and social needs, the courts have sometimes stepped.

Conclusion

The modern judge of the common law, in India, Australia and far beyond, is controlled in any excessive temptations to activism. The judge's boldest ambitions are held in check by opportunity, need, the inclination of most and the judicial method.[76] Of judges, the community expects detachment, honesty, integrity and learning. Increasingly, it also expects efficiency, timeliness and attention to case management. Prejudice and partiality have no place in the judicial function. The people have a right to expect the judge to be independent, professional and neutral.[77]

---

74 Sorabjee (1996) p 48.

75 AM Ahmadi (1996) *Zakir Hussain Memorial Lecture* (unpublished paper).

76 FG Brennan, 'The Judicial Method' (1996) 8 *Judicial Officers' Bulletin* (NSW) 73.

77 R Cooke, 'The Courts and Public Controversy' (1985) 5 *Otago Law Review* 357 at 356.

Society is slowly and somewhat reluctantly coming to realise the 'fairytale' of the declaratory theory of the judicial function. But there is no clear divide that marks off the limits of acceptable judicial creativity and activism. Informed observers have come to understand that some measure of judicial activism is not only permissible but is traditional in our system of law. Moreover, it is beneficial to the noble cause of justice under the law. The challenge for modern judges is to find where the line lies in a particular case, at a particular time and place. Each judge knows that limits exist. Most would agree with the remarks of Justice Anthony Kennedy, of the United States Supreme Court, that a society that leaves all or most of its hardest decisions to the courts is a weak society.[78] The burdens which society casts on its judges are greater today than ever before. We, the judges, are the servants of the law and of our societies. We must continue to find the sources of our discipline in legal authority. But when new problems arise, when the common law has no exactly analogous decision or when (as is so often the case) the Constitution or the legislation is ambiguous, we must also look to legal principle and legal policy.

Judges do not usually have the privilege to decline the obligation of decision. Sometimes we will err, for that is inherent in the human condition. But if we search for the solution to the particular case with the illumination of legal authority, legal principle and legal policy and are sometimes called 'judicial activists', we must accept that label with fortitude. Our activism has limits as every one of us knows. But in a real sense the common law itself is the product of judicial activists. The most we can hope is that we are successors, worthy in our time, to the great spirits who have preceded us.

Let me finish with the words of one of the finest of those spirits, Oliver Wendell Holmes Jr. Nearing his 60th birthday, and unaware that he was shortly to be elevated from Chief Justice of Massachusetts to the Supreme Court of the United States, Holmes said:

> I ask myself, what is there to show for this half lifetime that has passed? I look into my book in which I keep a docket of the decisions of the full court which falls to me to write, and find about a thousand cases. A thousand cases, many of them upon trifling or transitory matters, to represent nearly a half a lifetime. A thousand cases when one would have liked to study to the bottom and say his say on every question which the law has presented ... I often imagine Shakespeare or Napoleon summing himself up and thinking: 'Yes, I have written 5,000 lines of solid gold and a good deal of padding – I, who would have covered the Milky Way with

78 J Rosen, 'The Agoniser', *New Yorker*, 11 November 1996, p 90.

> words that outshone the stars'. We are lucky enough if we can give a sample of our best and if in our hearts we can feel that it has been nobly done.[79]

May each of us, lawyer and judge, evidence the same humility and aspire to the same noble contribution as that great jurist made to the living law.

79 Cited in JH Wootten, 'Creativity in the Law' (1972) 4 *Australian Journal of Forensic Sciences* 107 at 118.

Chapter 10

The Mason High Court: A Study of Change in Judicial Technique[1]

The following text is an abridged version of a speech given by Michael Kirby to the Melbourne University Law Students' Society on 6 September 1996, originally entitled 'Sir Anthony Mason Lecture 1996: AF Mason – From *Trigwell* to *Teoh*'. In this speech, he traces the recent evolution of the High Court of Australia and its jurisprudence by examining Justice Mason's development as a Justice and then as Chief Justice. According to Michael Kirby, Justice Mason's changing judicial technique cannot be explained simply by reference to personal factors. Instead, his 'judicial metamorphosis' came about largely because of changes to Australian society associated with a growing sense of independent nationhood, and institutional and cultural changes within the judiciary and court system itself. An understanding of these changes is a crucial tool in any analysis of the High Court of Australia today.

A Judicial Metamorphosis

Sir Anthony Mason participated in a significant period of change in Australia's federal supreme court. I wish to pose a question as to how this change came about under the leadership of a man who had earlier been extremely cautious about the role of an Australian appellate judge in relation to the alteration of settled principles of the common law or of established constitutional and statutory construction. The question that I pose is not an exercise in amateur psychology. It is a question that is not intended to be entirely personal to Sir Anthony Mason – every human being changes and develops during his or her lifetime. It would be remarkable if we were so impervious to personal, professional and social conditions as to be completely unaffected by them. It is rather a question directed at our judicial institutions, the people who inhabit them and their capacity to develop and change during their years in office.

1 This paper was first published in its original format as 'Sir Anthony Mason Lecture 1996: AF Mason – From *Trigwell* to *Teoh*' (1996) 20 *Melbourne University Law Review* 1087.

Something certainly happened between Sir Anthony Mason's early decisions in the High Court and those for which his period as Chief Justice is celebrated. In *State Government Insurance Commission v Trigwell*,[2] Justice Mason applied a 1947 House of Lords decision, itself based on ancient case law, that land owners were under no liability in negligence or nuisance for the escape of their animals onto the highway.[3] The Court rebuffed the suggestion that the rule, fashioned by the English courts concerning liability for animals, was either unsuitable to Australian conditions (and so not received into Australian law) or, if it were, that it should be overruled as inappropriate to the different circumstances of Australia. Justice Mason appealed to the political doctrine that judges apply the law, with relatively little scope to change it. He concluded that change, especially major change, must be left to Parliament.[4]

However, in later cases, such as *Papatonakis v Australian Telecommunications Commission*[5] and *Bryan v Maloney*,[6] Justice Mason embraced a new conceptualisation of the law of negligence. In the place of rules expressed in the English courts there was a heightened sensitivity to the need to establish and express rules of negligence suitable for the rather different social conditions of Australia. There are many other examples of the change in judicial technique that occurred between the appointment of Sir Anthony Mason to the High Court on 7 August 1972 and his retirement on 20 April 1995.[7] What occurred to occasion this judicial metamorphosis? In my opinion, there are at least ten institutional reasons for the change, many of which are based upon broader developments in Australian society.

---

2 (1979) 142 CLR 617. See J Doyle (1996) 'Implications of Judicial Law-Making' in C Saunders (ed) *Courts of Final Jurisdiction - The Mason Court in Australia*, Federation Press, pp 84-90, where the author refers also to *Gala v Prescott* (1991) 172 CLR 243 at 255.

3 *Searle v Wallbank* [1947] AC 341.

4 *State Government Insurance Commission v Trigwell* (1979) 142 CLR 617 at 633.

5 (1985) 156 CLR 7 at 16-20. See also *Australian Safeway Stores Pty Ltd v Zaluzna* (1987) 162 CLR 479 at 481-488 with Wilson, Deane and Dawson JJ.

6 (1995) 182 CLR 609 at 615 with Deane and Gaudron JJ. See also *Burnie Port Authority v General Jones Pty Ltd* (1994) 179 CLR 520 at 526, with Deane, Dawson, Toohey and Gaudron JJ.

7 Compare *McInnis v The Queen* (1979) 143 CLR 575 with *Dietrich v The Queen* (1992) 177 CLR 292; *Dugan v Mirror Newspapers Ltd* (1978) 142 CLR 583 with *McKinney v The Queen* (1991) 171 CLR 468; and *Miller v TCN Channel 9 Pty Ltd* (1986) 161 CLR 556 with *Australian Capital Television Pty Ltd v Commonwealth (No 2)* (1992) 177 CLR 106.

The Reasons for Change

Constitutional Trinity

The early Mason years were served during the Chief Justiceship of Sir Garfield Barwick. Chief Justice Barwick did not retire until February 1981. Whilst he sat on the Barwick court, Justice Mason's silence in court was legendary. Barwick was a dominant figure in any courtroom. He was an exponent of the power of human will, strongly directed. It is said that, with the move of the High Court to its permanent seat in Canberra, Chief Justice Barwick endeavoured to persuade the Justices to participate in more formal conferences over cases than had previously been their practice. This is, after all, the settled practice of the great federal court upon which the High Court of Australia was modelled, the Supreme Court of the United States of America.[8] But Barwick's attempts did not succeed.[9] Independent and (almost) equally opinionated colleagues resisted.

Nevertheless, the power of Chief Justice Barwick's influence, and his disapprobation of heterodox legal approaches, appeared to have had an impact upon Justice Mason in those early years. As counsel, he had appeared in Barwick's Court as Solicitor-General for the Commonwealth. He knew the power of the man and of the other Justices about him. All of the Justices enjoyed, before the constitutional amendment in 1977, life tenure. So indeed did Mason under his commission as a Justice. This assured the very long service of the Justices. It resulted in relatively little turnover in the Court's membership. It was into this world that the new Justice, after a short period of service on the New South Wales Court of Appeal, came to the High Court at a relatively young age.

There is an irony in the power of Barwick's will. Its chief enduring legacy, so far as the High Court is concerned, lay in his persuasion of successive governments that they should establish a permanent home for the Court in Canberra and place it, where it now stands, on Lake Burley Griffin. The irony is this. Whilst the High Court, and the mostly elderly gentlemen who constituted it, moved around Australia in regular contact with the judiciary and the Bar in the scattered communities of the Commonwealth, their self-image was, I think, very largely that of circuit judges after the traditions of the working courts whom they supervised. But when the Court was moved to its permanent home in Canberra and

---

8 BJ Cooper (1995) *Battles on the Bench – Conflict Inside the Supreme Court*, University of Kansas, pp 91-110.

9 GE Barwick (1995) *A Radical Tory – Reflections and Recollections*, Federation Press, pp 249, 251.

placed so obviously in the constitutional triangle, with its close physical relationship to the Parliament and to the offices of the executive government, a new and powerful symbolism was established.

The role of the Court as the constitutional court of Australia was made plain in its earliest years under the brilliant Chief Justiceship of Sir Samuel Griffith. But, for the most part, they were years of strict and complete legalism when, to some extent at least, constitutional interpretation was seen as closely related to the function (and therefore needing only the techniques) of statutory interpretation generally. Once the Justices of the High Court could see, so visibly and physically, that their Court was inescapably part of the trinity of the governmental organs of the country, a new national vision of the Court was likely to follow. I have little doubt that Chief Justice Mason's outlook on his role as a Justice and Chief Justice would have been deepened and strengthened by the move of the seat of the High Court of Australia to Canberra. It reinforced some of the other factors to which I will refer.

Colleagues

Next I would cite the impact on Justice Mason of the colleagues with whom he worked. Although he jested at Murphy's notion of implied constitutional rights,[10] the very jest betrays, perhaps, a depth of feeling that needed to be voiced in a strong and dismissive way because of a lurking sentiment that ultimately revealed itself in the free speech cases. Justice Mason would probably, to this day, reject the notion that Lionel Murphy's writing had greatly influenced him. They were two very different personalities. Their judicial styles were very different. Their techniques of opinion writing were quite distinct. But the fact is that Murphy's ideas became a catalyst for all of the Justices. More than his individual opinions, or his manner of writing them, his legal nationalism, proneness to question received English authority and fascination with the text and implications of the Constitution came to influence the other members of the Court.[11]

Perhaps of more direct impact on Justice Mason's intellectual evolution was the appointment of Justice Deane on 25 June 1982. He replaced Sir Ninian Stephen when the latter retired to become Governor-General. Justice Deane was also a product of the Sydney Bar. His considerable intellect was deployed in some of the very areas where Justice Mason was an acknowledged expert – particularly in the fields of

10 *Miller v TCN Channel Nine Proprietary Ltd* (1986) 161 CLR 556 at 579.

11 See Kirby, Chapter 11.

equity, trusts, intellectual property and the growing notions of unjust enrichment. Sir William Deane's creative intellect undoubtedly revived and stimulated the intellectual perceptions of Justice Mason. By co-operation and competition it stimulated him into patterns of judicial thought which became most evident in his writing on cases raising issues on fair dealing and good faith.[12] It spilled over into cases in the field of public law, including the expanding concept of procedural fairness.[13]

Justice Deane arrived at the High Court a year after Sir Garfield Barwick's departure. It was at about that time that the opinions of Justice Mason began to take on a new character, less hidebound by past doctrine. It was Justice Deane, in *Fay v Ocean Sun Line Special Shipping Company*,[14] who expressed succinctly the function of a judge of an ultimate appellate court in approaching a case before the Court. The primary duty of any judge in a society governed by the rule of law is the application of legal authority. But often legal authority is unclear. The Constitution or the statute may be ambiguous. The presented cases may not be readily stretched by the tools of analogical reasoning to afford a solution to the case in hand. Then, the judge in the tradition of the English legal system may call in aid legal policy and legal principle. If Lionel Murphy's techniques were somewhat uncongenial to the practised Mason, those of Sir William Deane were more appealing. They invited his concurrence and stimulated his further professional development.

The End of Privy Council Appeals

By the time that Justice Mason was serving his early days on the High Court, there was little opportunity for appeal from his decisions.[15] However, he had grown up in a legal and judicial world in which the superintendence of the Privy Council was an everyday reality. There may have been relatively few cases in fact. On the whole, the contribution of the Privy Council (outside constitutional issues, for federalism is rarely understood by Englishmen) was, in my view, beneficial. It rescued the

12 I Renard (1996) 'Fair Dealing and Good Faith' in C Saunders (ed) *Courts of Final Jurisdiction – The Mason Court in Australia*, Federation Press, p 63.

13 RA Finkelstein (1996) 'Procedural Fairness' in C Saunders (ed) *Courts of Final Jurisdiction – The Mason Court in Australia*, Federation Press, p 47.

14 (1988) 165 CLR 195 at 252.

15 Appeals to the Privy Council from the High Court of Australia had concluded with the passage of the *Privy Council (Limitation of Appeals) Act* 1968 (Cth) and *Privy Council (Appeals from the High Court) Act* 1975 (Cth). All that was left was the anomalous vestige of appeals as expressly provided in s 74 on constitutional questions *inter se* the constitutional powers of the Commonwealth and of the States. The High Court has made it plain that no such certificates will again be granted. The provision is now regarded as spent: *Kirmani v Captain Cook Cruises Pty Ltd (No 2)* (1985) 159 CLR 461.

Australian judiciary and legal profession from the risk of provincialism. But the existence of appellate superintendence provides an impetus towards caution. Those who are supervised must always keep in the back of their minds, at least, the possibility that their opinions will be reviewed, reversed or adversely remarked upon.

Whilst they survived, the existence of Privy Council appeals from Australia tied the jurisprudence of the High Court to the jurisprudence of the appellate courts of England. This was not only for fear of reversal. It was also because the Privy Council, overwhelmingly an English court, was still part of the Australian judicial hierarchy. Thus the books of the English judicial decisions were on the shelves of every judge and virtually every advocate in Australia. The English Court of Appeal was '*the* Court of Appeal'. Shifts and turns in English jurisprudence were felt far away in the courthouses of Australia. So long as an alternative avenue of appeal to the Privy Council remained, even if not by way of appeal from the High Court, that distinguished imperial tribunal retained its power to influence Australian legal decisions. Complete intellectual freedom of the Australian judiciary could not occur. At least in theory the Privy Council could criticise, distinguish and not follow decisions of the High Court of Australia.[16]

With the passage of the *Australia Act* 1986 (Cth) and its State and United Kingdom counterparts, Privy Council appeals ended forever.[17] The High Court of Australia was no longer in any way, directly or indirectly, answerable to a court of judges sitting in Whitehall. Sir Anthony Mason became the first Chief Justice of Australia who was not appointed to the Privy Council. He never took a seat on that tribunal before the appeals finally ended. The result was the development of a judicial attitude that could no longer be discouraged by the constraints of Privy Council jurisprudence.

Independent Nationhood

Coinciding with the foregoing developments, there occurred during Sir Anthony Mason's service on the High Court an imperceptible but distinct growth in the Australian sense of nationhood and independence. This included intellectual independence in the law. Strangely enough, I

16 In fact the Privy Council had long recognised and respected the right of the Australian High Court to take its own direction in a particular branch of the law. See *Geelong Harbour Trust Commissioners v Gibbs Bright and Co Ltd* [1974] AC 810; and (1974) 129 CLR 576. See now *Invercargill City Council v Hamlin* [1996] AC 624 at 642, 648.

17 *Australia Act* 1986 (Cth), s 11(1). The very last appeal from an Australian court was one from a decision I gave in the New South Wales Court of Appeal: see *Austin v Keele* (1987) 61 ALJR 605; 10 NSWLR 283 (PC).

think the rather low-key celebration of the bicentennial of British sovereignty in 1988 afforded a watershed: contributing to a reflection on where Australia had come from and where it was going. The mood coincided with a growing realisation that the political rhetoric of Australia's independence was true and that the challenge of the nation's future (as well as its opportunities) lay in Asia, the Pacific and the Indian Ocean regions that surround Australia. The notion of Australia as a country of Oceania, as distinct from as a nation of transplanted settlers from Northern Europe, began to affect the approach to the law of the nation's highest court.

The perception of national unity can be seen in the decision of the Court in *Street v Queensland Bar Association.*[18] But it was also to be found in the instruction that the High Court gave on the use to be made of foreign court decisions. In *Cook v Cook*[19] it was made clear, even for slow or reluctant learners, that no Australian court was to regard itself as bound by the legal holdings of any court in England, however distinguished, with the possible exception of the Privy Council during the period that it was part of the Australian judicial hierarchy. In *Nguyen v Nguyen*,[20] the High Court emphasised the reality that it could not hear appeals from the Full Federal Court or from the State Courts of Appeal or Full Courts, even in all of the cases which were interesting or important. Those courts were given a charter, and reminded, to play their own role in the development of Australia's law. In *Australian Securities Commission v Marlborough Gold Mines Ltd*,[21] the Federal, State and Territory courts from which appeals lay to the High Court were encouraged to search, wherever possible, for harmony in their construction of federal or uniform laws.

These messages were clear and confident. They emanated from a Court with a fresh vision of the nation it served and a clearer understanding of the opportunities and limitations upon it at the apex of the Australian judicial hierarchy. They portray a Court repositioning itself in its relationship with the Australian courts system following the end of the formal link with the English judiciary. These moves involved Chief Justice Mason. They reinforced his notion of his own role and that of the other Justices of the High Court in a new national and judicial environment.

---

18 (1989) 168 CLR 461.

19 (1986) 162 CLR 376. See also *Taikato v The Queen* (1996) 186 CLR 454 at 484-485 per Kirby J.

20 (1990) 167 CLR 245.

21 (1993) 177 CLR 485.

Special Leave

The introduction of the procedure for special leave to appeal to the High Court also profoundly affected the mix of business in the Court.[22] According to Mr David Jackson QC, a barrister of great experience in such matters, writing in the book of essays to celebrate Chief Justice Mason's service:

> The fact that for the first time the High Court was the only possible final court of appeal in all cases, taken with the fact that the exercise of all appellate jurisdiction had come to require the grant of special leave, meant that the Mason Court was operating under a charter significantly different from those of its predecessors.[23]

Gone was the obligation to deal with the large workload of original jurisdiction, with tax and patent cases. Gone also were the many tax appeals, testamentary cases and the range of public and private law matters that can be found throughout the early volumes of the *Commonwealth Law Reports*. The change was imperative if the High Court was to cope with the flow of appeals and applications coming to it. But it inevitably meant that the 'docket', as the United States judges call it, changed significantly. The Court would henceforth choose the cases it would hear and it would do so from a growing number of applications.

Virtually all of the cases that are chosen involve finely balanced issues where there are powerful arguments for both sides. Quite frequently they are expressed in the majority and minority opinions of the court under appeal. But the result of the faculty of choice has been an increase in the number of cases involving the Constitution, the interpretation of federal Acts, public law and, interestingly, criminal law. It was really during the service of Sir Harry Gibbs as Chief Justice that the growing involvement of the High Court in criminal cases expanded. This may not originally have been a development especially congenial to Justice Mason, with his background in the law far from the criminal courts. But he warmed to the task. He brought to it, in his later service, a strong sense of procedural fairness. He also brought a practical determination to ensure that compliance with the requirements of justice went beyond words and was translated into clear protective action where

---

22 *Judiciary Act* 1903 (Cth), ss 35 and 35AA; *Federal Court of Australia Act* 1976 (Cth), ss 24 and 33; *Family Law Act* 1975 (Cth), s 95; and *Industrial Relations Act* 1988 (Cth), s 432, repealed by the *Workplace Relations and Other Legislation Amendment Act* 1996 (Cth) (see now *Federal Court of Australia Act* 1976 (Cth), s 33) See also D Jackson (1996) 'The Role of the Chief Justice: A View from the Bar' in C Saunders (ed) *Courts of Final Jurisdiction – The Mason Court in Australia*, Federation Press, p 22.

23 Jackson, ibid, p 21.

that was necessary. The decision in *McKinney v Commonwealth*,[24] and the way its principles were made known to the legal and judicial community in Australia, is a good illustration of this.

Submissions

Another change which came upon the Court, and which flowed from the special leave system, was the introduction of strict time limits upon oral argument in special leave applications and effective time limits upon such argument in other cases, as by the requirement of written submissions. When the time for oral argument was limited, it became imperative for counsel appearing before the High Court to go as quickly and economically as possible to the heart of the matter. This has a tendency to encourage the identification of the issues of legal principle and legal policy which will attract the interest (and therefore the special leave) which the applicant seeks or which the respondent opposes. This is not to say that, during Chief Justice Mason's time, consideration of judicial policy was allowed to obscure the dividing point between the role of the Court as a judicial organ of government and the role of politicians on the hustings.[25] But with new techniques came a new willingness on the part of the judges to address, in the short time available, not only the authority that was available to assist on the point but also the broader arguments that tended to advance, or impede, the success of the application.

Judicial Choice

Chief Justice Mason's service also coincided with the decline and fall of the declaratory theory of the judicial function in Australia. His own professional career was as a child of that theory which every law student then learned. In 1972, Lord Reid had declared it to be a 'fairy story'.[26] But it still had many adherents in Australia, long after it was rejected as a fiction elsewhere. Two features of his life rescued Justice Mason from a

---

24 (1991) 171 CLR 468. *McKinney* established the principle that a jury in a criminal trial should be instructed by the judge to give 'careful consideration as to the dangers involved in convicting an accused person in circumstances where the only (or substantially the only) basis for finding that guilt has been established beyond reasonable doubt is a confessional statement allegedly made whilst in police custody, the making of which is not reliably corroborated' (at 476). See *Savvas v R* (1991) 55 A Crim R 241 at 289-290.

25 FG Brennan (1996) 'A Tribute to Sir Anthony Mason' in C Saunders (ed) *Courts of Final Jurisdiction – The Mason Court in Australia*, Federation Press, p 13.

26 Lord Reid, 'The Judge as Law-Maker' (1972) *Journal of the Society of Public Teachers of Law* 22 at 22.

blind faith in the declaratory theory. The first was that, as a student, he had been taught by Professor Julius Stone in the Law School of the University of Sydney. Like Justice Deane and many other contemporaries, as well as those appointed since, he was influenced by Stone's exposition of appellate decision-making.[27] He was affected by the explanation of the leeways for choice which present themselves to judges, especially in the highest courts. Whereas this would probably have been regarded as heresy in the High Court which Justice Mason joined, it became much closer to the accepted reality in the Court which he left as Chief Justice.

The other element in Sir Anthony Mason's life, apart from critical self-analysis, which made him open to Stone's view of the function of appellate judges, was his profound acquaintance with the jurisprudence of the Chancery Courts in England and the doctrines of equity in Australia. In a foreword to Professor Patrick Parkinson's *The Principles of Equity*,[28] Sir Anthony wrote of the way that 'the broad concepts' and 'discretionary remedies' of equity were able to adjust to the different demands and conditions of modern society. He went on:

> Indeed, much of the work of the High Court of Australia in recent years exhibits the historical characteristics of equity. As the authors point out, equity judges were not subscribers to the quaint common law fiction that the rules of law have survived from time immemorial and that judges merely find and declare the pre-existing law. We are reminded of Sir George Jessel's salutary reminder in *Re Hallett's Estate* (1879) 13 Ch D 696 that equitable doctrines and principles were 'established from time to time, altered, improved and refined from time to time'. Why the paramountcy of equity over the common law, established by the *Judicature Act*, did not prevail also in this matter of how principles of law came to be shaped, continues to astonish me.[29]

There is quite a contrast between these remarks and his earlier comments in *Trigwell*. It shows that beneath the surface was an intellectual doubt about the fiction upon which the declaratory theory rested. Once that doubt began to be shared by an increasing number of judges,[30] both in the High Court and elsewhere, its demise followed quickly. Its passing

---

27 MD Kirby, 'Julius Stone and the High Court of Australia' (1997) 20 *University of New South Wales Law Journal* 239.

28 (1996) Law Book Company, p x.

29 Ibid, p x.

30 MH McHugh, "The Law-making Function of the Judicial Process – Part I' (1988) 62 *Australian Law Journal* 15; and 'The Law-making Function of the Judicial Process – Part II' (1988) 62 *Australian Law Journal* 116.

helps to explain the open-mindedness and some, at least, of the judicial creativity which so marked Justice Mason's period as Chief Justice.

Parliamentary Disillusionment

It will be noted that, in *Trigwell*, Justice Mason expressed the conventional view that a legal development of the kind there proposed could and should be left to Parliament. However, this was clearly not a view that he held with the same conviction at the end of his judicial service. What happened? In part, I think the explanation must be that, over the years, Justice Mason came to see this view as yet another fiction that should not be erected, unjustifiably, in the path of legal justice. A period observing the Australian judicial and parliamentary scene – particularly from close hand when the Court moved to Canberra – would convince even the doctrinaire that the idea that Parliament can be relied upon to make all of the necessary amendments to private law is as fictional as the notion that judges do not make law and never have. Or that the High Court itself can repair every mistake or injustice that occurs within the Australian judicial hierarchy.

In fact, our system of justice, inherited from England, is a brilliant symbiosis between the formal mechanisms of lawmaking and the incremental lawmaking entrusted (amongst others) to the judges. This is a trust that has come with the Constitution and with the great system of law and justice which the Constitution affirms. If the judges never made law how, it was later asked by Sir Anthony Mason, did the 40 volumes of *Halsbury's Laws of England* come about?[31]

But something else happened. It was the advance of general education and heightened expectations of justice in the community. The community is now much less willing to accept judicial decisions, even of the High Court of Australia, abjectly with resignation and without criticism. There was always a measure of criticism. But it was nowhere as robust as has become in recent times. The same may be true of the institution of Parliament where there is even greater public disillusionment. As to the courts, on his retirement, Chief Justice Mason said:

> I would add one comment, echoing [Canadian Supreme Court] Justice McLachlin's remarks, that the community today expects just and principled outcomes from court decisions. The community is uneasy with the notion that the courts are somehow concerned with law, but not with justice.[32]

---

31 AF Mason (1996) 'A Reply' in C Saunders (ed) *Courts of Final Jurisdiction – The Mason Court in Australia*, Federation Press, p 115.

32 Ibid.

Clearly arriving at this conclusion, both of community expectations and of parliamentary incapacity to deliver them, encouraged Chief Justice Mason along the path of judicial creativity that marked his last years of judicial service.

Outreach

As Chief Justice, Sir Anthony Mason reached out to the community as no predecessor had done. His curiosity and inclination took him to countless conferences to which he contributed a vast range of papers on legal, judicial and associated themes. He became familiar to, and more comfortable with, the media than any of his predecessors. Most of them had ignored the media completely or regarded journalists as enemies of the High Court. All of this brought Chief Justice Mason into contact with community opinion in a way that an isolated life in the citadel on Lake Burley Griffin would not ordinarily allow. He heard at close hand scholarly and community criticism of the law, of its ways and of its results. I have no doubt that this exposure to the bracing sentiments of fellow citizens, whilst not perhaps influencing particular decisions, readied the mind of a most experienced judge to accept new ideas.

It probably also encouraged in him a feeling about the central importance of freedom of expression which can be seen in the free speech cases[33] in particular but which were evident in his earlier decision in *Commonwealth v John Fairfax and Sons Ltd.*[34] The potentiality of the later cases can be seen in several of the earlier decisions. The intellectual foundation to push forward the law of fiduciary obligations, of contract, tort and administrative fairness can also be found in his earlier professional experience. Thus it was as Mr AF Mason QC, Solicitor-General, that he persuaded Federal Attorney-General Nigel Bowen to establish the Commonwealth Administrative Review Committee. This led ultimately to the remarkable statutory reforms found in the new federal administrative law. I think it was Sir Anthony Mason's ascendancy as Chief Justice and the increased contact he then had with the outside world that freed him from some of the constraints which he had earlier felt. It allowed him to express views which, if he previously held them, he had largely kept to himself.

---

33 *Australian Capital Television v Commonwealth* (1992) 175 CLR 1; *Theophanous v Herald and Weekly Times Ltd* (1994) 182 CLR 104; and *Stephens v West Australian Newspapers Ltd* (1994) 182 CLR 211.

34 (1980) 147 CLR 39. Cf *John Fairfax Publications Pty Ltd v Doe* (1994) 37 NSWLR 81 at 100 and comment by J Miller, '*John Fairfax Publishing Pty Ltd v Doe*' (1996) 20 *Criminal Law Journal* 288.

International Links

Beyond Australia, as Chief Justice, Sir Anthony Mason took part in Commonwealth judicial and law conferences. Although a seat on the Privy Council was denied to him by historical developments, he had always been interested in international law. During his service as Solicitor-General for the Commonwealth he had taken part, as that office-holder usually does, in many international meetings, including of the United Nations Commission on Trade Law (UNICTRAL). His familiarity with international law and his sympathy for the inevitable changes that are necessary to secure the adjustments between Australian municipal law and international law can be seen in his decisions in *Tasmania v Commonwealth* (the *Tasmanian Dams Case*)[35] and also in *Teoh*,[36] the latter of which he wrote with Justice Deane.

Teoh was the writing of judges at the end of their service as the most senior of their country's highest court. It was the writing of judges who, instead of looking backwards nostalgically, were looking forward to some of the challenges facing Australian law in the century ahead. Sir Anthony took the same type of approach in *Mabo v Queensland (No 2)*[37] where Justice Brennan (with his concurrence and that of Justice McHugh) gave the clearest exposition to that date of the inevitable impact which Australia's adherence to international human rights treaties would have on the development of Australian law.[38]

The foregoing considerations may not wholly explain the change that occurred in the perception by Justice Mason of his judicial function as a Justice of the High Court of Australia. That there was a change seems clear by contrasting not only the results of early decisions with those that came later but also by comparing the judicial technique found in *Trigwell* with the exposition of so many leading decisions in later years.[39] The early decisions and expositions are entirely orthodox reflections of Sir Owen Dixon's 'strict and complete legalism'. In the

---

35 (1983) 158 CLR 1.

36 *Minister for Immigration and Ethnic Affairs v Teoh* (1995) 183 CLR 273. The majority of the High Court held that entry into a treaty by Australia creates a 'legitimate expectation' that an administrative decision-maker will act in accordance with the terms of the treaty, even where those terms have not been incorporated into Australian law. Thus procedural fairness required that the person affected by a decision inconsistent with such a legitimate expectation be given notice and adequate opportunity to put arguments on the point. However, a legitimate expectation cannot arise where there is statutory or executive indication to the contrary.

37 (1992) 175 CLR 1 at 120ff.

38 Ibid, at 42.

39 See AF Mason, 'The Use and Abuse of Precedent' (1988) 4 *Australian Bar Review* 93 at 106, 111.

later decisions and in their methodology of reasoning, Sir Anthony Mason had launched out on a new path. In doing so, he has instituted certain changes which, I believe, cannot and will not be reversed. He pointed in the direction of further changes that it will fall to others to continue.

The Future

Let me identify some of the changes which came about during Chief Justice Mason's service which seem unlikely to be reversed.

Australian Character

The High Court of Australia is now a distinctly Australian institution. A separate Australian jurisprudence was a natural direction for the Court at the head of the third branch of government in a wholly independent country. The judicial wigs and robes of the English tradition have been replaced by a simple robe, variously described as business-like and austere. Quite apart from these external symbols, Chief Justice Mason and other Justices of the High Court have embraced the principle that the people of Australia are ultimately the legal foundation for the legitimacy of the Australian Constitution under which all laws are made.[40]

Democracy

Chief Justice Mason contributed to the High Court's rejection of simplistic notions of democracy as involving no more than majority votes in Parliament intermittently elected. Modern Australian democracy is more complex. It involves a respect for the human rights of minorities, a new sensitivity to the position of the indigenous peoples of Australia (Aboriginals and Torres Strait Islanders) and an awareness of the important developments which are occurring, at an international level, in the field of human rights and fundamental freedoms.

Human Rights

The High Court's decisions under Chief Justice Mason also reflect an awareness of international human rights developments and a willingness to see Australia's constitutional and legal principles in relation to them. This is not to bring international treaties on human rights into Australia's

40 *Australian Capital Television Pty Ltd v Commonwealth* (1992) 177 CLR 106 at 138. Cf *McGinty v Western Australia* (1996) 186 CLR 140 at 230 where McHugh J refers to 'considerable theoretical difficulties' in this view. See Kirby, Chapter 12.

municipal law by 'a backdoor means' where not incorporated by Parliament.[41] It is simply to recognise that most of the important international human rights treaties were drawn by Anglo-American lawyers. They reflect concepts which are entirely familiar to those brought up in the traditions of the common law. They may provide a setting in which approaches to Australia's problems can be aided by an awareness of the way in which other jurists, grappling with analogous problems, arrive at their solution.

Policy

Whilst the dividing line between judicial principle and policy, on the one hand, and political policy on the other, is never bright, there will be no going back to the declaratory theory of the judicial function. The identification of legal principle and legal policy, and the candid discussion of it between judges and advocates, will help to achieve decisions which are better informed and more transparent.[42]

Society

The High Court operates in a society that is increasingly complex and affected by technological change and by a changing population with new and different ethnic, religious and cultural imperatives. If the Court is to continue to respond, as a branch of government, to a society undergoing such profound changes, it is essential that it should continue on the path that Sir Anthony Mason identified. It seems unlikely that the Court will ever return to the Court of my youth. Too much has altered in Australia, in the law and in the High Court itself.

Conclusion

The development in Justice Mason's outlook and the enlargement of his sense of permissible creativity are in themselves signals of the persistence and strength of the independence of the Australian judiciary. They came about as a consequence of the personal convictions of an appointed Justice of the High Court of Australia. Those convictions ultimately took him down new and sometimes untrodden paths. Such byways in the law can, as in life, be exciting and even, on occasion, a little dangerous. The easy response to change is usually to stick to the well-worn paths and to reject those that are new. Sir Anthony Mason

41 *Minister for Immigration and Ethnic Affairs v Teoh* (1995) 183 CLR 273 at 288 per Mason CJ and Deane J.

42 See Kirby, Chapter 9.

saw the changing times. He boldly struck out upon new ways. He embraced new ideas in a fresh and confident manner. If this had been his approach to life and the law throughout his professional service, it would have been unremarkable that it reached new heights when he took the central seat in the nation's highest court. But the fact that his professional life demonstrates significant change and development makes it the more fascinating and worthy of study: not only for Anthony Mason, the individual, but also for the consequences of such change for the institutions in which he served.

It is the search for the law as it serves justice that has been the hallmark of the legal system that we have inherited from England and developed for ourselves. Sir Anthony Mason's life is an example of how great legal skills and high judicial technique can be brought together, with an increasing sense of urgency, to discover and develop the law and to ensure, so far as we can, that the law is just.

Chapter 11

The Power of Lionel Murphy's Ideas[1]

Justice Murphy was a creative and unconventional Justice of the High Court of Australia during a period when any departure from established legal orthodoxy was frowned upon and exposed decision-makers to public, and certainly professional, ridicule. At the Annual Conference of the Australian Society of Labor Lawyers in Hobart on 1 October 1993, in a speech originally entitled 'Lionel Murphy and the Power of Ideas', Michael Kirby spoke of Justice Murphy's courage as a lone dissenter in many decisions and his unique contribution to the development of a forward looking and uniquely Australian jurisprudence. He describes the enduring influence of Justice Murphy's intellectual thought upon new generations of Australian lawyers who are more willing than ever before to question old rules in the light of changing social circumstances.

In his remarks at the ceremonial sitting of the Full High Court in Canberra soon after Justice Lionel Murphy's death, the then Chief Justice of Australia, Sir Harry Gibbs, spoke of Justice Murphy's remarkable achievements as Attorney-General. He also spoke of the great band of admirers whom Justice Murphy had gathered around him and who were steadfast during the dangerous days that preceded his death. Not many judges, not many public figures, could attract such support and sympathy. Accurately, Sir Harry Gibbs recorded Justice Murphy's desire to continue, as a judge, the process of legal reform for which he had striven in his years as a barrister, a Parliamentarian and as a Federal Minister. Accurately too, he discerned Justice Murphy's desire to 'bring about a more democratic and equal society' – something he carried over into his judgments.[2]

It would be hard to conceive a more dramatic contrast in the style of Justice Murphy and his last Chief Justice, Sir Harry Gibbs. In many ways, Justice Murphy was more similar to Garfield Barwick, whose life had been less cloistered, whose technique was equally robust and whose will was just as determined. The differences between Justice Murphy and Sir Harry Gibbs during those last years were well known. But in carefully chosen words, Sir Harry looked to the future:

---

1 An earlier version of this paper was published as 'Lionel Murphy and the Power of Ideas' (1993) 18(6) *Alternative Law Journal* 253.

2 'The Late Mr Justice Murphy' (1986) 160 CLR v at vii.

> It cannot be denied – and he would not have wished to deny – that he was at times the subject of controversy and that his judicial method was one which did not command universal assent. However, the value of the contribution made by any judge to the law and the extent of his influence upon it cannot be assessed by his contemporaries; judgment on those questions must be left to history.[3]

Others can review Justice Murphy's contributions to the parliamentary system, the role of the Senate and to legislative reform. What interests me is the way in which so many of the judicial opinions written by Justice Murphy (often in dissent) are being accepted today in Australia as legal orthodoxy. During his 11 years on the High Court, he wrote 632 decisions. In 137 of them he was in dissent. This is an average of nearly 22 per cent dissenting opinions – hugely higher than that of any other High Court Justice to that time[4] and well up in the league of the American dissenters.[5] I do not pretend that, in all of these dissents, Justice Murphy has been, or will be, vindicated by later judicial authority. But in a great number, the power of his ideas is already being felt. Three features of this development are worthy of note.

The first is that it shows how powerful ideas, simply expressed, can work away within our legal system to plant their seeds of doubt until, in due time, the once dissenting view becomes accepted. This is the beauty of our common law tradition with its judicial right to dissent. Most lawyers of the civil law tradition are shocked at the right of judicial dissent. It does not typically exist in the more autocratic traditions of the Napoleonic code and in the civil law judiciary.[6] Justice Murphy, like myself, would have found appointment to a court of single opinions completely uncongenial, and indeed inconsistent with the obligation of judicial and personal integrity. Intellectual integrity was an imperative of his life.

Secondly, it is worth noting how the influence of Justice Murphy's ideas has begun to have its effect despite the almost universal disdain, even contempt and scorn, in which he was held within the established

---

3 Ibid.

4 In the published Full Court opinions of the author between his appointment in 1996 and 1999 he was in the majority in 103 decisions (68%) and in dissent in 48 decisions (32%).

5 See MA Kadzielski and RC Kunda 'The Origins of Modern Dissent: The Unmaking of the Judicial Consensus in the 1930's (1983) 15 *University of West Los Angeles Law Review* 43; and S Goldman (ed) (1985) *Judicial Conflict and Consensus: Behavioural Studies of American Appellate Courts*, Uni Press Kentucky.

6 See RB Ginsburg, 'Remarks on Writing Separately' (1990) 65 *Washington Law Review* 133 at 134; and R David and JC Brierley (1978) *Major Legal Systems in the World Today*, Stevens, p 129.

legal profession during his judicial service, and upon his death. I can speak of these things because I saw them at first hand. Counsel reading a case to me in the Court of Appeal would completely ignore his opinion – and do so even when Justice Murphy was part of a majority and thus part of the binding rule of the High Court. When gently coaxed to venture upon it, counsel would resist or proceed with reluctance and with thinly veiled amusement. This was the intellectual arrogance of a closed society. The power of Justice Murphy's ideas is the more remarkable because of the positive dislike held for him by most members of the legal establishment in his lifetime. It should not have been so. He had, after all, a brilliant career at university and an outstanding life as a barrister and in high public service. But it was his unorthodoxy which troubled an intensely orthodox profession. Many felt threatened by it. It is, therefore, not a little pleasant for those of us who knew the power of his intellect and felt the warmth of his personality to see the way in which the scorn, previously targeted at him, has now been turned, full circle, towards the adoption of many of his ideas.

Thirdly, it is worth noting that full acknowledgment of Justice Murphy's influence is even today a reluctant commodity in the Australian legal profession and judiciary. Where his thoughts are accepted, they are often adopted without attribution. The essence of his reasoning finds its way into later judgments without so much as a footnote or citation. This could, of course, be accident. It could be embarrassment in facing squarely past error, or acknowledging openly a change of heart. Or it could be the lingering feeling that full attribution of ideas to Justice Murphy will somehow bring down the wrath of the orthodox and the calumny of the critics. Anyone who doubts the existence of such calumny should reflect upon the savage treatment meted out to the majority in the *Mabo* case.[7] One example is that of the former Justice Peter Connolly, who once delighted his colleagues in Brisbane by vehement attacks upon my Boyer Lectures,[8] and turned his criticism upon the High Court post-*Mabo*.[9]

Let me, therefore, take a few selected cases where Justice Murphy's judicial ideas have been adopted, with or without acknowledgment. My list will not be exhaustive. But it will, I hope, be sufficient to bear out my thesis.

---

7 *Mabo v Queensland (No 2)* (1992) 175 CLR 1.

8 MD Kirby (1983) *The Judges*, ABC Boyer Lectures.

9 PD Connolly (1993) 'Should the Courts Determine Social Policy?' in *The High Court of Australia in Mabo*, Association of Mining and Exploration Companies, p 1.

True Intellectual Freedom

A common theme running through many of Justice Murphy's opinions, and through the techniques which he used to expound his ideas, was the need for Australian lawyers to free themselves from imprisonment in the English line of precedent. Justice Murphy was specially irritated by the then still surviving links to the Judicial Committee of the Privy Council in London. Those links had persisted for most of his legal lifetime. He did his best, in Parliament, to terminate appeals of a federal character. But appeals from the State Supreme Courts, as an alternative to the High Court of Australia, remained.

The inappropriateness of accepting the legal authority of a court, comprised of judges of another nation, for resolving the practical disputes of concern to Australians was voiced in many of Justice Murphy's judgments. He complained of the intrusion of the Privy Council into Australian constitutional affairs 'even though it has no jurisdiction'. He saw its errors on display in *Oteri and Oteri v The Queen.*[10] He declared the continuance of the participation of English judges in laying down the law of Australia to be unacceptable. In *Viro v The Queen*,[11] in an elaborate critique of the Privy Council, he said in very direct words:

> I should add that no court in Australia is bound by the decisions of the House of Lords or the courts below it in the English system. The expression 'not technically bound' is often used, but it should be clear that Australian courts are not bound by such decisions, however persuasive they may be.
>
> In times of rapid social change, the creative role of appellate courts naturally expands to adapt decisional law to the new social environment. The Australian judicial system is not assisted in the definition and development of Australian law by the existence of a tribunal acting as a rival to the High Court. The members of the Privy Council have not been appointed by Australians, are not responsible to anyone in Australia and cannot be removed by any Australian procedure. ... The lesson of cases such as *Oteri* is that Australian courts should not be encouraged to look to the Privy Council for guidance on Australian law.[12]

At the time these things were said, they seemed to many to be needlessly offensive heresies. Or even amounting to insubordination. However, Justice Murphy, the former politician, saw clearly the role of the courts in the governmental decision-making of the country. He

10 (1976) 11 ALR 142.

11 (1978) 141 CLR 88.

12 Ibid, at 166-167.

therefore saw the continued subservience of Australian courts to the ideas of the judges in the English courts, in the exposition of local law, as totally unacceptable. It was not so much a matter of national pride. It was more a reflection of the integrity of our own judicial and legal system and the differing social conditions and community attitudes which existed as between Australia and England.

Whatever unorthodoxy existed when *Viro* was decided, it has been set at rest by the High Court's instruction, to similar effect, in 1986 in *Cook v Cook*.[13] There, Justices Mason, Wilson, Deane and Dawson went back over the old authorities of the High Court. In some of that authority, Australian courts had been urged 'as a general rule' to follow decisions of the English Court of Appeal. But by 1986 our highest court was saying:

> Whatever may have been the justification for such statements in times when the Judicial Committee of the Privy Council was the ultimate court of appeal or one of the ultimate courts of appeal of this country, those statements should no longer be seen as binding upon Australian courts. The history of this country and of the common law makes it inevitable and desirable that the courts of this country will continue to obtain assistance and guidance from the learning and reasoning of United Kingdom courts just as Australian courts benefit from the learning and reasoning of other great common law courts. Subject, perhaps, to the special position of decisions of the House of Lords given in the period in which appeals lay from this country to the Privy Council, the precedents of other legal systems are not binding and are useful only to the degree of the persuasiveness of their reasoning.[14]

Justice Murphy would have seen no reason for exceptions either for the Privy Council or the House of Lords at any time. The force of his exposition about the independence of Australian lawmaking – including in the judicial branch – is really unarguable. Yet it is comparatively easy to lay down the rule. Much more difficult is it to get judges and lawyers to free their minds from capture by the English case books. In part, this is because those books are still on the shelves of most judges and lawyers in Australia. Indeed, most of them still have an English series in preference to a series from another State of Australia. These physical impediments to true independence of the mind will diminish over time. As the next generation embraces the new information technology and uses the Internet, it will be much less likely that Australian lawyers of the future will draw so heavily upon English precedent. The growth of statute law will also encourage mental freedom. Already, in the decisions

13 (1986) 162 CLR 376.

14 Ibid, at 390.

of the High Court and of other Australian courts, we see a turn back to the earlier use of United States jurisprudence and the decisions of other common law jurisdictions beyond England. I doubt if, in the future, we will see the same condescending rejection of common law decisions outside England as was expressed by the High Court in its review of my reasons in *Public Service Board of New South Wales v Osmond.*[15]

On matters of judicial technique, some of what Justice Murphy did would still be regarded as controversial. Not every Australian lawyer – even of the radical variety – would necessarily agree with all of his techniques. But about his notion of the integrity of the Australian legal system within its own internal hierarchy and of the need for the removal of intellectual subservience to the working judicial hierarchy of another country, there can now be no real dispute. Yet the winning of the minds of the legal profession first to local jurisprudence and then to the great treasure house of common law principle that lies overseas, beyond England, remains a battle for the future. It is one which, daily, I fight, but, I am bold enough to think, with a growing measure of success. For every House of Lords decision read to me, I ask whether counsel have looked to the New Zealand Court of Appeal or the Supreme Court of Canada or to other great courts of the common law. This, I believe, is what Justice Murphy would be doing today, were he alive. I remember that, when he was appointed to the High Court, he gave instructions to the astonished officers of the Attorney-General's Department, who looked after these things, to 'get rid of' the English Reprint Reports housed in the chambers at Darlinghurst which he had inherited from Justice Menzies. In their place, he called for the reports of the Supreme Court of the United States of America. There it was that he doubtless found *Gideon v Wainwright*,[16] which he was to follow in *McInnis.*[17]

There are still lessons to be learned from Justice Murphy's approach concerning the enduring impact of legal imperialism upon the psyche of the Australian legal profession. It is still common to see the English Court of Appeal referred to in Australian cases as '*the* Court of Appeal'. Decisions in England, centuries ago, are still frequently accepted as stating the law for modern Australia, without a moment's hesitation or thought concerning the alterations in social conditions and community values since those decisions were handed down. Throwing off capture to foreign jurisprudence, Justice Murphy felt free to discuss more candidly

15 (1986) 159 CLR 656 at 668. A reference to the use of *Siemens Engineering and Manufacturing Co of India Ltd v Union of India* AIR (1976) SC 63; SCI 1785 at 1789.

16 372 US 335 (1963).

17 *McInnis v the Queen* (1979) 143 CLR 575 at 587.

the values of policy and principle which informed his decisions. In this, too, he has had an impact on the contemporary reasoning techniques of the High Court of Australia. Policy came to be increasingly perceived and sometimes candidly acknowledged, although without mentioning Justice Murphy's name or admitting to the stimulus which he gave to the process.[18]

Constitutional Cases

As the guardian of the Constitution, the High Court of Australia enjoys enormous power to influence the nature of the Australian polity. In his constitutional judgments, Justice Murphy revealed himself both as a civil libertarian and as a person committed to the attainment of the communal good, through laws adopted by democratic legislatures.[19] He offered a distinct and historically based view of the meaning of s 92 of the Constitution. This section promises that trade, commerce and intercourse amongst the States of the Commonwealth should be 'absolutely free'. Read in whole, and in context and against the purposes for its introduction, s 92 commanded no more than free trade in the restricted sense of 'freedom from customs duties or similar taxes on trade, commerce and intercourse'. Justice Murphy rejected the then orthodox view of the High Court that s 92 permitted mere regulation of such trade, commerce and intercourse and forbade much else, however rational and beneficial to the community. He expressed his opinion in *Buck v Bavone*.[20] He there called in aid the 'dramatic recantation' by Lord Wright of the judgment which he wrote for the Privy Council in *James v Commonwealth*.[21] In 1954, Lord Wright had said in a law review article:

> The idea of s 92 as a power in the air brooding and ready in the name of freedom to crush and destroy social and industrial or political experiments in Australian life ought, I think, to be exploded. In truth, as I said, s 92 is both pedestrian and humble, though very essential from the point of view of the founders of the Constitution, who wished to establish internal inter-State free trade in fiscal matters for all time.[22]

---

18 See AF Mason, 'The Role of a Constitutional Court in a Federation' (1986) 16 *Federal Law Review* 1 at 5.

19 JA Scutt (ed) (1987) *Lionel Murphy – A Radical Judge*, McCulloch, pp 79-83. See generally J and R Ely (eds) (1986) *Lionel Murphy: The Rule of Law*, Acron.

20 (1976) 135 CLR 110 at 132-138.

21 (1936) 55 CLR 1; [1936] AC 578 (PC).

22 Lord Wright of Durley, 'Section 92 – A Problem Piece' (1954) 1 *Sydney Law Review* 145 at 157.

This was Justice Murphy's view of s 92. He clung steadfastly to it – often to the derision of others who criticised both his naiveté and his rejection of the authority of the Court which had long established the contrary view. But he persisted.

In *Cole v Whitfield*,[23] two years after Justice Murphy's death, a unanimous High Court handed down a new principle for the application of s 92 to suggested cases of interference by State law in freedom of interstate trade and commerce. The Court held that the object of the section was simply the elimination of protection. It was addressed to discrimination against interstate trade and commerce in the protectionist sense. This was essentially what Justice Murphy had suggested in his series of opinions about the section. Lord Wright's remarks in his later recantation were reproduced in *Cole*.[24] The old doctrine was declared to be 'highly artificial'.[25] Justice Murphy's views in *Buck v Bavone* were criticised.[26] But the Court, like him, turned to embrace an interpretation based upon the original history, purpose and context of s 92. It is one which concentrates upon its object of preventing protection and infringing the guarantee of free trade and the absence of protection. In a sense, although Justice Murphy's thesis was not wholly endorsed – it was indeed castigated – its central idea carried the day. Lord Wright's recantation was vindicated. The over-reach of s 92 was trimmed back. Its true meaning was to be found from the context of all of its words and from its history as a shield against protectionism. Blind adherence to the unsatisfactory judicial doctrine of the past was to be overthrown. A new rule was henceforth to be applied. Both in content and in technique, *Cole v Whitfield* was much influenced by Justice Murphy's ideas, his approach and his persistence, however much the text might suggest otherwise.

There are many other cases in the constitutional field where his influence has been felt. But nowhere so dramatically as in *Australian Capital Television Pty Ltd v Commonwealth*[27] and *Nationwide News Pty Ltd v Wills*.[28] Implied constitutional rights were one of Justice Murphy's recurring judicial themes. In fact, he looked at the Constitution as any good lawyer should. It is a written document. Therefore, meaning must

23 (1988) 165 CLR 360.

24 Ibid, at 397.

25 Ibid, at 401.

26 Ibid, at 407.

27 (1992) 177 CLR 106.

28 (1992) 177 CLR 1. See now *Lange v Australian Broadcasting Corporation* (1997) 189 CLR 520 and *Levy v Victoria* (1997) 189 CLR 579.

be given to the writing – not only to the words but to the implications to be derived from the words and structure, read in their context. Even more, meaning was to be attributed to the words because of the very nature of the instrument as an enduring constitution, difficult to amend and meant to govern the political life of the nation, indefinitely. All of this was orthodox lawyering. Yet it was heresy for so long, at least, as Justice Murphy expressed it.

In *Ansett Transport Industries (Operations) Pty Limited v Commonwealth*,[29] Justice Murphy espoused the opinion that the provisions of the Australian Constitution for the election of the Federal Parliament necessitated freedom of movement, speech and other communications not only between the States but in and between every part of the Commonwealth. He asserted that the system of representative government itself, without more, required the same freedoms between elections. He described such freedoms as 'not absolute, but nearly so'. Although these freedoms were not expressly spelt out in the Constitution, he was of the opinion that they were necessarily implied in the language of the Constitution and in its structure and purpose. In a series of decisions, Justice Murphy expounded and reinforced these views.[30]

His colleagues on the High Court either ignored these opinions as irrelevant heresies or positively objected to them and rejected them. Most pointed was the sharp comment of Justice Mason in *Miller v TCN Channel Nine Proprietary Limited*.[31] He gave short shrift to the argument of implied guarantees:

> There was an alternative argument put by the defendant, based on the judgment of Murphy J in *Buck v Bavone*, that there is to be implied in the Constitution a new set of freedoms which include a guarantee of freedom of communication. It is sufficient to say that I cannot find any basis for implying a new s 92A into the Constitution.[32]

Imagine, then, the surprise of Justice Murphy's admirers when they read the reports of the High Court's judgments in *Australian Capital Television* and *Nationwide News*. In both of these decisions, the majority of the High Court upheld the argument that the federal legislation there attacked was invalid by reference to freedoms embodied in

---

29 (1977) 139 CLR 54 at 88.

30 See *Buck v Bavone* (1966) 135 CLR 110 at 137; *McGraw-Hinds (Aust) Proprietary Limited v Smith* (1979) 144 CLR 633 at 670; and *Uebergang v Australian Wheat Board* (1980) 145 CLR 266 at 312.

31 (1986) 161 CLR 556.

32 Ibid, at 579.

constitutional implications which amounted to implied guarantees of public and political discussion and criticism.[33]

As a number of observers at the time suggested, this was virtually pure Murphy doctrine.[34] Somewhat disappointing was the lack of candid acknowledgment in the opinions of the majority of the impact of Justice Murphy's ideas. Thus, in Chief Justice Mason's opinion there are numerous references to statements about implications in the judgments of earlier Justices who, some might feel, did not come nearly as close to the doctrine embraced on this occasion as Justice Murphy had done. But this point did not escape the eagle eye of Justice Dawson, in dissent. In a careful passage, presumably deriving from the arguments of the Commonwealth relying upon the repeated rejections of the Murphy doctrine, Justice Dawson went through each of Justice Murphy's decisions in turn. Turning the knife (figuratively speaking) he quoted back at Chief Justice Mason the scorn which the latter had earlier directed in *Miller* to the suggestion that a 'new s 92A' should be imported by judicial construction into the Constitution.[35]

It is interesting to speculate upon what Justice Murphy would have made of the *Australian Capital Television* case and the later decisions in *Lange* and *Levy*. He would, of course, have been sympathetic to the notion of an implied constitutional immunity from laws inhibiting political or other expression essential to the operation of the system of representative government which the Constitution establishes. After all, he had repeatedly expressed such ideas in a series of decisions where they were derided, as I have shown. But I suspect that he might have been more affected by his communitarian view and respect for the right of the Parliament to regulate broadcasting at the time of elections (ostensibly to respect their integrity). Any piece of legislation which, like the limitation on paid political advertising, could get through the divided Australian Senate and introduce a régime not dissimilar to that operating in numerous overseas democracies, might have seemed to Justice Murphy a positive contribution to informed discussion and choice. It might have been thought to be within the margin of appreciation left to a democratic legislature to derogate from an absolute freedom of expression uncontrolled by any law. After all, the Parliament's objectives

33 In the later decisions in *Lange v Australian Broadcasting Corporation* (1997) 189 CLR 520 and *Levy v Victoria* (1997) 189 CLR 579, none of the Justices questioned the basic proposition that implications of free speech arise from the language, structures and purposes of the Australian Constitution.

34 See 'Come Back Lionel' (1992) 17 *Alternative Law Journal* 206. See also the author's comments in 'Current Topics' (1992) 66 *Australian Law Journal* 775.

35 *Miller v TCN Channel Nine Pty Ltd* (1986) 161 CLR 556 at 581-582.

were arguably tolerable – the reduction of superficial electoral jingles; the enhancement of real news and opinion; and the prevention of people with deep pockets manipulating public opinion by trivialising the political debate through expensive paid advertisements. I suspect that he would have affirmed his view about implied rights but denied that this was an occasion where they had been breached. However that may be, as Justice Dawson plainly discerned and stated, this was a most important breakthrough for Justice Murphy's basic idea. Its consequences for the future constitutional law of Australia are potentially enormous. If implications may be drawn of necessity from the Constitution, there is no reason why they should stop with the legislative branch. In Chapter III, dealing with the judicature, there are many necessary implications and some of them have already been discovered.[36]

Perhaps equally important is the decision in *Mabo*.[37] I do not wish to concentrate on the legal error (the doctrine of *terra nullius*) which had long endured in Australia's settler society, although it had earlier been repaired in others. Instead, I want to mention the way Justice Brennan, in the course of his reasoning, embraced the utilisation of international law for the purposes of developing Australian common law and interpreting ambiguous Australian statutes. Justice Brennan referred, in *Mabo*, to the *International Covenant on Civil and Political Rights*, which Australia has ratified without relevant reservations. He went on:

> The common law does not necessarily conform with international law, but international law is a legitimate and important influence on the development of the common law, especially when international law declares the existence of universal human rights.[38]

This passage was written with the concurrence of Chief Justice Mason and Justice McHugh. Years earlier, often alone and usually in dissent, Justice Murphy had referred to the *International Covenant on Civil and Political Rights* and other principles of international law in the course of his reasoning. He did so in constitutional cases.[39] He was the most clear-sighted in rejecting the narrow construction of the external affairs power under the Australian Constitution. In the *Tasmanian Dams Case*,[40] he made it plain that, in his view, any other approach to the expression of the power of the Federal Parliament in this regard would permanently

36 *Kable v Director of Public Prosecutions (NSW)* (1996) 189 CLR 51.

37 *Mabo v Queensland (No 2)* (1992) 175 CLR 1.

38 Ibid, at 42.

39 See *Dowal v Murray* (1978) 143 CLR 410 and *Koowarta v Bjelke-Petersen* (1982) 153 CLR 168.

40 *Commonwealth v Tasmania (The Tasmanian Dams Case)* (1983) 158 CLR 1.

cripple Australia's capacity to play its proper role in the community of nations. This is the view which has ultimately prevailed in the High Court of Australia.

An important element of Justice Murphy's legacy is the heightened interest in international law and in the closer relationship between that body of law and our municipal law in Australia. In my own way, I have been endeavouring to carry on this important legacy.[41] I consider it to be one of the most important lessons to emerge from the insights of Justice Murphy in his role as a judge. I confess that, at first, I regarded his attitude of internationalism in law as unorthodox, and even heretical. I cannot, therefore, be too critical of those who remain of that view. I now acknowledge that I was wrong. Lionel Murphy merely saw a great truth before most others did. But it is encouraging that, in *Mabo*, and in earlier and later decisions of the High Court, there is increasing attention to international law and, in particular, to universal human rights norms as touchstones for the expression and development of our own common law in Australia.[42]

Murphy and the Underdog

In many of his decisions, Justice Murphy displayed an appreciation of the position of the disadvantaged operating within the legal system of Australia. In *Dugan v Mirror Newspapers Limited*,[43] he rejected the antique principles of English law held by the majority to be suitable for the law of Australia in respect of denying the rights of prisoners. In *Moffa v The Queen*,[44] he accepted, as a test for the reasonable person in multicultural Australia, a need to have regard to the culpability of the particular accused person and to avoid the stereotype of a single cultural response based upon assumptions of the ethnic uniformity of earlier times. In *Neal v The Queen*,[45] he defended, in ringing terms, Mr Neal's right to be an agitator. There is, I am afraid, a natural tendency for courts and lawyers to dislike agitators and to insist on bringing the whole weight of the law down on those who do not conform or, as Justice Vaisey once

41 See MD Kirby, 'The Australian Use of International Human Rights Norms: From Bangalore to Balliol – A View from the Antipodes' (1993) 16 *University of New South Wales Law Journal* 363. See now *Newcrest Mining (WA) Ltd v Commonwealth* (1997) 190 CLR 513 and *Kartinyeri v Commonwealth* (1998) 195 CLR 337.

42 See eg *Dietrich v The Queen* (1992) 177 CLR 292.

43 (1979) 142 CLR 583.

44 (1977) 138 CLR 601.

45 (1982) 149 CLR 305.

put it, to bring into line the 'only man in the regiment out of step'.[46] Justice Murphy, often himself being the 'only man out of step', had a natural sympathy for such persons. He had an instinctive view that the law should protect their rights, for that was when the law was really tested.

I suppose that the most clear-cut example of the adoption of a Murphy dissent as the new binding rule of the High Court of Australia is to be found in *Dietrich v The Queen*.[47] It was in that case that the Court finally overruled its earlier decision in *McInnis v The Queen*.[48] That decision was explained as based upon 'the absence of any argument directed to the existence of a right to be provided with counsel'.[49] It was said that the Court had simply assumed the correctness of the proposition that such a right did not exist. After a review of Australian, overseas and international human rights law, the High Court majority set aside the conviction of Mr Dietrich on a serious charge. It did so because it concluded that such conviction had followed a trial rendered unfair by the lack of legal representation of the accused. This was a clear rejection of the doctrine of Chief Justice Barwick, which had carried the day in *McInnis*. Yet it was not the inevitable outcome of an examination of the law, as a contrary decision of the Appellate Division of the Supreme Court of South Africa demonstrates.[50] Clearly, *Dietrich* is in tune with Justice Murphy's use of international law and of foreign jurisprudence. It is also in harmony with Justice Murphy's repeated perception of problems from a human rights angle, and his open-mindedness about the need to throw over old doctrine when it no longer accords to the social conditions and community attitudes of justice and fairness in Australia today.

In the Nooks and Crannies of the Law

A multitude of other cases could be cited to demonstrate the abiding impact of Justice Murphy's ideas, in dissent, during his period as a Justice of the High Court of Australia. It would be tedious to go over them all. I will mention just a few.

---

46 *Re Sussex Brick Co Ltd* [1961] Ch 289 at 293; cf *Acron Resources Ltd v Catto* (1992) 8 ACSR 219 at 230.

47 (1992) 177 CLR 292.

48 (1979) 143 CLR 575.

49 *Dietrich v The Queen* (1992) 177 CLR 292 at 303 per Mason CJ and McHugh J.

50 *S v Rudman* 1992 (1) SA 343 (AD).

Justice Murphy was very familiar with the operation of industrial laws. This was an area in which he had practised and risen to the top of the Bar. He knew only too well the artificialities and the unreality of some of the binding decisions of the High Court which intruded into the field of federal industrial relations. When he had the opportunity, as a Justice of the High Court, he did not hesitate to lend his voice to a removal of these artificialities. Thus, in *R v Bain; Ex parte Cadbury Schweppes Australia Limited*,[51] he expressed his views and expanded the meaning of a 'dispute' for constitutional and legal purposes in words which were regarded as astonishing at the time:

> The Commission has power to determine what in fact is the industrial dispute and is not circumscribed by the procedures for rejection of paper for demands. Thus an industrial dispute may be diminished or ended or enlarged or altered during the course of the proceedings in the Commission.[52]

On this occasion, Justice Murphy carried with him Justices Brennan and Deane.[53] In the face of strong precedent to the contrary, his view was later to prevail in *Re Federated Storeman and Packers Union of Australia; Ex parte Wooldumpers (Victoria) Limited*.[54] Chief Justice Mason followed it, in terms, in that case. The new rule encouraged industrial tribunals to concentrate upon the concepts of the dispute and ambit of the dispute in the context of general industrial matters. It permitted a gradual enlargement of the power of the federal arbitral body.

In the field of conciliation, too, Justice Murphy's judgment in *R v Turbet; Ex parte ABCE & BLF*[55] drew attention to the word 'prevention' in the Constitution. What he said in that case concerning conciliation was also regarded as radical and even heretical at the time. It challenged many old preconceptions and Court holdings. But it was another illustration of his capacity to look afresh at old language and to breathe life into the living Constitution. It is now a completely orthodox part of our constitutional and industrial law.[56]

In two cases upon which I was recently working I fell upon Justice Murphy's lonely dissent concerning the doctrine of presumptions in equity. What clearly began as rules of thumb to assist judges of the

---

51 (1984) 159 CLR 163.

52 Ibid, at 168.

53 Ibid, at 175.

54 (1989) 166 CLR 311.

55 (1980) 144 CLR 335 at 354. See now *Attorney-General (Qld) v Riordan* (1997) 192 CLR 1.

56 See *Re Printing and Kindred Industries Union; Ex parte Vista Paper Products Pty Ltd* (1993) 113 ALR 421 at 433.

Chancery Court in England to determine disputed claims about duties of conscience settled, quite quickly, in the hands of lawyers, into fairly rigid rules of law. Justice Murphy rejected such rigidities. He expressed a preference for replacing them with rational evaluation, by the judge, of all of the evidence in the particular case. He gave reasons for this approach which, to my mind, are compelling: 'As standards of behaviour alter, so should presumptions, otherwise the rationale for presumptions is lost, and instead of assisting the evaluation evidence, they may detract from it'.[57]

Whilst, in the case before me, I was then bound to the contrary view, I expressed a clear preference for the opinion voiced by Justice Murphy.[58] In little and big things, in the large canvas of constitutional law and in the nooks and crannies of the law of equity, Justice Murphy's original mind can be found at work in the *Commonwealth Law Reports*. He did not accept that the role of the judge was mechanically to apply old rules. Instead, he turned the light of his intellect upon those rules, as they were presented to him. If he found them wanting, he did not hesitate to say so and to explain why. It is those explanations which continue to haunt our legal system. They are spirits agitating the minds of the lawyers and judges who follow.

The Ultimate Legacy

The ultimate legacy of Justice Murphy on the High Court of Australia may be even greater. I believe that he broke the spell of unquestioning acceptance of old rules where social circumstances and community attitudes have changed, rendering those rules inappropriate or inapplicable.

The fact that this is so can be seen by contrasting the earlier and the present approaches of the High Court of Australia to the judicial function. The last detailed exposition of restraint in a decision of that Court was given by Justice Mason, in another case in which Lionel Murphy dissented, *State Government Insurance Commission v Trigwell*.[59] That was the case about the liability of property owners for sheep straying from adjoining land. In an eloquent passage,[60] Justice Mason urged the reasons for judicial restraint: the limited legitimacy of the Court to alter

57 *Calverley v Green* (1984) 155 CLR 242 at 264.

58 See *Stivactas v Michaeletos (No 2)* [1993] NSW Conv R ¶55-683, [1993] Aust Contract R ¶90-031; *Brown v Brown* (1993) 31 NSWLR 582.

59 (1979) 142 CLR 617. See Kirby, Chapter 10.

60 Ibid, at 633.

the law and its limited facilities to decide upon what that altered law should be. Justice Murphy was equally eloquent in his dissenting opinion.

Contrast the attitude expressed on that occasion with the recent line of authority in the High Court of Australia where the High Court judges have made new law. Take, for example, the decision on privity of contract in *Trident Insurance*.[61] Take the strong stand adopted on the so-called police verbals in *McKinney*.[62] Take the view in that case on prospective over-ruling of a rule of court practice. Take the unanimous opinion on the abolition of the common law doctrine that a husband could not, in law, be guilty of raping his wife.[63] That was a doctrine that had stood in the common law from 1736 and was assumed to be the law in the expression of several of the criminal statutes of Australia. Take the implied rights to free speech found in the Constitution already mentioned. Take the alteration of the law governing the recovery of moneys paid or expended as a result of a mistake of law.[64] Take the right to legal representation upheld in *Dietrich*.[65] Take the explosion of the doctrine of *terra nullius* in *Mabo*.[66] These and many other decisions show a High Court of Australia with an approach to its functions quite different from that expressed in *Trigwell*.

Perhaps these are simply changes which conform to different times. Perhaps they are the inevitable result of the release of the High Court of Australia from the apron strings of the Privy Council. Freed from English supervision and accountability to English judges, we are now building our own Australian jurisprudence and our own common law. The other appellate courts of Australia have been encouraged by the High Court to play their part in this regard.[67]

There remain, of course, important questions of the rule of law, of the separation of powers, of the limit of judicial legitimacy in lawmaking; of the implications of these moves for judicial appointment and tenure of such a creative judiciary; and of the changes that will come about in the future, as the judiciary of Australia examines afresh principles long established and long accepted as binding rules of law.

---

61 *Trident General Insurance Co Limited v McNiece Bros Proprietary Limited* (1988) 165 CLR 107.

62 *McKinney v The Queen* (1991) 171 CLR 468.

63 *The Queen v L* (1991) 174 CLR 379.

64 *David Securities Pty Ltd v Commonwealth Bank of Australia* (1992) 175 CLR 353.

65 (1992) 177 CLR 292.

66 (1992) 175 CLR 1.

67 *Nguyen v Nguyen* (1990) 169 CLR 245 at 269.

Until Justice Murphy came onto the scene and started asking the searching questions, it was comparatively rare in Australia to have expounded such a challenging view of the judicial role. Certainly, it was virtually unheard of at such a high level of the judicial hierarchy. Now, it is not so rare. This may be Justice Murphy's most enduring legacy. He showed that it could, and should, be done – that it could, and should, be done within a legal and judicial framework that was far from anarchistic. One which accepted the institutional constraints within which legal reform can be achieved by judicial fiat.

I emphasise that Justice Murphy was no revolutionary. He was a man who valued the institutions within which he worked – the Bar of the legal profession, the Parliament, the Ministry and the nation's highest court. A revolutionary would have disdained these institutions. An anarchist would have sought to throw them over and change them. Justice Murphy was for change: but change for the better, which is the banner of true reform. He was not for change for change's sake. He worked within our Constitution and the institutions it establishes. He saw the way in which, with fresh perception, the Constitution could be adapted and could live as the guardian of basic rights and the protector of a democratic society.

One of the greatest pleasures I have enjoyed in my appointment to the High Court has been to follow in the footsteps of Lionel Murphy. In very many ways I am different. I confess that I was always somewhat puzzled about what it was about me that he liked. We were, in a sense, children of the contrasting communities of Ireland. He: ebullient, gregarious, a lover of parties and champagne, light of touch and quick of mind. I: serious, dutiful, applied – more at home in a library than at a party. Yet like me he certainly did. He undoubtedly gave me chances in my career, particularly by appointing me to the Australian Law Reform Commission.

So it is for personal as well as professional and national reasons that I remember the life of Lionel Murphy. I am proud to honour him as a Justice of the High Court of Australia and as a legislator of the Commonwealth, questing to interpret the soul of our people. And I am proud to remember him as his fellow citizen and as a friend. It gives me more than a little satisfaction to see the way in which the powerful ideas of this remarkable man are having a continuing, and even growing, effect upon the Australian legal and judicial system. And especially upon the thinking of the Court upon which he served for 11 turbulent years.

In my own estimation, it is likely that this process of Justice Murphy's intellectual influence will continue to expand. Judges and advocates of the future in Australia will reach, without hesitation, for his dissents. There they will find fresh ideas and questions which should be asked and answered. They will also find insights concerning the legitimate creative function of the judiciary of the common law. In dissent, judges will find encouragement. And they will understand how, in the long haul, ideas which have value may one day come to be accepted.[68]

Perhaps it is the ignominious fate, even of the creative lawyers of today, to become the sources of legal orthodoxy of the future – until their ideas, too, are out of date and must be overthrown by a new generation of lawyers and other citizens with new ideas. Justice Lionel Murphy was a change agent in Australia. After him, nothing was ever quite the same.

68 See *Fisher v Minister of Public Safety and Immigration* [1998] AC 673 at 686 per Lord Steyn (in dissent).

Chapter 12

Popular Sovereignty and the True Foundation of the Australian Constitution [1]

This is an abridged version of a speech entitled 'Deakin: Popular Sovereignty and the True Foundation of the Australian Constitution', which was given as the Deakin Law School Public Oration, 22 August 1997. Deakin was one of the most progressive of the founders of the Australian Constitution, supporting the referendum over other less direct means of securing popular assent to the adoption and amendment of the Constitution. Michael Kirby discusses the important issue of whether ultimate sovereignty in the Australian Commonwealth is vested in the Australian people themselves. He compares historical evidence suggesting the continuity of British authority with the view that Australia suddenly became a fully independent nation in 1901. Despite the implications of this issue for theories of popular sovereignty and underlying constitutional rights, he acknowledges that Australians now take it for granted that the Constitution is ultimately founded in the will and consent of the people of Australia, and calls upon the courts to respond in appropriate ways to this reality.

A New Grundnorm?

When the new Australian Constitution came into force in 1901 few would have questioned the source of its legal legitimacy. Indeed, this was symbolised quite vividly by the voyage of the leading founders of the Constitution, including Alfred Deakin, to London as suppliants to the United Kingdom government to persuade it to have the Commonwealth Bill enacted by the Imperial Parliament at Westminster. The notion of a wholly autochthonous constitution, made by the people of Australia at their conventions, would have seemed to most of the founders, and to the people of Australia at that time, to have been legally illegitimate, if not bizarre. The chain of legal validity, which could be traced back (with rare interruptions) a thousand years, had to be maintained, unbroken, as the Australian colonies became the new Commonwealth within the

1 An earlier version of this paper appeared in (1996) 3(2) *Deakin Law Review* 129.

British Empire. To do this, an Imperial Act was essential. This was no rebellion against British authority.[2] It was continuity.

An alternative proposition has been advanced by Justice Lionel Murphy. In *Kirmani v Captain Cook Cruises Pty Ltd (No 1)*, he said:

> On the inauguration of the Commonwealth on 1 January 1901, British hegemony over the Australian colonies ended and the Commonwealth of Australia emerged as an independent sovereign nation in the community of nations. From then, the British Parliament had no legislative authority over Australia. The authority for the Australian Constitution then and now is its acceptance by the Australian people.[3]

Although this theory has some emotional attractions to Australian nationalists, it scarcely fits in with the contemporary historical reality that saw the emergence of a completely independent Australian nation as something that happened much more slowly. It occurred by incremental steps in the usual way of systems of the common law, derived from England. Indeed, it should not be forgotten that it was the provenance of the Australian Constitution as an Imperial Act which encouraged Justice Isaacs and his supporters to adopt the literalist approach to interpretation expounded in *Amalgamated Society of Engineers v Adelaide Steamship Co Ltd*[4] in 1920 and substantially followed ever since. If the United Kingdom Parliament, after 1 January 1901, had no legal authority whatsoever to enact any laws in relation to Australia, as a separate sovereign nation, one might ask: what business was it of the Parliaments of Australia, federal and state, to request and consent to the enactment of the Australia Acts of 1986?[5] What business was it of the United Kingdom Parliament (except native British politeness) to respond to such Australian parliamentary requests, which did not directly involve, in the slightest, the request of the people of Australia themselves? Nevertheless, enact those statutes, the legislatures of Britain and

---

2 G Winterton (1996) 'Constitutionally Entrenched Common Law Rights: Sacrificing Means to Ends?' in C Sampford and K Preston (eds) *Interpreting Constitutions: Themes, Principles and Institutions*, Federation Press, p 134. This issue is discussed in HGA Wright, 'Sovereignty of the People – The New Constitutional *Grundnorm*' (1998) 26(1) *Federal Law Review* 165, to which the author pays tribute.

3 (1985) 159 CLR 351 at 383.

4 (1920) 28 CLR 129. See G Williams, 'Engineers is Dead, Long Live the Engineers!' (1995) 17 *Sydney Law Review* 62. Williams describes the *Engineers* case as 'the most visible symbol of the traditional supposedly non-political approach of the Court ... prescribing a literalist approach in interpreting the Constitution, that is, an approach based almost exclusively upon analysis of its text' (at 85).

5 See *Australia Act* 1986 (Cth); and *Australia Act* 1986 (UK), enacted pursuant to the *Australia (Request and Consent) Act* 1985 (Cth) and with the concurrence of each State of Australia. See *Australia Act Request Act* 1985 of each Australian State.

Australia certainly did. Amongst other things, they ended the residual appeals to the Privy Council from State Supreme Courts and renounced further imperial legislative designs on Australian lawmaking.[6]

At law schools throughout Australia, well into the 1960s and possibly much later, it was taught that the historical origins of the Australian Constitution, and they alone, gave that document its legal authority. The origins emphasised were the passage of the Commonwealth Bill through the Parliament at Westminster. Rarely, indeed, was there reference to the agonising process of meetings, conferences, conventions, enactments and referenda of the people conducted in this country. Reference to these materials had been disdained from the earliest days by the High Court.[7]

The Constitution has proved highly resistant to formal change. Far more so, I suspect, than Deakin and other founders of the Constitution who were referenda enthusiasts would have expected. It is as if all the discussion during the Constitutional Conventions of the 1890s about referenda involving the direct participation of the people was naive. In actuality, such 'changes' as have been brought about have occurred, in part, by political and legislative initiatives using the text of the document in ways that would not have been conceived and, in part, by court decisions endorsing and upholding legislation or occasionally finding rights and guarantees which the legislators themselves neither saw nor wanted. Of this process, Justice McHugh has said: 'The meaning that the Constitution has for the present generation is not necessarily the same meaning that it had for the earlier generations or those who drafted or enacted the Constitution'.[8] To the same effect is Justice Gummow's remark:

> [R]epresentative government is a dynamic rather than a static institution. ... [T]he Constitution continues to speak to the present and allows for development of the institution of government by changes which may not have been foreseen a century ago.[9]

But when one looks at the Australian Constitution, even separating it from the Imperial Act to which, like a slender legal umbilical cord, it is

---

6 *Australia Act* 1986 (Cth), s 11.

7 *Municipal Council of Sydney v Commonwealth* (1904) 1 CLR 208 at 213; *Attorney-General (Victoria); ex rel Black v Commonwealth* (1981) 146 CLR 559 at 577-578. See now *Cole v Whitfield* (1988) 165 CLR 360 at 385.

8 *Theophanous v Herald and Weekly Times Ltd* (1994) 182 CLR 104 at 197.

9 *McGinty v Western Australia* (1996) 186 CLR 140 at 280-281. Cf G Lindell, 'Why is Australia's Constitution Binding? The Reasons in 1900 and Now and the Effect of Independence' (1986) 16 *Federal Law Review* 29 at 44.

still attached, some things are immediately plain. Its history is indelibly written in every line. It does not begin, as the Constitution of the United States does in its preamble:

> We the people of the United States, in Order to form a more perfect union, establish justice, ensure domestic Tranquillity, provide for the common Defence, promote the general Welfare and secure the Blessings of Liberty to ourselves and our Posterity, do ordain and establish this Constitution.

On the contrary the direct voice of the people was limited in its origins and has been circumscribed in its history ever since.[10]

Notwithstanding the difficulty for theory and practicality that these facts of history present, it is impossible to ignore the growing movement in Australian legal debate which suggests that the ultimate sovereignty, reflected in the Australian Constitution, is now to be taken as reposing in the Australian people themselves. The line of authority on this point can probably be traced to early hints given by the original Justices of the High Court, for example, in *R v Smithers*.[11] But the modern impetus began with the then heretical expositions by Justice Murphy.[12] It gained support from repeated opinions of Justices Deane and Toohey.[13] More cautiously, Chief Justice Mason, in the *Australian Capital Television* case, observed that '[t]he *Australia Act* 1986 (UK) marked the end of the legal sovereignty of the Imperial Parliament and recognised that ultimate sovereignty resided in the Australian people'.[14] In *McGinty v Western Australia*,[15] Justice McHugh acknowledged the difficulties in the way of ready acceptance of the Australian people as the ultimate foundation of the legal legitimacy of the Australian Constitution. Yet the conclusion he reached was that '[t]he political and legal sovereignty of Australia now resides in the people of Australia'.[16]

For the most part, courts can deal with constitutional questions by focusing their attention on the text and structure and upon those

---

10 An attempt to graft a new preamble on to the Constitution failed abysmally in November 1999.

11 (1912) 16 CLR 99. Griffith CJ stated that 'the citizen ... has the right to come to the seat of government ... to seek its protection, to share its offices ... and this right is in its nature independent of the will of any State over whose soil he must pass in the exercise of it' (at 108). See Wright (1998) p 165.

12 *Kirmani v Captain Cook Cruises Pty Ltd (No 1)* (1985) 159 CLR 351 at 383.

13 *Leeth v Commonwealth* (1992) 174 CLR 455 at 483; and *Cunliffe v Commonwealth* (1994) 182 CLR 272 at 336.

14 (1992) 177 CLR 106 at 138.

15 (1996) 186 CLR 140.

16 Ibid, at 230.

documents (such as the Convention debates) which may now throw light upon the text's meaning.[17] It is rare that the bedrock of a Constitution is explored or even thought about. At least, it has been rare in Australia until now. However, an indication of the possibility of things to come may be found in some of the arguments that were advanced in *Levy v Victoria*.[18] One of the arguments advanced to support the invalidity of the regulation forbidding Mr Levy access to places of duck shooting was that any such regulation was invalid on the ground that the people of Victoria had not empowered their Parliament to take from them the rights of protest and other actions, the exercise of which Mr Levy and his supporters asserted. The argument was not successful.

'Deep Lying Rights' of the People

If it is accepted that the people of Australia are the source of the legitimacy of the Australian Constitution, does this mean that the people have reserved to themselves some rights that even the Constitution, and the laws made under the Constitution, cannot extinguish? The notion that there are some 'deep lying rights' which have never been ceded by the people in the Constitution or otherwise to Parliament (or to any of the other organs of government) may find some reflections in the extra-curial comments of Justice Toohey:

> [W]here the people of Australia, in adopting a Constitution, conferred power upon a Commonwealth Parliament, it is to be presumed that they did not intend that those grants of power extend to invasion of fundamental common law liberties.[19]

These and like remarks[20] may amount to nothing more than an interpretative presumption. There is nothing unusual in suggesting that a document such as a Constitution (or any other statute) should be construed with the assumption in mind that basic common law rights are only abolished or diminished by language expressed in the clearest of terms.[21]

---

17 Cf *Kartinyeri v Commonwealth* (1998) 195 CLR 337 at 401 where it was suggested that, in respect of provisions of the Constitution altered with the concurrence of the electors of the Commonwealth by referendum, regard could be had to debates on the referendum proposal in the Federal Parliamentary debates and elsewhere.

18 (1997) 189 CLR 579 at 634-635.

19 J Toohey, 'A Government of Laws, And Not of Men?' (1993) 4 *Public Law Review* 158 at 170.

20 See *Nationwide News Pty Ltd v Wills* (1992) 177 CLR 1 at 69.

21 *Black Clawson International Ltd v Papierwerke AG* [1975] AC 591 at 638; *Sorby v Commonwealth* (1983) 152 CLR 281 at 289, 309, 311; *Baker v Campbell* (1983) 153 CLR 52 at 96-97, 104, 116, 123; and *Corporate Affairs Commission (NSW) v Yuill* (1991) 172 CLR 319 at 348.

Across the Tasman in New Zealand, without a written constitution, Justice Cooke (as Lord Cooke of Thorndon then was) repeatedly propounded the 'deep lying rights' thesis. For him, this went beyond an interpretative principle. He sought to rest the thesis upon the suggestion that laws made by Parliament are ultimately binding only because courts say they are. If Parliament purported to make a law which, for example, took away the rights of New Zealand citizens to resort to the courts of law for the determination of their rights, such a law would (he suggested) be of dubious validity.[22] This would be so although it had passed all the formal tests, carried on its face the royal assent and bore all the other apparent hallmarks of an Act of Parliament.

In *Fraser v State Services Commission*,[23] Justice Cooke put it quite vividly. 'This is perhaps a reminder that it is arguable that some common law rights may go so deep that even Parliament cannot be accepted by the Court to have destroyed them'.[24] In judicial writing and elsewhere I have doubted this thesis, suggesting that our true guarantee against such an unthinkable law lies in the collective wisdom of our Parliaments and in their regular accountability to the people.[25] Rather ungraciously perhaps, I repeated my hesitations at a conference convened to celebrate Lord Cooke's many contributions to the jurisprudence of the common law world.[26] I suggested that, in this regard, his view was heresy, even dangerous heresy. He took it all with good grace and patient fortitude.

However, several developments are occurring which should be noted and which are relevant to the thesis of 'deep lying rights'. They include the greater willingness of constitutional courts to construe the constitutional instrument and other legislation against a presumption of respect for fundamental human rights; their greater willingness to invoke the international law of human rights to lend support to this endeavour;[27] their greater sensitivity to constitutional implications found in

22 *New Zealand Drivers' Association v New Zealand Road Carriers* [1982] 1 NZLR 374 at 390.

23 *Fraser v State Services Commission* [1984] 1 NZLR 116.

24 Ibid, at 121.

25 *Building Construction Employees and Builders' Labourers Federation of New South Wales v Minister for Industrial Relations* (1986) 7 NSWLR 372 at 406-407.

26 MD Kirby (1997) 'Lord Cooke and Fundamental Rights' in P Rishworth (ed) *The Struggle for Simplicity – Essays for Lord Cooke of Thorndon*, Butterworths, p 331.

27 *Tavita v Minister of Immigration* [1994] 2 NZLR 247 at 266; *Minister for Immigration and Ethnic Affairs v Teoh* (1995) 183 CLR 273 at 291. Cf MD Kirby, 'The Impact of International Human Rights Norms: A Law Undergoing Evolution' (1995) 25 *University of Western Australia Law Review* 1 at 10-11; and S Donaghue, 'Balancing Sovereignty in International Law: The Domestic Impact of International Law in Australia' (1995) 17 *Adelaide Law Review* 213.

the language and structure of the document;[28] and their insistence upon the protection of the integrity of the judicial process, the independence of the judiciary[29] and the availability of constitutional judicial review.[30]

In the old days, it was easy to find the fundamental basis – the *Grundnorm* for the Australian Constitution. It lay in the legal authority by which the document was clothed when the Imperial Act endorsing it passed through the Commons, was approved by the Lords Spiritual and Temporal and had affixed to it the sign manual of Queen Victoria. However, as the twentieth century has passed, such explanations of the legitimacy of our Constitution no longer command universal acceptance. Increasingly they seem inappropriate and out of date.

That is why Australians are now looking to themselves for the authority of their Constitution and for the reason why they accept it as governing them. Is it, like many other features of Australian national life, just apathy that explains this acceptance? Do people not really care: considering that time should not be wasted upon such theoretical quandaries? Is the Constitution obeyed because the police and perhaps the army would ultimately enforce its provisions against those in Australia who objected to it? Do Australians turn away from these debates because they realise that 'the people', who are said to be sovereign, have only the slightest inkling of how constitutional democracy operates? A recent study in the United States revealed that 59 per cent of the public could name the Three Stooges; however, only 17 per cent could name three Justices of the Supreme Court of that country.[31] In Australia, the percentage would probably be much smaller, at least on the latter statistic. Perhaps it is a constitutionally contented people that know the Three Stooges and not three Supreme Court judges.

---

28 *Kable v Director of Public Prosecutions (NSW)* (1996) 189 CLR 51. For interesting Indian analogies, see *Golakanath v State of Punjab* AIR (1967) SC 1643 and *Kesavananda Bharati v State of Kerala* AIR (1973) SC 1461. Cf CC Aikman, 'Fundamental Rights and Directing Principles of State Policy in India' (1987) 17 *Victoria University of Wellington Law Review* 373; and DG Morgan, 'The Indian "Essential Features" Case' (1981) 30 *International and Comparative Law Quarterly* 307.

29 *Wilson v Minister for Aboriginal and Torres Strait Islander Affairs* (1996) 189 CLR 1.

30 This was illustrated by proceedings before the High Court in *Ellman v Commonwealth* (unreported, July 1997), per Brennan CJ. See also *Levy v Victoria* (1997) 189 CLR 579.

31 J Biskupik, 'Has the Court Lost its Appeal?', *Washington Post*, 12 October 1995, p A23, citing SB Smith, 'The Constitution of Jurisprudence' (unpublished paper).

Consequences of Popular Sovereignty

If the Australian people are (as is suggested) now the ultimate foundation of the legitimacy of the Constitution, we must realise that this hypothesis has consequences. They may lie not only in the arguments that will be advanced about the fundamental 'deep lying rights' which the people have reserved themselves but also in the work of the courts. If the Australian people, and not the notional legality traced back to an imperial statute, are the ultimate source of constitutional authority in Australia, may it not be the duty of the courts in their mode of reasoning to be more accessible to the people? If judicial officers are not simply demonstrating to the professionally skilled the legal authority of their decisions, but must also speak to the people from whom their legal authority ultimately comes, should different modes of reasoning and explanation be adopted? A different judicial method? A greater attention to 'reconnecting jurisprudence' to ordinary people?[32]

One American scholar has recently made this point in words that deserve our attention in Australia:

> Judicial opinions serve as the primary link between the courts and the populace. Presumably, opinions are written to assure the people that legal judgments are reasoned, not capricious. As forms of communication, opinions must therefore be widely intelligible if the judiciary is to maintain popular credibility. For the United States Supreme Court, this responsibility is paramount. 'Constitutional law is not pronounced principally for the benefit of the legal profession but for the American people as a whole'. 'The Court maintains its constitutional authority in part by reinforcing the political principles and political bonds of the country'. Expositions of constitutional meaning ultimately must address the fundamental commitments of the populace. To do so, they must be easily understood. When constitutional opinions become unintelligible to the ordinary citizen, one of our nation's three central supports begins to crumble.[33]

The United States Supreme Court has recognised this for itself. In a recent decision it remarked that 'the Court's concern with legitimacy is not for the sake of the Court, but for the sake of the Nation to which it is responsible'.[34]

---

32 M Kammen (1986) *A Machine That Would Go of Itself: A Constitution in American Culture*, Knopf, reviewed in RB Bernstein, 'Charting the Bicentennial' (1987) 87 *Columbia Law Review* 1565, at 1618, 1622.

33 SB Smith, 'The Constitution of Jurisprudence' (unpublished paper), p 19.

34 *Planned Parenthood v Casey* 505 US 833 at 842-844 (1992).

We could content ourselves in Australia by saying that none of this applies to us. Ours is a Constitution without ringing phrases, with no Bill of Rights. It can safely be left to judges and lawyers to handle its problems. If, in the United States, only a small fraction of the people reads judicial opinions and a smaller one consults law reviews,[35] the number is obviously smaller still in Australia. This makes the people highly dependent upon the media for coverage of the courts' work. Perhaps, recognising this, the High Court of Australia may need to adapt its procedures so that the people understand better what it does and why it does it. If it fails to do this, the Court may be exposed, even more than it presently is, to misunderstanding and even to misrepresentations which are inadequately answered. The Court should not, in my opinion, lose sight of the truth that 'if society no longer identifies with the law, then its constitutional democracy is at risk'.[36]

Taking the Centenary Seriously

So long as the foundation of the Australian Constitution was nothing more than an imperial statute enacted in 1901 and an ancient chain of legal title going back (with a few 'embarrassing interruptions') a thousand years, and so long as the declaratory theory of the judicial function reigned, the exposition of the Australian Constitution could be safely left to technically expert lawyers skilled in construing bills of sale and contested wills. The point I want to make is a simple one. To the extent that Australians now accept that the ultimate foundation of their Constitution is the will and consent of the people, and not its imperial statutory provenance, courts must adapt their thinking. If the people are the foundation, are there rights, even when not expressed, implied in the text and structure of the Constitution that the courts must uphold? Are there rights which the people, through their representatives, may declare in a Charter of Rights enforceable in the courts? Are there rights that the people have never surrendered to Parliament but reserve to themselves? If the people are the ultimate source of all legal authority, does that have consequences for the way courts reason? And for the way they explain their reasons to the people of Australia who are, on this hypothesis, the source of all legal and governmental power – including that of the courts themselves?

We cannot naively assert that the Australian people are sovereign without considering the consequences of this assertion for a

35 SB Smith, 'The Constitution of Jurisprudence' (unpublished paper), p 24.

36 Ibid, p 26. See the comments on the judgments of Murphy J in J Hocking (1997) *Lionel Murphy – A Political Biography*, Cambridge, pp 247-249.

Constitution which, in many ways, was framed upon quite a different hypothesis. Political phrases acclaiming popular sovereignty come cheap. But a deeper reflection on constitutional governance is what Australians should be attempting as the centenary of the federation approaches. This event is, or should be, a serious and constructive reflective event in the life of a people and a nation. In my humble view, it is infinitely more important than the Olympic Games which, however ennobling of the human spirit, are transient and concern the whole world – not Australia's peculiar constitutional destiny.

If the people are truly sovereign, politicians and other decision-makers should seek to engage all of the people in the celebration of the centenary of Australian nationhood. Otherwise the bread and circuses of the Olympics will overshadow a truly great Australian achievement – the century of federation. We will slide back to the view that government is really a matter for the experts and that the law is truly a disembodied science for lawyers and others in the elite. This would be a profoundly disappointing outcome. It would consign the so-called sovereignty of the Australian people to a mere fiction – a thing of legal theory. Deakin, who did more than anyone else to bring about the Federation, stated that 'its actual accomplishment must always appear to have been secured by a series of miracles'.[37] But are Australians up to miracles today?

37 Cited in R Evans et al (1997) *Our Future's Past*, Macmillan, p 92.

Chapter 13

Attacks on Judges: A Universal Phenomenon[1]

At the American Bar Association's Meeting at Maui, Hawaii, on 5 January 1998, Michael Kirby examined recent attacks on the judiciary by the media, politicians and academics in a number of common law countries. Although he recognises the useful nature of some of these criticisms, he points out that an increasing number are primarily political or personal in nature. He examines the implications for judicial independence and possible strategies to combat this phenomenon, including increased community education about what the judiciary does and how important it is to the protection of basic freedoms in society.

In the past decade, in many countries of the common law, the general deference formerly paid to judges has been eroded. Attacks on judges have now become commonplace. Many are now made by politicians who see mileage in that course. But beyond politicians, the attacks have been made by the media, public commentators, academics and members of the legal profession, the last sometimes even omitting to dress up their words in the respect for the judicial office which they formerly professed.

To illustrate the universality and contemporaneity of this phenomenon, I will give a few recent illustrations of what has been occurring. They will bear out, I believe, my proposition that attacks on the judiciary are a universal phenomenon.

United Kingdom

In the United Kingdom, from whose judiciary common law countries ultimately derive their model, the deference paid to Her Majesty's judges has lately begun to decline. Increasingly, political leaders of succeeding governments have publicly criticised judges in ways that would have been unthinkable in earlier times.[2] The media of Britain have fallen upon these differences, notably those which emerged between the Major

---

1 An earlier version of this paper was published in (1998) 72 *Australian Law Journal* 599.

2 See Lord Irvine of Lairg, House of Lords, *Hansard*, 5 June 1996, 1254 at 1255.

government and the senior judiciary, taking 'delight in both highlighting – and, one suspects, fuelling – the split between judiciary and government'.[3] The Beaverbrook press claimed that there was a 'sickness sweeping through the senior judiciary – galloping arrogance'.[4] With just a little *hubris*, the editorialist declared that '[w]hile European Human Rights judges, some from countries which once sent political prisoners to Siberia, are venting their spleen on Britain, legal weevils here at home are practising their own brand of mischief'.[5] The Rothermere press joined in with comments that seem astonishing to lawyers from the United States and Australia, brought up in the tradition of constitutional review:

> Now it seems that any judge can take it on himself to overrule a Minister, even though Parliament might approve of the Minister's action. This is to arrogate power to themselves in a manner that makes a mockery of Parliament. ... The judges are giving the impression that they are acting on a political agenda of their own.[6]

The Times, once the bastion of the Establishment in Britain, under new ownership, demanded that a new Chief Justice be appointed who could 'steer his profession away from the sound of gunfire'.[7]

The more courageous and articulate members of the English judiciary, such as Sir Stephen Sedley, answered back. They reminded those who had forgotten about the peril of supine judges. They called in aid Sir Edward Coke's assertion of the sovereignty of the courts in the face of the Crown's prerogatives.[8] They cautioned against mob rule, nowadays increasingly dressed in the guise of tabloid newspapers and talkback commentators. These courageous judges draw on United States experience in the refurbishment of the constitutional institutions of Britain.[9] Sometimes their leaders rise in the House of Lords to defend the judiciary from attack and to espouse its causes.[10]

---

3 R Stevens (1995) 'Judges, Politics, Politicians and the Confusing Role of the Judiciary' in K Hawkins (ed) *The Human Face of Law: Essays in Honour of Donald Harris*, Clarendon, p 264.

4 *Daily Express*, 4 November 1995, cited in Stevens, ibid.

5 *Sunday Express*, 1 October 1995, cited in Stevens, ibid.

6 *Daily Mail*, 2 November 1995, cited in Stevens, ibid.

7 *The Times* (London), 4 May 1996, p 3.

8 Sir Stephen Sedley 'Human Rights: A 21st Century Agenda' in R Blackburn and JJ Busuttil (1997) *Human Rights for the 21st Century*, Pinter, p 1. Cf Lord Ackner, 'The Erosion of Judicial Independence' [1996] *New Law Journal* 1789.

9 Lord Steyn, 'The Weakest and Least Dangerous Department of Government' [1997] *Public Law* 84.

10 See Lord Bingham LCJ, House of Lords, *Hansard*, 3 November 1997, p 1245. Because of our notion of the separation of powers, that facility is unavailable to judges in the United States and Australia. The forums available to us are rather less grand.

New Zealand

In New Zealand, in recent times, the old deference has also taken something of a battering. Judges have been castigated ferociously for bail decisions that went wrong. They have been prosecuted for false travel claims. They have been attacked for failing to respond to media criticism. When the Chief Justice, in a public speech, cautioned that

> The increasingly strident cries of the well heeled sector of the community, pressuring Government and the judiciary as to the particular brand of justice they seek, are not a pretty sight ... nor are the supportive noises made by acolytes in the profession.[11]

he was denounced in the *New Zealand Law Journal*, of all places, for getting into politics, damaging the independence of the judiciary and insulting the legal profession.

Australia

The debates in Britain and New Zealand seem positively genteel by comparison to those which have engaged the Australian judiciary in recent times. The problem is a general one. But it came to the fore after the High Court of Australia decided in 1996 that the native title to land of Australia's indigenous peoples was not, as a matter of law, necessarily extinguished by the pastoral leases granted over vast areas of the Australian continent beginning in the nineteenth century.[12] The decision was by a majority of four to three of the Justices of the seven-member Court.[13] Subsequent to the decision, politicians in both Federal and State Parliaments appeared to compete with each other to attack the Court and especially the majority judges. Few, indeed, demonstrated any familiarity with what the judges had actually written. A senior Federal Minister singled my reasons out for special castigation, declaring that he was 'underwhelmed by them'. A State Premier described them as nothing more than 'rantings and ravings'. The attacks, the like of which we have never seen before in Australia, continued for months, unrepaired by an effective defence of the Court by the traditional political guardian of judicial independence, the Attorney-General. The Attorney-General stated that he did not agree with the convention that it

---

11 Sir Thomas Eichelbaum, cited in 'Judges and Politics' [1996] *New Zealand Law Journal* 361 at 361. See also Editorial, 'Dismissal of Judges' [1997] *New Zealand Law Journal* 333.

12 *Wik Peoples v Queensland* (1996) 187 CLR 1. See also *Mabo v Queensland (No 2)* (1992) 175 CLR 1.

13 Toohey, Gaudron, Gummow and Kirby JJ; Brennan CJ, Dawson and McHugh JJ dissenting.

was his role to defend the courts from criticism. They must, he declared, find ways of defending themselves.[14] For this, he, in turn, was criticised by judges and retired judges.[15] The politicians maintained their attack. Some did so long after the decision.[16]

The derogatory comments of politicians soon became the springboard for academic and media castigation. Recent High Court decisions, the Court and the Justices were labelled 'bogus',[17] 'pusillanimous and evasive',[18] guilty of 'plunging Australia into the abyss',[19] a 'pathetic ... self-appointed [group of] Kings and Queens',[20] a group of 'basket-weavers',[21] 'gripped ... in a mania for progressivism',[22] purveyors of 'intellectual dishonesty',[23] unaware of 'its place',[24] 'adventurous',[25] needing a 'good behaviour bond',[26] needing, on the contrary, a sentence to 'life on the streets',[27] an 'unfaithful servant of the Constitution',[28] 'undermining democracy',[29] a body 'packed with feral judges',[30] 'a

---

14 D Williams (1996) 'Who Speaks for the Judges?', Address to Australian Judicial Conference, November; and D Williams (1997) 'Judicial Independence, the Courts and the Community', Address to South Australian Chapter of the Australian Institute of Judicial Administration, February.

15 Sir Gerard Brennan (1997) 'State of the Australian Judicature', Address to the Australian Legal Convention, September.

16 See, for example, D Cass, 'Constitutional Debate Puts the High Court in the Dock', *The Age*, 7 November 1997, p A17.

17 *Canberra Times*, 9 March 1997, p 4, referring to comments of Professor G Craven.

18 B Mandle in *Canberra Times*, 9 March 1997, p 9.

19 Senator R Boswell, reported in *The Age*, 4 March 1997, p A4.

20 Premier R Borbidge (Qld), *The Age*, 4 March 1997, p A4.

21 G Richardson, 'Oh, What a Tangled Web They've Weaved', *The Bulletin*, 4 February 1997, p 31.

22 G Craven, 'The High Court: An Abuse of Power', 31st Alfred Deakin Lecture, Melbourne, noted in *Australian Financial Review*, 10 October 1997, p 29.

23 Ibid.

24 WR Hassell, 'High Court Must Know its Place', *The Australian*, 24 September 1997, p 12.

25 JM Fraser (former Prime Minister), *The Australian*, 24 September 1997, p 13.

26 G Milne, 'Government Puts Judges on Good Behaviour Bond', *The Australian*, 9 June 1997, p 11.

27 L Kavanagh, 'Sentence Judges to Life on the Streets', *Courier Mail*, 14 June 1997, p 25.

28 G Craven (1997) 'The High Court and the Founders: An Unfaithful Servant', in Australian Parliament, Senate, Papers on Parliament, *The Constitution Makers*, Australian Parliament, p 63.

29 Sir John Gorton (former Prime Minister) quoted in P Akerman, 'Telling the Truth', *Sunday Telegraph*, 16 November 1997, p 63.

30 P Akerman, *Daily Telegraph*, 20 November 1997, p 11.

professional labour cartel'.[31] There were many more epithets of a like character, many stronger.

These attacks eventually called forth defences of the High Court by judges and retired judges,[32] the organised legal profession,[33] leading members of the Bar,[34] a former Governor-General,[35] legal academics,[36] a few members of Parliament,[37] selected editorialists[38] and even a law student who felt compelled to write.[39] One professor warned of the consequences of such a prolonged confrontation between the executive government and the judiciary in Australia. He did so drawing upon the experiences of the land of his birth, Malaysia, where in 1988, the most senior judge was driven from office.[40] The then Chief Justice of Australia, Sir Gerard Brennan, in an unusual move, wrote a private letter to the Acting Prime Minister to correct the erroneous suggestion, made publicly, that the Court had deliberately delayed its decision in the pastoral leases case. Promptly, this letter was secured by journalists

---

31 'Dilute the Judges' Cartel', *Australian Financial Review*, 12 May 1997, p 20.

32 S Jacobs, 'Judge Warns of Short-Cut to Tyranny', 26 March 1997, *The Advertiser*, p 5; Judge Anthony Smith, 'Attacks by Senior Politicians on the Integrity of the High Court of Australia', *Judges' Forum Newsletter*, August 1997, p 3; and RD Keal, 'Stop Attacking the Judges', *West Australian*, 10 March 1997, p 12.

33 C Pullin, 'From the President', *Australian Bar Gazette*, March 1997, p 1; PJ Short, President, Law Council of Australia, 'Who Speaks for the Judges?', *Australian Lawyer*, April 1997, p 6; 'Attacks on the High Court by People Who Ought to Know Better', *Bulletin* (Law Society of South Australia), May 1997, p 6; and C Merritt, 'LCA Backs High Court', *Australian Financial Review*, 19 March 1997, p 6.

34 Sir Maurice Byers QC, 'Doubtful Political Wisdom', *Sydney Morning Herald*, 20 March 1997, p 16; R Castan QC, 'Judge-Bashing Reveals an Ignorance of Legal Principles', *The Australian*, 1 October 1997, p 13; J Cain, 'A Low Attack on our High Court', *The Age*, 25 February 1997, p A15; M Tobias QC, 'I Beg to Differ', *Sydney Morning Herald*, 30 October 1997, p 18.

35 Sir Zelman Cowen (1997) Address to the Rotary Club of Richmond, March.

36 D Skapinker, 'Gross Over-reaction', *Sydney Morning Herald*, 7 March 1997, p 14; G Williams, 'Attacks Undermine Role of High Court', *Sydney Morning Herald*, 9 March 1997, p 11; D Cass, 'Constitutional Debate Put the High Court in the Dock', *The Age*, 7 November 1997, p A17.

37 See Senator Helen Coonan, *Commonwealth Parliamentary Debates (Senate)*, 18 June 1997, p 3974.

38 See 'Besieging the Bench', *The Age*, 22 February 1997, p A14; 'Diversionary Attacks on the High Court', *Courier Mail*, 19 February 1997, p 20; 'High Court Plans are Sour Grapes', *West Australian*, 20 February 1997, p 12; and 'In Defence of Judges', *Sydney Morning Herald*, 22 September 1997, p 16. Cf JR McClelland, 'Criticism of Courts Unfounded', *Sydney Morning Herald*, 27 January 1997, p 13.

39 S Ioannou, 'Professor and High Court', *Australian Financial Review*, letter to the editor, 14 October 1997, p 18.

40 Professor Hoong Phun Lee, 'Why We Must Protect the Protectors', *Sydney Morning Herald*, 13 June 1997, p 17.

(presumably knowledge of its existence was leaked in Parliament) under the freedom of information legislation. It was given widespread publicity.[41] Later, at a series of legal conferences in Australia[42] and overseas,[43] the Chief Justice spoke of the dangers of such sustained attacks on the judiciary. From the United States, Kathryn Graham wrote to the Australian press to castigate the 'disappointing lack of understanding of the role of the Court'.[44] In October 1997, Chief Justice Gleeson, at that time Chief Justice of New South Wales, called for a truce and for mutual respect between the branches of government.[45] However, the debate and the attacks persisted. Only the chosen means varied. Too many critics were having too much fun in a new game to stop prematurely.

The feature of the Australian debate which has concerned many observers has been the complete shift from bipartisan political acceptance of constitutional and other important decisions of the Court which had marked Australia's history in the past, even when those decisions were extremely important and controversial.[46] There is also a concern that such an unrelenting barrage of criticism and denigration will, if unabated, undermine the community's confidence in the courts and acceptance of court decisions.[47] Editorialists might declare that 'robust legal debate [is] good for [the] country'.[48] But a lot of judges and lawyers, unused to such unrelenting assaults, had their doubts.

United States

The prize for the worst examples in a developed country in this *genre* of political attack on the judiciary must, however, go to the United States of America. Of particular concern to outsiders (and possibly to citizens of the United States as well) has been the appearance of federal political leaders, looking around for themes for their electoral campaigns, and

41 Noted in A Ramsay, 'High Court Gets Short Shrift', *Sydney Morning Herald*, 8 March 1997, p 43.

42 Brennan (1997). See also Chief Justice Brennan, 'Address to the Twelfth South Pacific Judicial Conference', noted in *The Australian*, 15 April 1997, p 3; and *Sydney Morning Herald*, 15 April 1997, p 3.

43 Chief Justice Brennan (1997) 'The Third Branch and the Fourth Estate', Second Address in the Series *Broadcasting, Society and the Law*, April.

44 K Graham, 'Judges obliged to take a stand', *The Age*, 4 March 1997, p A14.

45 AM Gleeson, 'Who Do Judges Think They Are?' (1998) 22 *Criminal Law Journal* 10.

46 A Ramsay, 'High Court Gets Short Shrift', *Sydney Morning Herald*, 8 March 1997, p 43.

47 Cf B Smith, 'Craven Attack on Court Dubbed "Alarming" ', *Australian Financial Review*, 17 October 1997, p 26.

48 *The Weekend Australian*, 15-16 February 1997, p 22.

selecting the easy targets of the judiciary as a means of promoting themselves as tough on law and order.[49]

The retiring President of the American Bar Association, Mr N Lee Cooper, stated, on the eve of leaving office, that the biggest challenge to the legal profession and justice system of the United States was 'the continuing attack upon our federal judiciary'.[50] While Senator Robert Dole's call for the impeachment of Judge Harold Baer of the United States District Court[51] and his consignment of United States Appeals Judge Rosemary Barkett to his 'judicial hall of shame'[52] did not work very well as an electoral theme once it was pointed out that Dole had voted in the Senate to confirm 97 per cent of President Clinton's judicial nominees, these attacks continue. Mr Cooper could have widened his focus to the State judiciary as well. The gravest attacks in the United States have been made by State politicians seeking to punish judges for decisions in criminal, and particularly death penalty cases, cases which tend to engender strong public passions. At least the federal judiciary enjoys constitutional protections provided by the wisdom of the Founders of the United States Constitution who, even 200 years ago, saw the dangers.[53] Many State judges in the United States are especially vulnerable to removal from office. Some have suffered that fate for performing no more than their judicial duty.

The Governor of Tennessee (Mr Don Sundquist), after effectively securing the removal of Justice Penny White from the Supreme Court of that State by electoral recall, declared that judges *should* be looking over their shoulders to see whether the same would happen to them.[54] This assertion drew a retort from Justice John Paul Stevens of the United States Supreme Court, speaking at the 1996 ABA annual meeting. 'It was never contemplated that the individual who has to protect our individual rights would have to consider what decision would produce the most votes'.[55]

---

49 SB Bright, 'Political Attacks on the Judiciary' (1997) 80 *Judicature* 165. See PJ White, 'An America Without Judicial Independence' (1997) 80 *Judicature* 174.

50 L Cooper, 'On Independence, Once and For All', *ABA Journal*, August 1997, p 8. See also American Bar Association (1997), Report of the Commission on Separation of Powers and Judicial Independency, *An Independent Judiciary*, American Bar Association.

51 Bright (1997) p 166.

52 Ibid, p 169.

53 A Hamilton et al, *The Federalist: A Commentary on the Constitution of the United States*, Modern Library edition (1941), No 78. See GP Joseph 'Judicial Imperfection and Judicial Independence' (1997) 23(4) *Litigation* 1; cf Lord Steyn (1997) p 84.

54 Bright (1997) p 166.

55 Ibid, p 169.

There have been a number of cases in other States. They include the removal of Chief Justice Rose Bird and two other Justices of the Supreme Court of California, and Justice James Robertson who was voted off the Mississippi Supreme Court in 1992.[56] The action of Judge Baer, in changing his ruling after the heat of political pressure was applied, may have been unconnected with that pressure. But it certainly did not look good.[57]

Fundamental human rights defend the right of every person in a cause affecting them to be heard by an independent, neutral and competent judge. The Declaration of Independence of the United States listed amongst the grievances against King George III that 'He has made judges dependent on his Will alone, for the tenure of their offices'.[58] Constitutional decisions uphold the promise of judicial independence.[59] This core value of constitutionalism is also guaranteed in international law by the *International Covenant on Civil and Political Rights*.[60] Political pressure, sometimes applied with a fair measure of brutality to secure particular results from sitting judges, undermines the principle of independent, neutral and competent justice according to law. It is no more to be tolerated where the brutality is verbal than where it is physical.

As discussed, one of the most disturbing features of the attacks on the judiciary in the United States is the way they have been followed up by removal of judges from office, or threats of impeachment. Another concern is the complete misrepresentation of judicial opinions and serious over-simplification of complex issues.[61] The truth and detail about controversial cases tend to elude headstrong politicians on the campaign trial. Yet another is reports of elected judges in the United States running for office or re-election on the boast that they are '*too* tough on criminals'.[62]

---

56 Ibid, p 170.

57 Ibid, p 172.

58 Ibid.

59 In the United States see *Chambers v Florida* 309 US 227 (1940) per Black J. See American Bar Association (1997) pp 9-12.

60 Article 14.1 provides that '[a]ll persons shall be equal before courts and tribunals. In the determination of any criminal charge against him or of his rights and obligations in a suit at law, everyone shall be entitled to a fair and public hearing by a competent, independent and impartial tribunal established by law'. Cf *Liteky v United States* 510 US 540 at 555; 114 S Ct 1147 at 1157 (1994).

61 Bright (1997) p 173.

62 Advertisement to re-elect Judge Mike McCormick, a Circuit Judge in Alabama, in SB Bright, 'Political Attacks on the Judiciary: Can Justice Be Done Amid Efforts to Intimidate and Remove Judges from Office for Unpopular Decisions?' (1997) 72 *New York University Law Review* 308 at 323.

Also of concern is the failure of leading political office-holders in the United States to speak up to defend judicial independence. An American commentator has asked, in relation to Senator Dole's call for the impeachment of Judge Baer: 'Where was Senator Orrin Hatch, a lawyer and the Chairman of the Senate Judiciary Committee, when this attack was made?' The answer given is:

> Unfortunately, he was not defending the independence of the judiciary. After Baer reversed his ruling, Hatch told reporters 'Unfortunately this sort of attention cannot be brought to bear on all of the other soft-on-crime decisions issued by other activists that President Clinton has appointed'.[63]

The author went on:

> Similarly, those in the Democratic Party should have taken President Clinton – a former constitutional law professor – to task for the suggestion that he might call for Baer's resignation because he disagreed with Baer's decision.[64]

For anyone wanting to read the catalogue of United States equivalents to the Australian list of verbal denigration recently hurled at the judiciary, a good starting point is the article by Judge JW Bellacosa of the New York State Court of Appeals.[65] 'Screwballs'[66] is the kindest of the epithets. Judge Bellacosa concludes that '[j]udges can take criticism, I am very confident, but whether the public interest can stand and absorb mal-informed, drum-beaten and heated attacks on the judicial process is worth pause and reflection'.[67]

Assessment of the Storm

What can be said about the period we are living through, illustrated by the examples that I have cited from several countries?

Always Some Criticism

It is wrong to think that criticism of the judiciary is completely new. In the United States, under the protection of the First Amendment, the media and politicians have commonly said nasty things about particular

---

63 Bright (1997) p 173.

64 Ibid.

65 JW Bellacosa, 'Remarks – Judging Cases v Courting Public Opinion' (1997) 65 *Fordham Law Review* 2381.

66 Ibid, p 2385.

67 Ibid, p 2388.

judges. For example, when President FD Roosevelt nominated Hugo Black to the Supreme Court, the *Chicago Tribune* declared that 'If he wanted the worst man he could find, he has him'.[68] In *Newsweek*, a commentator was quoted as saying: 'There have been worse appointments to high judicial office; but, ... I can't remember where or when'. The *Washington Post* said that the nomination combined 'lack of training ... and extreme partisanship'.[69] Black went on to distinguished service on the Court. It is a little ironic (but not perhaps entirely surprising) that it was he who said in *Chambers v Florida* that courts serve 'as havens of refuge for those who might otherwise suffer because they are helpless, weak, outnumbered, or because they are ... victims of prejudice and public excitement'.[70]

In England, a memorandum from the Permanent Secretary to the Lord Chancellor's Department, recently disclosed, asserted:

> In recent years ... it has been difficult for the State to obtain justice from the judges of the High Court. It is not too much to say that in recent years, the weight of prejudice against the State in the minds of many members of the Court of Appeal and judges of the High Court has been such as seriously to affect the administration of justice.[71]

This was not written during the current debates. It was penned in March 1929 to the first Lord Hailsham, who was Lord Chancellor in Stanley Baldwin's first administration. However, in the England of that time the opinion was privately expressed and kept so for decades.

In Australia, as in Britain, the law of contempt, in the form of 'scandalising the court', has imposed a measure of restraint on attacks on judges,[72] particularly where it is considered that the statement is an attempt to influence specific court proceedings.[73] However, from the outset, this power was used cautiously in Australia.[74] It has faded in most developed common law countries during the course of the century in harmony with expanded notions of free speech.

One liberal High Court judge in Australia, Justice Lionel Murphy, suggested many years ago that there was actually insufficient, and not excessive, attention to the courts and their importance to the

68 WE Leuchtenberg (1995) *The Supreme Court Reborn*, Oxford, p 186.

69 Ibid.

70 309 US 227 at 241 (1940).

71 Stevens (1995) pp 245-246.

72 See *Gallagher v Durack* (1983) 152 CLR 238; and *Lewis v Judge Ogden* (1984) 153 CLR 682.

73 See *Hinch v Attorney-General (Vic)* (1987) 164 CLR 15.

74 See *R v Nicholls* (1910) 12 CLR 280.

government of the country.[75] Going back to the good old days when politicians, the media and others would show respectful obeisance to the judges, confining their criticisms to private mutterings is now an impossibility. In any case, when explored, those old days included some political and personal attacks, admittedly rather more muted than of recent times.

Inevitability

In a free society some criticism of the judiciary is inevitable. This is especially so at a time when there is a growing appreciation of the inescapable choices which fall to judges (particularly in the highest courts). It is naive to expect that commentators will be silent about such choices. Just as decisions of the other branches of government attract criticism and occasional calumny, important and controversial decisions of the courts will inevitably do the same. Into this milieu has been injected the technology of modern communications. In his lecture on this subject, Chief Justice Gleeson, then Chief Justice of New South Wales, said of the politics of law and order:

> It has been said that the public attitude to war in the USA underwent a great change when American families sat down each night to watch television programmes depicting casualties with unprecedented visual and emotional impact. To an extent, a similar phenomenon may account for the fact that modern citizens have become convinced that they are living in the middle of a crime wave. Night after night they see, on their TV screens, victims or relatives of victims of violent crime, telling their stories and being asked whether they are satisfied with the sentences imposed on convicted offenders. Talkback radio programmes are filled with people expressing feelings of insecurity and demanding ever-increasing severity of penalties. To all of this politicians respond by competing with each other to be seen to be tough on crime.[76]

The same phenomenon imposes unrealistic expectations on police.[77] It is an inescapable feature of the world we live in. The media encourage conflict, dramatic visual images, demands for instant solutions. Uncomfortably for the judiciary, theirs is a profession whose mission is to serve the ages, not the instant sound-bite or 'spin' considered appropriate to most of the actors in the other branches of government and in the contemporary media.

---

75 J Hocking (1997) *Lionel Murphy – Political Biography*, Cambridge, pp 267-268, citing Justice Murphy's Address to the National Press Club of Australia in 1973.

76 Gleeson (1998) p 10.

77 JR Wood (1997) 'Address to NSW Police Academy by Royal Commissioner', cited in Gleeson (1998) p 10.

Some Good

Some of the heightened attention to the courts and their doings is justifiable; some even desirable. The principle of public justice and open courts is designed to constantly submit the judges themselves to public scrutiny. Incompetent, dilatory, ill-tempered, prejudiced judges may deserve to be exposed so long as the object is truth, not just entertainment at the behest of a disgruntled litigant whose views are given currency at the expense of one who cannot effectively answer back. Much criticism of courts and of the legal profession itself is perfectly healthy.[78] Judges are citizens too. They live in their communities. It is right that they should be alert to community feelings. It would be naive to declare that they are completely unaffected in their professional decisions by the public debates that swirl around them.

However, what is expected is that, when the crunch comes and a serious attack is made on vulnerable people, the courts will uphold the law and the Constitution. The High Court of Australia did exactly this in 1951. In the midst of the Korean War, the Red scare and an enormous public fear of communists and communism, the Court struck down as unconstitutional the *Communist Party Dissolution Act* 1950 (Cth).[79] That statute had been proposed and enacted by a government that had a specific electoral mandate to do so. A referendum to authorise amendment of the Constitution to overcome the decision was defeated.[80] Although the Court was criticised by some at the time, the politicians faithfully accepted the decision. There was none of the ferocity of comment that has lately been voiced against the Court. And the criticism that was voiced would have been of the decision or the reasoning, not of the judges personally.

Some Too Far

Having acknowledged the legitimacy of public debate about cases and issues, of criticism of decisions and attention to judges who are lazy, slow, incompetent or rude, it remains to be said that the recent level of political and personal attacks on the judiciary is unacceptable. It has gone too far. Unless there is a measure of restraint, the judicial institution will be damaged and judicial integrity undermined. It is because courts are obliged to protect the rights of unpopular individuals and minorities that they are exposed, in elected democracies, to political castigation.[81] If

---

78 Ibid. Cf Bellacosa (1997) p 2389.

79 *Australian Communist Party v Commonwealth* (1951) 83 CLR 1.

80 MD Kirby, 'HV Evatt, The Anti-Communist Referendum and Liberty in Australia' (1990) 7 *Australian Bar Review* 93.

81 Bright (1997) p 165. Cf *Falbo v United States* 320 US 549 at 555 (1944) per Murphy J.

judges are to perform their functions when the going gets rough, they need tenure to underwrite their independence. Personal courage may not always be enough. Even with tenure, ambition or thirst for popularity may sometimes get in the way. Judges may sometimes wilt under the barrage of criticism, as Judge Baer appeared to do.

When judges reverse their decisions in the wake of political or media criticism, the judiciary as an institution is presented as supine or malleable. When judges are exposed to removal from office at the behest of politicians who dislike their decisions, they are highly vulnerable to improper pressure that diminishes their real neutrality. When judges are submitted to unrelenting political attacks by people who should know better, there is a danger that the public will draw from the silence of the judges an implication that the criticism is justified.[82] Yet silence is ordinarily imposed by judicial convention. Judges, ordinarily, cannot answer back. At least, most cannot do so in effective forums. Because of inexperience any attempts to respond may result in compounding their problems and demeaning their office.

In Australia, where neither federal nor State judges are subject to election, recall or popular removal, new developments have been occurring which are a source of added concern. State courts and State and federal tribunals have been abolished and targeted members not re-appointed to the successor body.[83] Independent office-holders who criticise governments may find that their statutory powers are diminished. In the wake of the recent controversies in Australia, proposals have been made, for the first time, that judges should be appointed for a term of years or chosen with participation of the people. The retirement from the High Court of Australia of two of the seven Justices and the pending retirement of the Chief Justice on attaining the constitutional retiring age of 70 years led to a declaration by the Deputy Prime Minister of Australia that the government would appoint three 'capital C conservatives' to replace the retirees.[84]

---

82 HL Sarokin, 'The Dangers of Judge-Bashing – Politicians are "Willie Hortonizing" the Bench', *Legal Times*, 27 October 1997, p 25. Judge Sarokin resigned from the US Court of Appeals (Third Circuit) to convey the 'gravity of [the] dangerous course [and] in protest over the politicization of attacks on the federal judiciary in the United States'. He conceded that his 'grand gesture' was a 'complete fizzle' which actually emboldened further attacks and calls for impeachment.

83 See *Attorney-General (NSW) v Quin* (1990) 170 CLR 1; and cf MD Kirby, 'Abolition of Courts and Non-reappointment of Judicial Officers' (1994) 12 *Australian Bar Review* 181 at 189-204.

84 *The Age*, 6 March 1997, p A6; Courier *Mail*, 5 March 1997, p 1. Cf 'Politicising High Court appointments', *Courier Mail*, 10 March 1997, p 10; and 'Merit the best judge', *Canberra Times*, 8 March 1997, p 17.

Governments in Australia are not subject to Senate confirmation hearings for their judicial appointments. They can appoint whom they choose. They have always been entitled to make judicial appointments with reference to what they hope may be the appointee's philosophical inclinations. But in Australia we have not, until now, had such a clear indication that ideological leaning, rather than professional reputation or intellectual merit, will be the chief criterion for appointment to judicial office. The Deputy Prime Minister's comment drew much criticism. The Federal Attorney-General, by an unprecedented procedure of consultation about High Court appointments, has subsequently tried to repair the impression that the political inclinations of candidates, rather than their ability and independence, will be the chief criterion for appointment to the nation's highest court.

Some Bad

Distinctly bad have been the following features of recent attacks on the judiciary: the personal targeting of identified judges; attempts to intimidate them or to deflect them from fidelity to their oath to decide each case strictly on its merits; and the unrelenting character and partisan political aspect of the attacks. Little wonder that some good judges prefer to resign. Small surprise that good people of independent mind now refuse judicial appointment. Once proud and famous courts are criticised for buckling under to political pressure.[85]

Another feature of the barrage which should not pass unnoticed is the way in which women judges have tended to be singled out for special attack, whether in the United States,[86] New Zealand[87] or in Australia.[88] Targeting judges, identifiable because of their sex, race or other personal considerations, attacking them by over-simplified and often inaccurate generalisations, panders to public prejudice. It reinforces stereotypes about the judiciary. Such conduct is unworthy of countries that claim to uphold fundamental rights and the rule of law.

---

85 Bright (1997) p 172.

86 Ibid.

87 Editorial, 'Judges and Politics' [1996] *New Zealand Law Journal* 361 at 362 (a reference to Dame Sylvia Cartwright of the High Court of New Zealand).

88 R Campbell, 'Personal Attacks Gone Too Far – Kirby Hits at Critics', *Canberra Times*, 6 January 1998.

What Can Be Done?

In the face of the barrage there are a few strategies available to the judiciary. It is worth listing them. Some of them can be put out of account as unworthy or impossible of attainment.

Unacceptable Responses

An unworthy response would be to just cave in to the pressure and to do exactly what the politicians, editorialists and other powerful interests want. This would be a complete abdication of the judicial function. It would be out of line with constitutional and legal requirements and with judicial traditions. Although other judicial models exist (for example, in China), those countries, like Australia and the United States, which have chosen the path of a strict separation of the judicial power assert that the judiciary, and not the legislature, is the ultimate arbiter on political power. For judges of this tradition, caving in is out of the question.

So is ignoring the barrage in the hope that it will diminish or go away. There are limits to what the judiciary itself can do to respond to its critics. Within those limits, judges should certainly try to correct misapprehensions and insist upon the truth. Collectively and individually they have an ultimate duty to protect the integrity and independence of the judicial institution. Because they spend their days hearing both sides of a conflict and searching for the rational resolution of difficult problems, judges and other lawyers tend to feel especially uncomfortable in simply putting up with one-sided criticism and misinformation.[89]

Yet putting one's head above the ramparts can be risky for a judge. An interesting article on law review publications by judges of the United States Court of Appeals compared the pattern before and after the Senate confirmation hearings concerning Judge Robert Bork's nomination to the Supreme Court of the United States.[90] The analysis concludes that publishing by such judges declined significantly following the Bork hearings. Judges with established reputations, particularly, appear to have observed and learned.

The desirability of such a result is questionable. Is it better to appoint a silent and unproductive nominee whose value system is a complete mystery rather than one who has contributed to intellectual debate, exposed his or her ideas and demonstrated courage in sharing jurisprudential opinions with the legal profession and beyond? Driving

---

89 Bellacosa (1997) p 2383.

90 SS Gaille, 'Publishing by US Court of Appeals Judges: Before and After the Bork Hearings' (1997) 26 *Journal of Legal Studies* 371.

candidates for judicial preferment into silence may have undesirable results. When the Pandora's box of judicial appointment or promotion is reached along a silent road, uncomfortable surprises may lie in wait.

Court Defences

One solution, increasingly used, is the recruitment of media and public affairs officers to the service of the courts. They can help journalists, often working to strict deadlines, to accurately report important court decisions and to correct factual or legal mistakes where they occur. They can also promote more accurate and informed media commentary about the law in general and its personnel.

However, there are dangers in playing the media's game. Courts have no business cultivating political or public favour. They will always lose in a competition with the political branches, which inevitably enjoy greater experience and resources. Equally, courts would be diminished if they felt obliged to defend their decisions beyond their published reasons by employing media 'spin doctors' for that purpose.[91] But it must be admitted that judicial reasoning is often obscure and highly technical. Perhaps, by failing to provide user friendly summaries and by insufficient attention to the necessities of communications in the age of multi media, judges have brought on themselves some of the confusion which they criticise so readily in others.[92]

Response of Chief Justices

It seems now to be an accepted obligation of Chief Justices and other senior judges to respond to attacks on the courts, their judgments, their personnel or the administration of justice itself. Chief Justice Rehnquist did so during the last United States presidential campaign.[93] Justice Stevens did so at the American Bar Association meeting in August 1996, already mentioned. Chief Justice Brennan did so in Australia, joined from time to time by Sir Anthony Mason, his predecessor. Such statements may quieten the barrage for a time. But judges are generally too busy; usually lack the skills to mix it with political or other critics; and typically share a concern that an endeavour to do so would diminish them and their office. This concern is not misplaced. Reticence in public debate and controversy is what citizens generally expect of their judges.

---

91 'No court of knaves', *Canberra Times*, 23 September 1997, p 8.

92 SB Smith, 'The Constitution of Jurisprudence', unpublished, pp 66-67.

93 Bright (1997) p 172.

The Bar

It therefore rests increasingly on the organised legal profession to defend the judiciary, to correct blatant misinformation and to remind politicians, the media and others of the precious heritage of judicial neutrality and independence which common law countries have enjoyed until now.[94] For the United Nations, I have worked in a number of countries where independence and incorruptibility are not ordinary features of the judiciary. It is important that institutional protection for those features be maintained. Political attempts to undermine them should be rebuffed. Leaders of the legal profession, whatever their own general political persuasion, should speak up where judges are unfairly criticised by politicians and others for doing their independent duty. The Attorney-General, as the traditional leader of the legal profession, should speak out in appropriate cases.

In Australia, the Federal Attorney-General has, at least in part, evidenced a willingness to return to this traditional role and even to criticise his ministerial colleagues in the process.[95] In the United States, Attorney-General Janet Reno has, somewhat belatedly, expressed her concern at 'the increasingly heated rhetoric surrounding the debate' about judicial activism.[96] Attorney-General Reno acknowledged that judges today 'must have thick skins' and condemned the way recent debates had not sought to argue 'the rightness of an issue but to undermine the very credibility of the judiciary'. The temperature of the debate elicited 'alarm' on her part. She noted delays by the Senate in considering the large number of judicial nominations awaiting confirmation. Those delays appear to have become caught up in partisan political issues. So perhaps has the related question of maintaining judicial remuneration.

Political Mutual Respect

Statements of this kind from a leading political figure such as the Attorney-General are to be welcomed. But generalities voiced months after an attack are no substitute for specific defence of particular judges

---

94 American Bar Association (1997) p 59. There are a number of relevant recommendations, including that steps be taken to inform the Bar and the public of regular ways of handling complaints against and disciplining judges under the *Judicial Conduct and Disability Act* 1980 (US).

95 See 'Attorney Pleads for Peace in Court Row', *The Age*, 1 March 1997, p A5; 'Williams Calls for High Court Restraint', *Australian Financial Review*, 23 September 1997, p 6.

96 Attorney-General Reno's remarks addressing the ABA House of Delegates, 5 August 1997, unpublished. Cf B Galligan, 'Do we want activist courts?', IPAA (Victoria) Government Law Series, unpublished, 11 November 1997, p 2.

when they are under political or personal attack for performing no more than their judicial duties. It is then that strong political leadership of a principled kind is required. The increasingly adversarial and combative nature of our societies should not become endemic to the damage of the relationship between the judiciary and the other branches of government. Legislators, members of the executive government and the judiciary should all realise that each branch has its own part to play, without which constitutional government would be impossible.[97] What the political branches of government have to understand (as formerly, I believe, their members generally did) is that it would be an abdication of their constitutional function for judges to court popular opinion or to swing abjectly in the wind of the latest popular mood.

It was out of recognition of that danger that, when the people of England banished King James II from the Kingdom in 1688, they only invited his successors, William and Mary, to take up the Crown upon conditions. One of the conditions was judicial tenure and independence. When this principle, accepted for Britain, was not extended equally to the English colonies, the colonists and settlers complained. In America, they rose in revolution. They instituted, at least in the federal judiciary of the United States, a firm guarantee of tenure and independence. We in Australia are the happy beneficiaries of these two revolutions of 1688 and 1776. But it is necessary for judges and lawyers to remind their fellow citizens of the causes of those revolutions long ago, the importance of maintaining the principles which were thereby secured and the dangers involved in expecting judges to decide cases based on whether their decisions will be popular.

Education in Civics

Observations of this kind will not repair the mischief that years of concerted attack on the judicial institution and individual judges can cause. Such attacks often portray a fundamental lack of understanding of what judges do, what they do not do and even why they exist in our kind of society. Such basic misapprehensions may not be curable in mature adults. The remedy should therefore start in the schools and through the media. It should not be confined to law faculties and institutes of learning. A renewal in the teaching of civics for all citizens would be timely.[98] Let it be a goal of the new century that we re-teach the lessons of our Constitution and engender an informed appreciation of

---

97 Galligan (1997) p 17.

98 MD Kirby, 'Teaching Australians Civics', (1997) 13 *Queensland University of Technology Law Journal* 149. This is also a suggestion of Judge Sarokin. See Sarokin (1997) p 25.

the judges and of their vital importance for the peaceful government of us all. Not blind or uncritical faith. Not confidence extracted by the ever present threat of legal enforcement.[99] Not appreciation won by clever public relations and media hype. But a deserved evaluation of faithful and honest service in a difficult profession, the alternative to which is anarchy and the power of guns.

---

99 Cf T Li-ann, 'An "i" for an "I"? Singapore's Communitarian Model of Constitutional Adjudication' [1997] *Hong Kong Law Journal* 153 at 181-185, referring to contempt and defamation proceedings in Singapore.

Chapter 14

Judicial Stress[1]

The following text is based on a speech given to the Judicial Commission of New South Wales' Annual Conference of the Local Courts, 2 June 1995. It incorporates additional case studies from a speech titled 'Judicial Stress Revisited', which was given at the Supreme Court and Federal Court Judges' Conference in Brisbane, 31 January 1997. Michael Kirby provides a fascinating insider's account of the loneliness of judicial office, the heavy and often unrealistic demands placed upon judicial officers, and the media intrusions and public scrutiny which all judges must now face. He suggests various ways of dealing with stress, and calls for greater resources to assist judges to cope with the unrewarding and unappreciated aspects of their daily work.

An Unmentionable Topic

Life in the courts can be a stressful business. Yet stress was, until very recently, a subject which neither judge nor advocate was supposed to admit – still less write about. This unwillingness to bring stress out into the open was partly due to the cultural inhibitions inherited from the English tradition of the Bench and Bar. The Australian phlegmatic self-image may have reinforced this inherited model. Judicial officers are subject to the role imperatives of an occupation still overwhelmingly made up of men, who share a conventional disinclination to recognise and to speak openly about occupational stress. Generally, in Australia, stress in the judiciary has been mentioned only obliquely: not spoken of directly.[2] It is a sign of the growing open-mindedness of the Australian judiciary that it is willing to tackle this formerly unmentionable topic. Is

1 This paper was first published in its original form in (1995) 12(3) *Australian Bar Review* 101 (Butterworths Australia). The paper also contains extracts from 'Judicial Stress – An Update' (1997) 71 *Australian Law Journal* 774.

2 An exception is Justice Thomas, of the Supreme Court of Queensland, who in 1991 wrote about the human problems of judicial life in rural Australia, which was published for the edification of American judges. JB Thomas, 'A Down-under Circuit: the Life of a Judge in the Remoter Parts of Australia' (1991) 74 *Judicature* 208. He has since expressed surprise that he was conscious of the stress of such judges and scepticism about the whole topic. See JB Thomas 'Get Up Off the Ground' (1997) 71 *Australian Law Journal* 785 at 789. Cf MD Kirby 'Judicial Stress – A Reply' (1997) 71 *Australian Law Journal* 791.

this just a fashion that will pass? Or is it recognition of a deeper malaise that we see in our institution and in ourselves and which we feel the need to talk about with each other?

Treatment of the topic overseas indicates that Australian judges are not alone. On 8 April 1996, the *National Law Journal*, a broadsheet published in the United States, carried a front-page article 'Judicial Crack-ups Fracture the Bench'.[3] The story appears under a baleful photograph of Justice James Heiple of the Illinois Supreme Court, featuring in a 'mug-shot', which sadly bears a credit 'AP/Wide World Photos'. Justice Heiple's humiliation was presumably shared with a wide world. He was described as awaiting trial on charges for resisting arrest by trying to outrun a police officer who claimed to have stopped him for speeding.

The article listed a number of other recent cases in the United States:

- A Los Angeles municipal judge, William Ormsby, who was severely and publicly censured on 20 March 1996 by a Judicial Commission 'for temperament problems, including the arrest of people who had been whispering in his court room';
- An elected civil trial judge in Illinois, Michael F O'Brien, who resigned on 4 December 1995 after it was disclosed that he had falsely pretended for 20 years to have received the Congressional Medal of Honour;
- A US District Judge, Andrew Hauk of Los Angeles (83 years of age), who was censured by the 9th US Circuit Court of Appeals for making 'outrageous remarks' about minorities and others;
- Former Pennsylvania Supreme Court Justice Rolf Larsen, who was convicted in 1994 for illegally obtaining anti-depressant drugs;
- County Court Judge William McClain in Indiana, dismissed with a ban on practising law for two years, for allegedly having 'participated in sending' a used condom to a courthouse secretary on whom he supposedly had a crush;
- Most news-making of all, the fall of the former Chief Justice of New York State, Sol Wachtler, convicted and imprisoned in 1992 for allegedly harassing his ex-lover, including by threatening to kidnap her teenage daughter, demanding $20,000 and mailing a condom to the girl.

In Australia, we have had nothing quite like these cases. The closest we have come has been the cases involving Justice Lionel Murphy's trials;

3 (1996) 18(32) *National Law Journal* A1.

the criminal conviction of the former Chief Magistrate of New South Wales, Mr Murray Farquhar; the allegations (never proved) against the former State judge David Yeldham, who tragically took his own life; and the hearing before the New South Wales Legislative Council of the proposal that Justice Vince Bruce of the Supreme Court of that State be removed from office following lengthy delays in the delivery of his decisions. The Council rejected the removal motion after Justice Bruce made a statement to it attributing his difficulties to depression which, for a long time, had been undiagnosed.[4]

As the article in the *National Law Journal* puts it: 'Getting to the top is thus no sure guarantee against falling into an emotional abyss'.[5] Chief Justice Wachtler was a widely respected judge. There was not much further that his career could have gone, except to the Supreme Court of the United States. But he hit a 'psychological wall' in 1991 which plunged him into deep depression, resulting in the disordered, dangerous and criminal activity which led to his professional destruction. In a 1993 interview with the *New York Law Journal*, after he had served 13 months in a federal prison, Wachtler said that he had not sought to see a psychiatrist during his period of profound turmoil 'because of the professional and social stigma attached, especially in the light of his gubernatorial aspirations'. Instead, he turned to a family doctor who prescribed a number of prescription drugs. Combined with his then mental pre-disposition, he entered upon a 'very very dangerous road'.[6] The former Chief Judge is now working in an alternative dispute resolution service in provincial New York. He has written a book on his prison experiences.

Press reports in October 1996 told of a Hong Kong judge, an ex-patriate New Zealander, who was 'delusional' and suffering 'an acute confused state'.[7] The then Governor of Hong Kong set up a judicial tribunal to determine whether that judge should be removed from office for allegedly making false claims that two other judges had attempted to influence him in the handling of a trial of an immigration consultant, also from New Zealand. The judge eventually disqualified himself from the case.

---

4 After further delays and delivering his reserved decisions, Justice Bruce resigned from judicial office on 22 February 1999.

5 'Judicial Crack-ups Fracture the Bench' (1996), p A20.

6 Ibid.

7 'Inquiry into "Delusional" Judge Stopped', *Sydney Morning Herald*, 16 October 1996, p 10.

Are these and like cases evidence of declining standards in the modern judiciary? Or are they evidence that events which once would have been dealt with 'discreetly' are now front-page news? Are the instances no more than examples of judges, who are human beings, straying from traditional and exceptional standards? Or do these cases evidence a larger problem which can be summed up as the impact of stress upon vulnerable members of an overstressed profession?

The Editor in the *National Law Journal* considered that there were deeper forces at work to explain the manifestations of bizarre judicial conduct in the United States. 'It's not very pleasant being a judge these days. Mental health professionals say they are seeing a lot of anger and anxiety in judicial clients, the apparent result of crushing case loads, novel and complex legal issues and increasing media scrutiny.'[8]

Beginning in the 1980s, it became relatively common in judicial training courses in the United States to provide a programme on judicial stress and how to handle it.[9] Dr Isaiah M Zimmerman, a psychologist, was first invited to speak on the topic at the 1980 conference of Chief Judges of the United States. His essay, reproduced in the *Judges Journal* of the American Bar Association, became a classic.[10] It was also provided to judges in Canada.[11] Stress invoked a rash of articles in the early 1980s, most of them by psychologists who lectured judges on their high levels of stress and how to manage them.[12] Even in England, as the rules against judicial comment were loosened in the 1980s, judges started to reveal the facts and causes of some of their feelings of stress.[13] However, this trend did not make it to the Antipodes.

The new attention to stress in judicial life is paralleled by a fresh concern about stress in the life of the practising lawyer. A major survey was carried out in the United States in 1985 to examine the role of legal education in producing psychological distress among law students and

8 Editorial, 'Judges at Risk' (1996) 18(32) *National Law Journal* 16.

9 M Middleton, 'Judges Told how to Deal with Stress' (1981) 67 *American Bar Association Journal* 1100.

10 IM Zimmerman, 'Stress – What It Does to Judges and How It Can Be Lessened' (1981) 4(8) *Judges Journal* 20.

11 IM Zimmerman, 'The Judge and Stress' (1984) 26 *Canadian Journal of Criminology* 6. See R Ray, 'Help is Available for Addicted Lawyers and Judges' (1991) 18 *Canadian Bar Association National* 26.

12 CR Showalter and DA Martell, 'Personality, Stress and Health in American Judges' (1985) 69(2) *Judicature* 83. See S Abrahams, 'Workshop Examines Way to Help Disabled Judges' (1982) 65 *Judicature* 327 and Middleton (1981) p 1100.

13 I regret to say that one of the chief causes disclosed by some judges is 'the sting of humiliation when [the judge's] sentences are overturned by the Court of Appeal'. R English, 'Judgment Days', BBC *Worldwide*, July 1994, p 16.

new lawyers.[14] It was found that, whereas law school should be the very place in which practitioners learn to cope effectively with the demands of the legal profession, the psychological well being of law students was actually stunted by the education process. At best, stress and how to cope with it were completely ignored.[15] At worst, excessive workloads, serious problems with time management, over-crowded, impersonal lecture rooms and concentrated attention on analytical skills, without equal regard to inter-personal development, produced very high distress levels. They were found to have actually prevented the alleviation of symptoms and the preparation of law students for good lawyering.

Given that Australian law schools, at least at the time when most judicial officers of today were trained, followed much the same model as those described in the United States study, it is little wonder that lawyers are so frequently criticised for their lack of skills in dealing with clients, witnesses and each other. The judicial officer in Australia is typically the product of a legal education system which, in the United States, produced extremely high levels of psychopathological symptomatology and recurring depression. Perhaps in our more robust and easy-going country, our lawyers were immune from some of these outcomes. But the parallels are uncomfortably close.

As evidence that Australian lawyers are beginning, belatedly, to turn their attention to this issue, one has only to look at the professional journals. In the Victorian *Law Institute Journal*, an article told of the breakdown of a lawyer who reacted to professional stress with sleeplessness and a constant sense of impending doom.[16] He eventually turned to alcohol. He could not escape for a time, because he refused at first to acknowledge the real causes behind his symptoms. In New South Wales, the *Law Society Journal* urged upon its members the ultimate lesson of *Donoghue v Stevenson*; namely, that lawyers should demonstrate a duty of care to themselves. They should be alert to their special susceptibility to the diseases of civilisation, including cardiovascular disease, diabetes and stress.[17]

In the United States, concern about the impact of stress upon the actors in the drama of litigation has now even extended to jurors. The National Center for State Courts has reported new initiatives to

14 G Andrew et al, 'The Role of Legal Education in Producing Psychological Distress Among Law Students and Lawyers' (1986) 2 *American Bar Foundation Research Journal* 225.

15 Ibid, p 226.

16 'Tom – One Lawyer's Story' (1990) 64 *Law Institute Journal* (Vic) 1020.

17 J Brown, 'Physical Fitness – The Duty of Care to Oneself' (1990) 28 *Law Society Journal* (NSW) 68. See MR Liverani, 'Mid-Life Crisis or Epiphany?' (1994) 32 *Law Society Journal* (NSW) 46 at 47.

cope with the stress-related symptoms suffered by jurors, particularly in long cases. Their symptoms range from the mild to the severe. They are most acute where jurors are cut off from their families and friends and exposed to repeated scrutiny of highly upsetting, haunting facts such as in a gruesome murder trial.[18]

At a conference of the International Bar Association in Melbourne in October 1994, another oft-forgotten group at last came into their own. The spouses and partners of lawyers (and one might add, judges) are also subjected to stress. It can come from shared anxieties, from the experience of lonely absences and from just empathising with a companion under seemingly inescapable pressure. For the first time, the International Bar Association included a session in its conference, addressed by psychologist Dr Richard Gates, on how the 1990s have led to increased demands on all professionals and on lawyers in particular. Dr Gates, it was promised, would 'lead the audience in general discussion about their own experiences of living or working with lawyers under pressure, how they have coped and perhaps some strategies for coping better'.[19]

So it will be seen that stress in the law, and even on the Bench, is out of the shadows. Save for cultural norms or *macho* inhibitions, there is no reason why stress should be hidden, being a reality of professional life. It is a little stressful for me to broach the topic. But nobody else in the Australian judiciary seems willing to do so. So here goes.

What is Stress?

The role of stress in human behaviour generally is increasingly the subject of scientific scrutiny. It is conventionally explained in terms of the body's response to danger when it makes its choice between 'fight or flight'. In part, the phenomenon has a positive role in heightening the ability of the judge and the lawyer to deal with what is often an issue of the greatest importance for the client or litigant. A so-called 'stress hormone' (corticotrophin) has been isolated as have glucocorticoids. As the mind signals the body to mobilise its resources in a situation of stress, glucose, simple proteins and fats pour out of storage to stoke the muscles. To increase this delivery of nutrients and oxygen the heart beats faster, blood pressure goes up and breathing rate increases. The stress hormone has been found in the placenta of the human neonate. It is said

18 'Juror Stress: What Price Do Jurors Pay?' (1992) National Center for State Courts Report No 10, p 3.

19 International Bar Association (1994) *Programme*, p 23.

to be associated with the human sleep cycle.[20] It seems reasonable to infer that lawyers and judges normally have a lot of this hormone rushing around their systems, simply because they are daily engaged in a form of combat. It may not be the kind of physical combat for which nature designed the hormone. But it is certainly, quite often, confrontational and challenging. On a regular basis, judges must summon up the emotional and physiological responses that have such a powerful effect on body and mind.

An article in a popular magazine identified three simple ways of testing whether you are as relaxed as you should be:

> First, feel the nape of your neck with the palm of your hand. If the area between your shoulder blades feels cooler than your forearms or hands you are in a state of stress. One of the direct physical affects of anxiety is to slow blood flow to the peripheral areas like the skin at the back of the neck. … Perhaps the old saying "hot under the collar" should have been "Cold under the collar".
>
> Your second test is to try to catch yourself at an unsuspecting moment. Are your jaws or teeth tightly clenched, is your brow furrowed or are your hands balled into fists? …
>
> Thirdly, try clearing your mind for 30 seconds. Stop any one thought dominating your consciousness. … If you can't keep specific things from returning and disturbing your respite, you score minus on this test.[21]

These homely tests, which we can all perform, are actually backed up by quite detailed research, including by Australian universities. In the Department of Physiology at the University of Sydney, experimentation has shown that animals become addicted to the natural opiates that their bodies release in response to stressful situations. Unfortunately, they then display a craving for the very stress that triggers the release of these natural opiates. According to Dr Nick Labidas of the University of Sydney, human subjects, exposed to stress, release body opiates to which they too can become addicted. Although such stress can be harmful to the body and psyche of the subject, people crave it because it provokes the release of the addictive chemicals described as 'similar to those resulting from the use of chemical opiates such as morphine and heroin'.[22] What an irony it would be if this new research eventually were to prove that judges, who are required by law to punish severely people who become embroiled in the use of addictive illegal drugs, were

---

20 'Science Probes Key to Stress', *The Australian*, 13 August 1990, p 9. See also RM Sapolsky (1994) *A Guide to Stress, Stress-Related Diseases and Coping*, Freeman.

21 Ansett Airlines, *Panorama*, August 1996, p 36.

22 *University of Sydney News*, 12 September 1996, p 2.

themselves victims of 'the ultimate addiction' – to the stress of their work.

At the time of my first judicial appointment in 1974, a jest was told, ascribed to Justice Bernard Riley. It suggested that the judicial life had advantages. Those anointed would find that 'the tension went out the window with half their income'. The part about the income was certainly true. But the part about the drop in tension has not been true for all judicial officers.

At the outset it is necessary to put stress in the Australian judiciary in proper context and perspective. In many countries, judicial officers are subjected to daily perils and risks to their lives and safety – and to that of their families. In contrast, the stress faced by Australian judges is generally less intense and dangerous. But it is serious enough. I will analyse the typical causes of judicial stress before turning to some of its features and a few suggested solutions.

Causes of Judicial Stress

Nature of the Work

The transition from practising lawyer to judicial officer involves a journey to loneliness, at least to some degree. Many new appointees tell of their dread of the official welcomes and professional inaugurations where the critical spotlight is unswervingly placed on them as individuals, not as advocates or the representatives of parties.

Loneliness of office is, to some degree, inescapable. An element of distance and remove are a usual part of the judicial life. There is a definite role expectation for judicial officers in Australia. It governs even the most gregarious initiates. Justice Thomas paints a vivid picture of the ceremonial arrival of Mr Justice Cooper at the Normanton Courthouse in the nineteenth century. In rustic surroundings, but in full judicial robes, the judge had to portray the assurance and confidence of the judicial office which he paraded before the people down the main street of the town.[23] Whether Cooper ever felt any self-doubt is not disclosed.

Until now, there has been little in the way of formal preparation for the judicial life. Most judicial officers came to the courts from the Bar, and their lives as advocates were seen as preparation enough for their lives as judges. It is a truism that expertise as an advocate might not necessarily fashion a good judge. Studying judges for decades might simply lead the observer to replicate common errors. In addition, many

---

23 Thomas (1991) p 209.

newly appointed judicial officers complain that there are few people to ask about the rudimentary problems of judging. This could be a further cause of uncertainty, self-doubt and stress.

When a solicitor was appointed from practice to judicial office in the Supreme Court of New South Wales, and took the highly sensible precaution of sitting for a time to observe a judge of his Division, there was much ill-considered criticism at the Bar. Yet at least two newly appointed judges of the Court of Appeal (Cripps JA and Powell JA), both very experienced judges, took the sensible course of sitting with the judge administering the motion list before embarking on that duty for themselves. Rationality and efficiency should overcome tradition where tradition increases stress, involves pretence and has no professional necessity. On the very day that I was sworn into office as President of the New South Wales Court of Appeal, I was required to preside in motions necessitating countless rapid decisions with the provision of accurate *ex tempore* reasons. Sitting on each side of me was a vigilant colleague. It was highly stressful. But in those days, that was what was expected.

As mentioned, a source of stress for many judicial officers derives from role expectation and role-playing. Judicial officers are expected, as Sir Robert Megary once put it, to be as wise as they are paid to look. A psychologist, Dr Walter Menninger, told United States judges of the judge who asked: 'What can I do on the Bench that will reduce the urge to scream?'[24] More often, the problem is yawning, not screaming. But the frustration can certainly build up. The judge is expected always to react in a way that is 'unobtrusive and acceptable'. The response must not interfere with the manifestly lawful and just solution to the problem before the court.

Some judicial officers, on appointment, complain about the immediate drop in their income.[25] Several fine judges in Australia have been lost both to Federal and State courts because of this problem. Although judicial salaries and benefits doubtless seem very high to most people in the community, it is usually said that they can only be compared with the judicial officer's alternative sources of income – namely, in the practising legal profession. A family accustomed to the income of a senior barrister or solicitor may complain about the drop. The pressures of unfulfillable demands, and even recrimination, may flow over to the judicial officer. Whether objectively warranted or not,

---

24 W Menninger, quoted in Middleton (1981) p 1100.

25 Thomas (1997) p 787.

this is certainly a source of anxiety for some. Complaints are often made about the severe discrepancies between the social status usually accorded to judicial officers, and the salaries and other benefits that they receive. A return to the profession, as an easy release from this source of stress, is likely to occur much more frequently in the future. Until the recent past, it was unthinkable.

Many judicial officers also complain about the lack of feedback concerning their performance. When practising as a lawyer, one has many colleagues who will speak with candour and with constructive suggestions. But practitioners and litigants are inhibited in what they can, and will, say to a judicial officer, except through the formal process of appeal and judicial review. The lack of feedback accentuates the feeling of loneliness which many newly appointed judicial officers experience. Unless they are members of an appellate court, it is the nature of their occupation to sit alone. I recall quite clearly how Sir Nigel Bowen, as Chief Justice of the Federal Court, would sometimes come and sit in the back of my courtroom – as of other new appointees – to observe the 'new' judge. This is rare, if not unique. For the most part, the judge receives little by way of day-to-day assessment. He or she is thrown back upon personal staff who tend to have a feeling of loyalty or, at least, discretion, which suppresses too much criticism. It is voiced, if at all, in professional gossip or in the measured opinions of appellate courts.

Another stressful feature of the work of judicial officers today is the increasing workload that they must bear. This is not a phenomenon confined to Australia. It has forced a kind of bureaucratisation on the judiciary in the over-worked courts of the United States. Throughout the common law world, judges are burdened and over-burdened.[26] For example, the workload of the New South Wales Court of Appeal where I previously served – which did not have the controls on its work flow afforded to the High Court by its facility to grant or refuse special leave to appeal – has increased three-fold since the establishment of the Court in 1966. Yet, for a very long time, the judicial strength of the Court was completely unchanged. The sight of the never-ending tide of cases, the increasing backlog and the perceived incapacity to do much to reduce it, is a stress that many judicial officers feel. A great source of that stress is the conviction of judges that, however hard they may work, they do not have the means to provide simple solutions. They are locked into legal and professional requirements which work to exacerbate the delays already inherent in the careful handling of individual cases.

---

26 See SN Silva, 'Interview' (1994) 19(1) *Dana* 5 at 7 (Sri Lanka Court of Appeal).

Another feature of the very nature of judicial work which adds to stress is the limited capacity of judicial officers to delegate their judicial functions. True, some functions may be given to judicial registrars or mediators. Administrative functions may be given to list clerks. Still other functions may be assigned to personal staff. But, at least in the tradition of the Australian judiciary, the personal obligation of consideration and decision-making rests upon the shoulders of the sworn judicial officer alone. It cannot be shifted. Most judicial officers have a strong sense of that responsibility. But it adds to the stress. Whereas middle-aged or older personnel in many other occupations can shed intolerable workloads, judicial officers have a strictly limited power to do so.

The pressure of increased judicial workloads has elicited from the judiciary (who have given up hope of securing substantial increases in numbers and resources) remarkable innovation in case management and alternative dispute resolution techniques.[27] The system could not have survived without these and other innovations devised by the judges. These changes themselves add somewhat to the stressful burdens placed upon judges today. Not only must they decide cases. They must 'manage' them. By constant directions they must shepherd them through the court system: marshalling to best advantage the very scarce judicial time. These innovations create stresses of their own, as judges must learn to master new managerial techniques. They must take into account not simply the interests of the parties before them but also the interests of other litigants waiting in the queue and of the public generally.[28] Whatever they do, judges seem destined to be subjected to more and more case load pressure. In an essay on the future of judicial life in Canada, Dennis Hauptly observed:

> The burgeoning case load, reduced resources, and emphasis on science-related cases in the docket will require judges in 2034 to be vastly more technically literate than today's judges. ... [T]he judiciary will have to handle not only more cases, but more complex cases, with diminished actual resources per case. Judges cannot work many more hours to accomplish this. ... Delaying the resolution of cases is not a real option, either. Anyone engaged in civil litigation knows that delays in some

---

27 See T Sourdin, 'Judicial Management and Alternative Dispute Resolution Process Trends' (1996) 14 *Australian Bar Review* 185; JRT Wood (1994) 'The Changing Face of Case Management: The New South Wales Experience', unpublished paper, cited in Sourdin, pp 187, 191; and PA Sallmann 'Life Beyond Caseflow Management' (1994) 3(2) *Journal of Judicial Administration* 143.

28 *Sali v SPC Ltd* (1993) 116 ALR 625; *GSA Industries Pty Ltd v NT Gas Ltd* (1990) 24 NSWLR 710; *Cohen v McWilliam* (1995) 38 NSWLR 476; *Ketteman v Hansel Properties Ltd* [1987] AC 189; and *Queensland v JL Holdings Pty Ltd* (1996) 189 CLR 146.

> districts have already reached intolerable levels because of the precedence that must be given to criminal cases. The only answer ... is for judges to develop the ability to handle more cases as well in less time.[29]

On top of these problems comes the social isolation. The judicial officer, after appointment, usually finds it harder to make firm friends. Some become anxious that signs of friendship, for example from the practising profession, are self-interested and not genuine. Friendships of the past are often diluted; both by the judicial officer's obligation to preserve manifest independence and by the profession's obligation to keep ever open the right of vigorous criticism and appeal which the defence of a client's interests may require. According to a leading Canadian advocate who admitted to long-term alcohol and drug dependence:

> In our society we isolate judges ... All of a sudden a lawyer at 40 goes from fraternising with friends to becoming a judge. He can't golf, go to dinner or socialise with his former colleagues. An active man [sic] is now isolated and lonely. It leads to the old expression – if you're hungry, angry, lonely and tired, you are one step from a drink.[30]

These are the reasons why the judicial office today carries the potential of presenting the incumbent with obligations and duties that are unusually stressful. Obviously, no one is obliged to accept judicial appointment. Nowadays, more than in the past, lawyers realising the disadvantages of judicial service quite frequently decline appointment. They preserve their professional independence and the higher income that goes with it. To this extent, the judiciary tends to be a self-selecting group of lawyers who have a general idea of what the work entails. The discovery of the detailed requirements of office awaits them. The isolation, the high role expectations, the financial disadvantages, the lack of feedback, the ever increasing workload and the limited power of delegation all add up to special sources of stress which are important to acknowledge if judicial life is to become tolerable, and even enjoyable.

Lack of Appreciation

One particular aspect of the social isolation and lack of feedback, referred to above, is another important source of judicial stress. This is the sense of a lack of appreciation for the enormous efforts that the judicial officer typically makes in order to be worthy of the high calling

---

29 DJ Hauptly, 'The Future of Judicial Education' (1996) 9(3) *Bulletin of National Judicial Institute (Canada)* 1 at 2.

30 See Ray (1991) 26.

and of the ancient tradition. For some, a feeling that he or she has been passed over for a higher office, when others seemingly less worthy have been preferred, is a source of pain and disappointment that adds to stress. Some judicial officers have been known to allow an exaggerated estimate of the importance of promotion to get the better of their temperament. Now that promotion within the Australian judiciary is more common than it formerly was, it is important that incumbents should preserve their own integrity and that of the judicial office. To be anxious about something over which the judicial officer can, and should, have no control or influence, is pointless. A healthy scepticism about political decision-making will help cope with this source of anxiety.

Some judicial officers become anxious about what they see as a decline in the niceties of respect for the Bench in general and themselves in particular. Justice Thomas's tale of the somewhat pompous Cooper arriving on a country circuit in Queensland is well targeted to deflate the pomposity of judicial officers of high expectation. As Justice Thomas observes:

> Sadly, a circuit visit these days is something of a non-event in the town. It is no longer safe for a judge to assume that he will be met by anyone upon his arrival. Some may feel a nostalgia for the golden era when the arrival of the judge was an important event.[31]

Once the newly appointed judicial officer appreciates the true limits of his or her own importance, the lessons of humility will not seem so painful.

One of the chief sources of anxiety about the lack of appreciation can arise because of the judicial duty to sit in court and dispense justice with a never-ending flood of cases approaching the court door and a strictly limited capacity to deflect or reduce it. Medical practitioners and dentists in emergency wards have similar obligations to cope with highly important and stressful moments in people's lives. But in our society such individualised responsibility is comparatively rare. Most vocations enjoy a much greater opportunity to share the load and thereby to cope. Many judicial officers, anchored in their courtrooms, face a sense of dread that the work keeps coming in ever-increasing amount, that they strive to do battle against the tide, and that most of their fellow citizens do not appreciate, or even notice, the efforts they put into their work on the public's behalf.

Whereas in the past, judicial officers, in Australia at least, could comfort themselves with the almost universal admiration in which they

31 Thomas (1991) p 208.

were held by the public and the media (and in which they held themselves), nowadays this can scarcely be said.[32] Judicial officers – from the High Court to the Local Court – are subject to the badgering attacks of the media, politicians and others. 'Judges may be told how to behave'; the *Sydney Morning Herald* intoned in September 1996.[33] 'DPP: Put Judges to the Test' was the report of the *West Australian* in October,[34] containing a call that judges should be made 'accountable for the quality of the service they provide':

> If a judge is lazy, inefficient, stupid or merely a procrastinator, why should there not be agreed methods of accountability and appropriate sanction? We have surrendered the right to make judicial officers accountable for the efficiency and quality of the service they provide as judges in the confused belief that accountability and independence are mutually inconsistent, and that requiring a judge to be efficient is an intrusion on the judge's independence of decision.[35]

There is an incongruity about the public's misconception of judicial work and the actuality that is known only too well by judicial officers themselves. There are few with whom the judicial officer can share these feelings of frustration and even resentment. The result is that judicial officers are typically obliged by convention to bottle up their frustrations and to continue the struggle against the growing tide of litigation. They must do so in the face of a highly critical media, indifferent politicians and an uncomprehending public. The champions who might once have helped to reduce or remove the causes, redress the balance and defend the institution are no longer there when they are needed. In large measure, today's judges are on their own. The combination of these realities can result in intolerable stress in some individuals. Or it can produce cynicism as the incapacity of the individual judicial officer to overcome the rising workload or to meet unwarranted calumny ultimately tames him or her to do the best that can be done, and to surrender the fruitless quest for perfection and appreciation.

Personal Factors

In addition to the foregoing features of the judicial life and its characteristics in Australia today, some mention should be made of the features of the personal lives of judicial officers which make them

---

32 See Kirby, Chapter 13.

33 *Sydney Morning Herald*, 5 September 1996. This is a reference to D Wood (1996) *Judicial Ethics: A Discussion Paper*, Australian Institute of Judicial Administration.

34 *West Australian*, 11 October 1996, p 5.

35 Ibid.

vulnerable to stress, often precisely at the moment when they are first ushered into their new judicial chambers.

Mid-life passage (or 'crisis') is a well-established psychological phenomenon. As described, it is usually associated with the death of parents, the departure of children from the home, deterioration in health, in physical self-image and in sexual activity. It frequently coincides with similar developments in the life of a spouse or partner. The much higher levels of marriage and relationship breakdown in contemporary Australian society probably mean that more judicial officers in the future will suffer the stresses of break-up and personal loneliness. Such features may reinforce the vulnerability of people appointed to judicial office.

Some elements of this passage can be positive. It may encourage an appreciation of the fragility of life and the importance of the small number of persons who matter to the judge as a person. But it can also be negative, resulting in questioning of long-term relationships and a retreat to work as a means of escape from the stressful business of personal emotional challenges. A newly appointed judicial officer may have enough stress in the courtroom, so that the addition of personal stress will present risks of burnout and even breakdown. These outcomes can manifest themselves in numerous ways: repeated loss of temper in the courtroom; gross delay in the delivery of reserved judgments; incapacity in decision-making and hostility to the world at large. At least one Australian judge, faced with some of these stresses, found escape in suicide. Fortunately, this is an extreme solution, and is rare. For most, the answer is redoubled effort, despite the fact that the judicial officer well knows that it will have a strictly limited impact on the sources of pressure.

Future Stress

As if the foregoing were not sufficient, a number of phenomena add to the stresses faced by Australian judges today. They include the amount of legislation which pours from our Parliaments and frequently changes the law, just when judges think they are beginning to understand it. New legal procedures demand new techniques of judicial control of the courtroom. New rules for the conduct of trials and new principles of sentencing produce an immediate obligation to keep pace with legislative and common law changes in a way that judicial officers of earlier generations would have found intolerable. Completely novel notions, such as the introduction of the jurisprudence of fundamental human rights, begin to intrude into the life of the Australian judge to an extent that would have been unimaginable in law school days.[36]

To the pressures of new law must also be added the pressure of new technology. Judicial officers today must learn, in middle age, to use computers, word processors and the Internet. Increasingly, they are exposed to telecommunications hearings and the use of video recordings in trials. Now we are on the brink of voice recognition software programmes. By the new century, most of us will probably dictate our opinions to a machine which will recognise our voices and reproduce, with near perfect accuracy, a written text. Training and adaptation to the new technology has added to the stresses of judicial life.[37]

There is now more changeover in the personal staff of judicial officers. The old convention of an elderly retainer, usually chosen from retirees from the defence services, has been replaced by the appointment of young law graduates. They can certainly add stimulus and new perspectives. But their service tends to be temporary. By the time they have been rendered most useful by their training, it is time for them to move on. They are then replaced by new staff, requiring the establishment of new personal relationships and training from scratch.[38]

Another peril and stress has been added to the judicial life. Judicial officers today are much more accountable to the public than they were in earlier times. Of course, this is not necessarily a bad thing. But it certainly adds to pressure when judicial officers are singled out and pilloried in the media for perceived mistakes or departures from popular or media wisdom. In 1993, the harassment of individual Victorian and South Australian judges by television interviewers, who confronted them in public streets and accused them of gender bias, added a pressure that would not have been imagined by the judiciary at the time of my first appointment two decades ago.[39] Better communication, through the media to the community they serve, will be enhanced by media liaison officers appointed to the courts. But sadly, the media is often interested only in an 'angle' or 'spin' and in combative entertainment. Few judges will escape entirely the wrath or derision of the media during their judicial career. Whilst they must remain alert in case the criticism is

---

36 See *Mabo v Queensland (No 2)* (1992) 175 CLR 1 at 42; *Kartinyeri v Commonwealth* (1998) 195 CLR 337 at 417; cf *Young v Registrar, Court of Appeal* (1993) 32 NSWLR 262 at 272; and *R v Sandford* (1994) 33 NSWLR 172 at 177.

37 MD Kirby, 'The Future of Courts – Do They Have One?' (1999) 8 *Journal of Judicial Administration* 185.

38 Thomas (1991) p 208.

39 See B Virtue, 'The Trial of a Gentle Man' (1993) 28(11) *Australian Lawyer* 8; and 'Focus on System, Not on the Judges' (1994) 29(5) *Australian Lawyer* 20.

justified, and lest they have truly lost touch with community values, they must equally preserve their fidelity to the law and to their own consciences. Our judiciary does not march to the drum of editorialists.

Finally, the Australian judge today must operate in a rapidly changing society where few of the values of youth remain unquestioned or unchallenged. Judges must learn to adapt to rapid change. They must become alert to the community's new sensitivity to the rights of women,[40] of Aboriginals, of ethnic communities, of homosexuals, bisexuals and transgender people, of the handicapped and so on. Most judicial officers, being themselves members of the community, respond sympathetically and positively to these changing perceptions relevant to the demands of justice. For some, however, there will be a generational, individual or cultural disinclination. Changes in long-settled ways of the law and the courts may often be beneficial. But it may also be stressful, particularly for older judges, bearing the attitudes and values of their generation and training. They should, and must, adapt to changing times. The judicial office is not theirs to pursue their own humours, but to serve the law and the community.[41] This said, the process of change in directions which may be personally uncongenial will undoubtedly be stressful. If the judicial officer is unwilling or unable to accept the changes, especially in the law itself, integrity will point in the direction of resignation or retirement, rather than the judicial version of Custer's last stand.

Special Categories of Judicial Stress

Rural

One category of judicial service that has been acknowledged as especially prone to high levels of stress in the United States is that in isolated rural communities.[42] For some, service in a country town might be congenial, particularly for a judicial officer with a young family, provided there are good educational facilities and, nowadays, occupational opportunities for the spouse or partner.

---

40 See B Cooney (1994) *Gender Bias and the Judiciary: Report by the Senate Standing Committee on Legal and Constitutional Affairs*, Senate Standing Committee on Legal and Constitutional Affairs.

41 See Lord Halsbury LC in *Sharp v Wakefield* [1891] AC 173 at 179; and *Dwyer v Kaljo* (1992) 27 NSWLR 728 at 744.

42 See BR White, 'The Special Role of State Judges' (1991) 30(2) *Judges Journal* 6 at 10 and K Fahnestock 'The Loneliness of Command – One Perspective on Judicial Isolation' (1991) 30(2) *Judges Journal* 12.

But for many judicial officers, assignment to a remote rural district can offer only acute isolation. He or she is unable to mix socially with a wide group of people, lest doing so causes embarrassment and necessitates disqualification from judicial decision-making for apprehended bias. The judicial officer must avoid the appearance of favouritism towards friends and acquaintances but must also avoid penalising them, or their clients, in order to be scrupulous and to appear as such. In rural districts, there is usually a loss of personal anonymity. These are reasons for adhering to the centralised organisation of the higher courts in Australia and to the provision of country circuits that many judicial officers actually find congenial. Circuits do not present the same sources of stress, at least in Australia, where the judge can usually stay in a modern motel rather than the gloomy 'judges' lodgings' which sometimes cast a lonely blight on judicial service in England.[43]

Aspects of circuit life in Australia are undergoing change, however, as noted by Justice Thomas. Whereas in the past, home hospitality with members of the profession was a common feature, now it has declined. Challenges of judicial bias have occurred arising out of social contact between the judge and local practitioners. Justice Thomas appears to lament the decline of this tradition:

> [P]rovincial towns large enough to attract a circuit are no longer isolated and there is little novelty in visitors. It is hard enough these days for the working spouse to persuade the home spouse to put on a dinner for any guest, let alone for a judge who is hardly likely to be a ball of fun. Whatever the reasons, home hospitality is a fairly rare benefit.[44]

Urban

The urban judicial officer is the most likely to experience the stress of judicial burnout and overwork. He or she will work during court hours under the unrelenting pressure of court lists. The coincidence of judicial working hours makes contact with peers difficult unless special efforts are made in the lunch hour or after court. According to the literature, this is the group of judicial officers which most needs attention to health and regular medical checkups.

---

43 Thomas (1991) p 209.

44 Ibid. In England, the Lord Chancellor in 1994 changed arrangements about 'judges lodgings'. This led to complaints and even letters to *The Times* by judges claiming that their assignment to discounted hotels presented security problems and reduced HM's Judges to little more than 'travelling salesmen'. Opinions about judicial accommodation on circuit are not uniform. See 'Woolfe Calls for Judges to Work in Teams', *The Times*, 28 September 1994, p 5; 'Judges Oppose a Review of Circuit Lodgings', *The Times*, 3 October 1994, p 10.

Appellate

The appellate courts, at least, have the advantage of professional collegiality. But they have their own sources of stress, including high competition amongst their members, frequent clashes of personality and even, occasionally, irrational behaviour. The record of the conduct of Mr Justice Starke in his dealings with Mr Justice Evatt in the High Court of Australia in the 1930s reveals the *nadir* to which the personal relationships of the court had sunk at that time.[45] There are similar tales in the House of Lords following the decision in *Liversidge v Anderson*.[46] Lord Atkin was isolated and ignored by his noble colleagues for suggesting that they had taken their principles from Humpty-Dumpty, not the law books.[47]

In any group of talented professional colleagues of high ability, working closely and continuously together on contentious business, tensions will occasionally surface. It then becomes the duty of the judges to sort out the stresses and pressures and to restore, so far as can be done, working arrangements which ensure the discharge of their duties in a proper manner. During my service in the New South Wales Court of Appeal, good collegial relationships were cemented by fortnightly meetings of all the judges to review the business of the Court. These meetings were supplemented by regular luncheons and occasional dinners. In the High Court of Australia there are monthly business meetings and some social occasions. Since the arrival of Chief Justice Gleeson in 1998 the more frequent meetings common in the Court of Appeal have been introduced. Group psychology presents paradoxes and pressures. The judiciary is not immune from these. Working so closely together can sometimes be stressful; but it can also be creative and enjoyable.

Chief Judges

A special class of judicial officers subjected to particular stresses nowadays are Chief Justices, Chief Judges and Chief Magistrates. They are often on the receiving end of complaints by the public, by the media, by politicians, by professional bodies and by disaffected litigants. Their capacity to effect change in an institution of highly motivated and highly opinionated individuals is limited. Much depends upon these chief

---

45 See CC Lloyd, 'Not Peace But a Sword – The High Court under JG Latham' (1987) 11 *Adelaide Law Review* 175.

46 [1942] AC 206 at 209.

47 R Stevens (1979) *The Law and Politics: The House of Lords as a Judicial Body 1800-1976*, Weidenfeld and Nicolson, p 287.

judicial officers. Before the community and the media they are increasingly perceived not only as working judges but also as the representatives of their courts. This, in turn, adds to their burdens. The skills that were required of Chief Justices in earlier times have radically changed in the past two decades. At least to some extent, Chief Judges are now expected to keep abreast of court management, social change, legal trends, judicial philosophy, law reform, macroeconomics, the law reviews, world events, cultural occasions, legal conferences and suitable charities. They must defend their judges' reputations and privileges whilst seeking to ensure reasonable increases in productivity and the informal handling of sources of complaint falling short of judicial misconduct. These duties add special pressures to the life of a Chief Justice, Chief Judge or Chief Magistrate in Australia today. The fact that many such office holders are themselves appointed to such offices directly from the practising legal profession, without prior judicial service, adds to the pressure, which they can share with relatively few. One way of easing that pressure is by adopting collegiate decision-making and sharing the responsibility of court governance – seeing it as a modern managerial exercise instead of an imperium of unyielding commands.

Characteristics of Judicial Stress

Every judge and lawyer knows the characteristics of judicial stress. They have been noted by a lifetime of watching the courtroom performance of others. But one's own reactions to stress may not be so well appreciated because no one may have been so rude as to mention them.

Judicial stress may be cognitive, resulting in difficulty of concentration and constant glancing at the clock, as much as to ask 'When will I be released from this burden?' Or it can result in a resigned lack of interest in the work, a fatalistic belief that every day will be the same and that nothing the judicial officer can do will much affect the unrelenting workflow and the crushing backlog.

Alternatively, stress can take a physical toll. It might attack the judicial officer's digestion. It might cause nausea, diarrhoea, a sense of agitation, or, in some, an uncontrollable urge to fall asleep and thereby to blot out the pain of an uncongenial life.

In relationships with others, both inside and outside the court, stress may produce outbursts of temper, an egocentric exhibition of self-confidence or the cynicism of a hardened pessimism, producing a lack of concern about the cases being heard and leaving the judicial officer relatively untouched by the pain of the parties involved.

Of course, these are exaggerated consequences of stress. Most judicial officers absorb it, directing it to creative activity, imagination and endless innovation, unerring politeness, accuracy and prompt decisions. Such people – and there are many – are paragons. They absorb what observers have described as 'appalling' personal stress. It is when the cognitive, physical or behavioural outcomes of stress begin to interfere with judicial performance that the judicial officer, the court and the community itself have a legitimate interest and an obligation to look for the cure.[48]

Coping with Judicial Stress

The cure, if there is one, is a subject upon which expert psychologists and others have written, with far more knowledge than I can offer. Typically, they make the point that the judicial reaction to the predicament of stress will depend largely upon the personality and characteristics of the particular judicial officer and his or her insight into the existence of stress and ways of coping with it.

The first step on the path to relieving stress in judicial life, as in life generally, is to admit its existence to oneself and to close friends. Thereafter, it is necessary, if stress is creating a problem, to look to personal and professional responses that will attack the sources of stress, both in the work environment and in the personal life of the judicial officer.

A judicial officer under stress will do well to resist the ego-tempting invitation to join yet another committee or to serve in some new and worthy public cause which adds to time deprivation. However, a deflection of the mind to outside interests, books outside the law, music and theatre, will often be beneficial to those who are stressed. Sometimes the judicial officer will need to reorganise his or her personal life. Some turn to transcendental meditation or yoga; others to relaxation techniques; others to religion; still others to physical exercise or tai chi; others to music-whilst-they-work; others to massage, flotation or other therapy. Some resort to overseas travel; others retreat to an intense home life. Almost always, true relief is found in non-verbal activities.[49]

48 Showlater and Martell (1985) p 85.

49 See JW Gardner (1990) *On Leadership*, Free Press, p 134. Gardner, who knew and worked with several United States Presidents and Congressional leaders, cites Montaigne's injunction: 'I endeavour to free this corner from the public storm, as I do another corner of my soul'.

Some develop hobbies and take an interest in bodies and causes compatible with their office, although not strictly professional or judicial.

All the books urge various physical responses to stress. Cutting down sugar and salt. Vitamin B supplements. Reducing the intake of caffeine, nicotine and alcohol. Taking adjournments to break the day. Walking out of the court building during the lunch hour. Clearing the mind of law, advocates and litigants with their stressful disputes and endless arguments.

Perhaps out of a belated recognition of the pressures imposed on judicial officers, court buildings of the future will include facilities for physical exercise and relaxation. Perhaps some corner of an ancient court building may be found that is forever stress free and provides stress-reducing exercise equipment. It is not without significance that the new Parliament House in Sydney included a gymnasium and a heated swimming pool. The lives of politicians are certainly stressful. But the needs of the judiciary in this regard should not be overlooked, as they have been in the past.

Within the judiciary initiatives can be taken to help to reduce stress arising from the workload. A careful diagnosis of the build-up of cases can lead to a programme for the efficient despatch of an accumulated backlog. The reorganisation of court business and change to time-honoured procedures should be contemplated in the effort to attack one of the major causes of judicial stress – the never-ending workload and the feeling of helplessness in reducing it. Judicial officers cannot be reduced to automatons. Nor can they provide true justice to a fixed timetable set by computers. But their efficiency can be improved by the provision of better equipment, improved library and research facilities, increased professional staff and better computer-aided listing and case monitoring. Properly mobilised, these resources can increase the judicial throughput. Doing this might itself help to reduce judicial stress.

Even if it seems unlikely that judicial salaries in Australia will much improve, other benefits of judicial office may be enhanced, notably by the provision of improved study leave, paid participation in judicial conferences, better technology and regular communication amongst judicial colleagues at all levels of the hierarchy concerning the work and the shared problems and frustrations. Just speaking of such matters can often provide some relief.

A New Beginning

It is in a spirit of open-mindedness and honesty that I have offered these thoughts on judicial stress. The era of silence and denial is over. The era of candour has begun. With the stress, in equal measure, there is in the life of a judicial officer in Australia excitement, intellectual stimulation, personal satisfaction, still a great deal of public esteem, a general sense of social utility, and a never-ending feeling of the privilege it is to be a judicial officer in a country ruled by the law. It is indisputably an exciting time to be a judicial officer even if the going is somewhat more perilous than it was for our predecessors. Today's judges are the latest servants in a tradition of 800 years. When judges keep that perspective, most of the pressures seem tolerable. But one of the greatest judicial virtues is unswerving honesty. And if we are honest, we will accept that stress is an inescapable feature of judicial service today. Once this reality is faced judges are already on the path of coping and helping colleagues who may need encouragement and assistance.

Chapter 15

Has the Legal Profession Lost Its Soul?

At an address on receiving the Honorary Degree of Doctor of Laws from the University of Sydney on 4 May 1996, Michael Kirby reflected on his early life at the University and the responsibilities of today's graduates about to embark upon careers in the law. He considers a book by Professor Kronman, Dean of Yale Law School, concerning the declining ideals of the legal profession in the United States. His message is that, important as Kronman's warning is for the future, the law's claim to nobility rests on a broader foundation than that recognised by Kronman. Rather than retreating to a nostalgic view of the past, lawyers should be looking for humanistic and modern solutions to complex modern problems.

Forty Years On

It is 40 years since I first walked up the Union steps to begin my life at Sydney University. Anyone wishing to have a description of that memorable day in March 1956 can read all about it in Clive James' *Unreliable Memoirs.*[1] Clive, Robert Hughes, Jon Bell, Murray Gleeson, Germaine Greer and others entered this, the oldest university in Australia, on that day. They came into this Great Hall for the first time to receive the welcome of the Chancellor, Sir Charles Blackburn, well into his 80s but with 10 years still to serve. Chancellors are survivors. Clive James remembers Robert Hughes that day, as I do, rushing everywhere, huddled in a long and heavy Oxford-type scarf, which was a trifle remarkable as Sydney was in the midst of a heatwave. He notes with retrospective embarrassment his own display of the School Christian Movement badge which betokened his spiritual convictions at the time. I am only grateful that our paths did not cross on that fateful day or I would be immortalised in his book for wearing, as I did, the blazer of a school prefect at Fort Street High School. How could I have done such an unsophisticated thing? Thank goodness, Clive did not notice. But it shows what a naive lot we were, growing up in a lucky country in the 1950s and privileged to attend its finest university.

1 C James (1980) *Unreliable Memoirs*, Cape, Chapter 13.

I earned four university degrees at this place. My brothers (who are with me today) earned four more. So we attended, as a family, eight ceremonies such as this. My parents were at them all. By God's grace they are with me today. So is my sister. She is a nursing sister who tenders to the seriously ill in the great hospital attached to this campus. These ceremonies become important milestones in the life of a family. Photographs freeze in time the joys of effort acknowledged and the love of those who sustain us, the graduates.

I express my heartfelt thanks to the University for honouring me in this way. I am proud to join today's graduates. I did not expect another graduation here. Gareth Evans, a colleague in student and in later days, once said of my collection of degrees (in contrast to his own of the Oxford variety) that I had concentrated on quantity rather than quality. I shall have to let him know, subtly and apparently nonchalantly, about today, for it is quality abounding.

By the sheerest chance, the letter inviting me to accept this high honour arrived on the very morning of the day on which, in the afternoon, I was called out of a meeting to be invited to accept appointment as the 40th Justice of the High Court of Australia. Little did I imagine, as I walked up Science Road in my battered school blazer, or as I sat in this Great Hall in 1962 at my own law graduation, that such events lay ahead. Life has an exquisite unpredictability.

My mind rushes back through the years to the dear family members who supported me, notably my grandmother and great-aunt Lillian who are not here today. I say to my fellow graduates to cherish this moment. Without embarrassment, they should acknowledge their love and debt to those who sustained them. Such love endures. Beyond the family members, the people we should remember include the kindergarten and school teachers, comrades in the classrooms and the scholars of the University to whom we will always be indebted. Thirty and forty years on may you all remember this day as I do the precious events in my life.

The Lost Lawyer

One thing only is sure about today. It is that in a few days (perhaps a few hours) no one will remember a single word of what I have said. In all truth, I cannot call to mind any of the wise sayings or jests of any of the eight occasional speakers of the graduations of my family or the hundreds which, as a Fellow of the Senate or as Chancellor at Macquarie University, I heard on these great occasions. The fledgling graduate is impatient to escape to photographs and family praise.

But it is a convention of these occasions that you must endure one last lecture in which a spoilt-sport of the older generation tries to caution you with admonitions to attempt to be almost as good as *they* were in life. It is the office of the ageing to press unbidden advice on the young. But what can I, bedecked in doctoral finery, say that will be of any use to the cogitations of young graduates who will have responsibilities for the law and for society into the new millennium, long after I am just an occasionally read page in the *Commonwealth Law Reports*?

One of the letters which was sent to me to congratulate me on my appointment to the High Court came from a friend of Law Reform days who is now a Professor of Law in the United States. Accompanying his letter was a book, *The Lost Lawyer*.[2] It is written by Professor Anthony Kronman, Dean of the Yale Law School: possibly now the most influential law school in the United States. The subtitle of the book is *Failing Ideals of the Legal Profession*. My correspondent urged that it was the most important text written on the legal profession in the United States in the past 30 years. In a typical Australian way, I found such a buildup off-putting. Can we ever escape the cynicism and scepticism that came with the convicts?

Kronman begins his book with assurance:

> This book is about a crisis in the American legal profession. Its message is that the profession now stands in danger of losing its soul. The crisis is, in essence, a crisis of morale. It is the product of growing doubts about the capacity of a lawyer's life to offer fulfilment to the person who takes it up. Disguised by the material well-being of lawyers, is a spiritual crisis that strikes at the heart of their professional pride.[3]

In his summation, Kronman looks back, in a way that we at this ceremony must look forward:

> The lawyers of my generation now find themselves in positions of authority and power. Twenty years after graduating from law school, we stand near the top of our profession. We are partners in our firms and senior professors in our faculties. And we are beginning to be appointed in large numbers to the courts. To a significant degree, the stewardship of these institutions, and of the legal profession generally, is in our hands. When we came to the law, it seemed mysterious and remote. Yet after an impossibly short time we find that it is we who are the guardians of our profession and responsible for its well-being. . . . This is our hour in the sun. But the profession we have inherited is not the one we joined.[4]

---

2 A Kronman (1993) *The Lost Lawyer*, Harvard University Press.

3 Ibid, pp 1-2.

4 Ibid, p 353.

If this book is causing such a fuss in the United States, we should perhaps pay heed to it. Experience teaches that what happens there has a tendency to happen, a decade or so later, here, in Australia. So why is Kronman so alarmed?

- Attorneys, he says, practise law in a different way now than did their forebears. The best gravitate to huge and impersonal law firms, where time charging rewards the slow and the irresolute. The original ideals of wise and dispassionate advice to clients are enfeebled by a mercantile attitude that lets the client dictate the course of disputes, without the cautionary words that lawyers once gave. The role of the lawyer in the old days, according to Kronman, involved compassion for the client's entire predicament, tempered by detachment and also concern for the public good.[5] The growing ascendancy of the economic view of the law, and the decline of its self-image as a helping profession, deeply concern Kronman as he surveys the places to which his best and brightest graduates from the Yale Law School go to seek their future.
- Advocates are also undergoing change, according to this book. The old days of complete honesty to the courts and candour and honour in dealings with colleagues have given way, according to Kronman, to a more ruthless effort to win cases upon which huge profits may hang, essential to the lawyer's business. The client becomes a 'punter'. The lawyer becomes too caught up in the client's speculation. Whereas in the past, the advocate would conceive of his or her role as being, like that of the judge, to maintain the rule of law, sharing the judicial attitude in that regard, now the advocate is just another businessperson and the client's cause, ultimately, an investment.
- Under the pressure of caseloads, he says, judges have become mere editors of opinion drafts drawn for them by their clerks. According to Kronman, very few judges in the United States still write all of their own opinions. The result is discursive opinion-writing, needless dissents and footnote battles as clerks struggle for their place in the lawbooks. Fuzzy reasoning reflects what Kronman calls the lack of wisdom and 'horse-sense'.[6]

---

5 Ibid, p 74.

6 Ibid, p 23, quoting Karl Llewellyn.

Not everyone in the United States agrees with all of Kronman's gloomy analysis.[7] One writer, recalling the stalwart work of Archibald Cox, Judge John Sirica and the unanimous opinion of the Supreme Court that brought down Richard Nixon,[8] is more optimistic:

> Some say our Law's in a sorry plight, and folly its fruition.
> The answer to that is to set it right, in the Common Law tradition.[9]

But there are enough similarities for Australian lawyers to heed the warning. Cases of outrageous overcharging have occurred. Time charging spreads its baleful influence. Pro bono work falls unevenly. Involvement in law reform and the other hallmarks of a public-spirited profession remains patchy. Commitment to complete honesty with the Bench and colleagues is occasionally missing. The mounting pressure on all courts in Australia demands solutions. But they must be solutions that still leave time for the advocate to persuade the decision-maker. And for the judicial officer to reason to his or her own conclusion – not a mere endorsement of the opinion of others.

A Parable

What is it that gives the law its claim to nobility? I know what gives the healthcare professions that claim. I have seen my sister's ministrations which can help to save life and reduce suffering. Do we in the law have such a claim?

In my speech at my swearing in at the High Court, I suggested that it was the law's contribution to the quest for justice that gives us such a claim. Justice, according to law, true. But justice is on our banner. As I reflected on Kronman's thesis, however, it seemed to me that the law's claim to nobility, at least in Australia, rests on a broader foundation. It depends upon the integrity of a profession which is not just another money-making business. It depends upon attorneys putting the client's interests always above their own. Upon advocates preserving scrupulously the culture of honesty and candour. Upon judges accepting the heavy burden of personal decision-making. Upon all of us retaining our respect for the people whom we serve.

Long ago, even before I entered this University in my prefect's blazer, an experience imprinted itself on my mind that taught me, in a vivid way, what it was to be a professional person. My mother fell ill.

---

7 MA Glendon (1994) *A Nation Under Lawyers – How the Crisis in the Legal Profession is Transforming American Society*, Farrar, Strauss and Giroux.

8 *United States v Nixon* 418 US 683 (1975).

9 Glendon (1994) p 253, attributed to Karl Llewellyn.

Her specialist was in practice in Macquarie Street, Sydney. A telephone call was made about her predicament. The specialist said it was no problem. He was going that night to the Repatriation Hospital nearby and would call on our home, as he did. He arrived, resplendent in full military uniform. It was quite a sight for a 12-year-old boy. Gently and skilfully he went about his consultation. He treated each one of us, in our small family group, with courtesy, kindness and understanding. He came into my room to look at my study chart and to give some words of encouragement. He went off into the dark. But he left an indelible memory on my impressionable mind. To take the extra step. To offer the extra help. To live by a professional golden rule. To treat every person under your professional attention as special, unique, a whole human being with a life extending far beyond the professional problem. To show compassion, tempered with detachment. To strive to be worthy of the highest ideals of those who have gone before. To offer the profession to the next generation not diminished, as Kronman fears. But enhanced and, in our case, more sensitive to justice for all under the law.

You may think this is hopelessly high-minded Polonian advice.[10] But I hope some of you will draw from my life parallels and a message of encouragement and guidance for a life in the law. There is much wrong to be righted. We should search for the tools and respond, whenever we can. We should listen every day for the call of justice under the law. And we should never forget that our profession is judged by the way we treat those who have no power and no importance, who may even be hated; but who come to us in need.

I close with the only words of an occasional speaker that I can summon to memory from the years I sat through a thousand ceremonies such as this. A Scottish theologian, speaking from this place, in an accent not unlike my grandfather's from Ulster:

> For what we have received
> And what we will receive by the precious gift of education, in the years to come.
> May the Lord make us truly thankful.

10 Kronman (1993) p 145.

References

Books and Articles

'Academy Joins Debate Over DNA Patents', *Science*, vol 277, 4 July 1997, 41.
'Attacks on the High Court by People Who Ought to Know Better', *Bulletin* (Law Society of South Australia), May 1997.
'Attorney Pleads for Peace in Court Row', *The Age*, 1 March 1997.
'Australia: A Non-Secret is Out', *The Canberra Times*, 22 April 1999.
'Besieging the Bench', *The Age*, 22 February 1997.
'China Fails to Block a UN Human Rights Vote' (1995) 6(1) *Tibet Press Watch* 1.
'Clone mammals … clone man?', *Nature*, vol 380, 13 March 1997, 119.
'Come Back Lionel' (1992) 17 *Alternative Law Journal* 206.
'Dilute the Judges' Cartel', *Australian Financial Review*, 12 May 1997.
'Dismissal of Judges' [1997] *New Zealand Law Journal* 333.
'Diversionary Attacks on the High Court', *Courier Mail*, 19 February 1997.
'Focus on System, Not on the Judges' (1994) 29(5) *Australian Lawyer* 20.
'High Court Plans are Sour Grapes', *West Australian*, 20 February 1997.
'In Defence of Judges', *Sydney Morning Herald*, 22 September 1997.
'Inquiry into "Delusional" Judge Stopped', *Sydney Morning Herald*, 16 October 1996.
'Judges and Politics' [1996] *New Zealand Law Journal* 361.
'Judges at Risk' (1996) 18(32) *National Law Journal* 16.
'Judges Oppose a Review of Circuit Lodgings', *The Times*, 3 October 1994.
'Judicial Crack-ups Fracture the Bench' (1996) 18(32) *National Law Journal* A1.
'Merit the best judge', *Canberra Times*, 8 March 1997.
'No court of knaves', *Canberra Times*, 23 September 1997.
'NTU Co-Conference on Chinese Press in China', *The Straits Times*, 22 March 1995.
'Opinions on Homosexuality', *Washington Post*, 26 December 1998.
'Politicising High Court appointments', *Courier Mail*, 10 March 1997.
'Prominent Chinese Dissidents Support Negotiations with Dalai Lama and Plebiscite in Tibet' (1995) 7(5) *Tibet Press Watch* 3.
'Renewed Fight Over Gene Patent Policy', *Science*, vol 276, 11 April 1997, 187.
'Science Probes Key to Stress', *The Australian*, 13 August 1990.
'Tom – One Lawyer's Story' (1990) 64 *Law Institute Journal* (Vic) 1020.
'UN Rapporteur on Religion Visits Tibet' (1995) 6(5) *Tibet Press Watch* 10.
'UN Visit A Farce', *Australia Tibet Council News*, February/March 1995.
'United Nations Backs Predominantly Chinese Industries in Tibet' (1995) 6(5) *Tibet Press Watch* 12.
'Williams Calls for High Court Restraint', *Australian Financial Review*, 23 September 1997.
'Woolfe Calls for Judges to Work in Teams', *The Times*, 28 September 1994.
1 Corinthians 13 xii.
Abrahams, S, 'Workshop Examines Way to Help Disabled Judges' (1982) 65 *Judicature* 327.
Ackner, Lord, 'The Erosion of Judicial Independence' [1996] *New Law Journal* 1789.
Adams, J, 'Encryption – The Next Big Thing?' (1998) *Computers and Law*, February, 39.
Aikman, CC, 'Fundamental Rights and Directing Principles of State Policy in India' (1987) 17 *Victoria University of Wellington Law Review* 373.
Akerman, P, 'Telling the Truth', *Sunday Telegraph*, 16 November 1997.

Akerman, P, *Daily Telegraph*, 20 November 1997.

Andrew, G et al, 'The Role of Legal Education in Producing Psychological Distress Among Law Students and Lawyers' (1986) 2 *American Bar Foundation Research Journal* 225.

Akerman, P, '"P" Marks a Spot in History', *Daily Telegraph (Australia)*, 22 April 1999.

Ansett Airlines, *Panorama*, August 1996.

Australian Privacy Charter Council, 'Privacy Charter' (1995) 2 *Privacy Law and Policy Reporter* 44.

Balz, SD, and O Hance, 'Privacy and the Internet: Intrusion, Surveillance and Personal Data' (1996) 10(2) *International Review of Law, Computers and Technology* 219.

Bartlett, P, 'Internet & the Legal Tangle' (1995) 1(4) *Computer Law and Practice* 110.

Barwick, GE (1995) *A Radical Tory – Reflections and Recollections*, Federation Press.

Bellacosa, JW, 'Remarks – Judging Cases v Courting Public Opinion' (1997) 65 *Fordham Law Review* 2381.

Beloff QC, M, Review of Joshua Rozenberg's *Trial of Strength*, *The Times Literary Supplement*, 22 August 1997.

Bernstein, RB, 'Charting the Bicentennial' (1987) 87 *Columbia Law Review* 1565.

Bickel, A (1986) *The Least Dangerous Branch. The Supreme Court at the Bar of Politics*, Yale University Press.

Biskupik, J, 'Has the Court Lost its Appeal?', *Washington Post*, 12 October 1995.

Bond, J, 'Telecommunications is Dead, Long Live Networking', *I-Ways*, Third Quarter 1997, 26.

Borella, MS, 'Computer Privacy vs. First and Fourth Amendment Rights', <http://www.eff.org/pub/Privacy/comp_privacy_4th_amend.paper>.

Brennan, FG (1996) 'A Tribute to Sir Anthony Mason' in C Saunders (ed) *Courts of Final Jurisdiction – The Mason Court in Australia*, Federation Press.

Brennan, FG, 'The Judicial Method' (1996) 8 *Judicial Officers' Bulletin* (NSW) 73.

Breyer, S, 'US Judge Puts the Case for Judicial Activism', *Australian Financial Review*, 29 October 1996.

Bright, SB, 'Political Attacks on the Judiciary: Can Justice Be Done Amid Efforts to Intimidate and Remove Judges from Office for Unpopular Decisions?' (1997) 72 *New York University Law Review* 308.

Bright, SB, 'Political Attacks on the Judiciary' (1997) 80 *Judicature* 165.

Brown, J, 'Physical Fitness – The Duty of Care to Oneself' (1990) 28 *Law Society Journal* (NSW) 68.

Byers QC, Sir Maurice, 'Doubtful Political Wisdom', *Sydney Morning Herald*, 20 March 1997.

Byk, C, 'Patenting Human Genes', in BBV Foundation (Spain) *The Human Genome Project: Legal Aspects*, vol 2.

Cain, J, 'A Low Attack on our High Court', *The Age*, 25 February 1997.

Campbell, R, 'Personal Attacks Gone Too Far – Kirby Hits at Critics', *Canberra Times*, 6 January 1998.

Cass, D, 'Constitutional Debate Put the High Court in the Dock', *The Age*, 7 November 1997.

Castan QC, R, 'Judge-Bashing Reveals an Ignorance of Legal Principles', *The Australian*, 1 October 1997.

Cavoukian, A and D Tapscott (1996) *Who Knows – Safeguarding your Privacy in a Networked World*, Vintage.

Clarke, R, 'Beyond "Fair Information Practices": A New Paradigm for 21st Century Privacy Protection', <http://www.anu.edu.au/people/Roger.Clarke/DV/BeyondFIP.html>.

Clarke, R, 'Profiling and its Privacy Implications' (1994) 1 *Privacy Law and Policy Reporter* 128.

Connolly, PD (1993) 'Should the Courts Determine Social Policy?' in *The High Court of Australia in Mabo*, Association of Mining and Exploration Companies.

Cook-Deegan, R (1994) *The Gene Wars*, Norton.

Cooke, R, 'The Courts and Public Controversy' (1985) 5 *Otago Law Review* 357.

Cooper, BJ (1995) *Battles on the Bench – Conflict inside the Supreme Court*, University of Kansas.

Cooper, L, 'On Independence, Once and For All', *American Bar Association Journal*, August 1997.

Cornish, E, 'The Cyber Future: 92 Ways Our Lives Will Change by the Year 2025' (1996) 30(1) *The Futurist* 27.

Craven, G (1997) 'The High Court and the Founders: An Unfaithful Servant', in Australian Parliament, Senate, Papers on Parliament, *The Constitution Makers*, Australian Parliament.

David, R and JC Brierley (1978) *Major Legal Systems in the World Today*, Stevens.

Davies, S, 'Strategies for Protecting Privacy in the New Information Structure' (1995) 2(2) *Privacy Law and Policy Reporter* 23.

Davies, S, 'The Australian federal government has abandoned its election promise to enact privacy legislation for business' (1997) 16(6) *Computer Law and Security Report* 429.

Dawson, D, 'Do Judges Make Law? Too Much?' (1996) 3 *Judicial Review* 1.

de Werd, M and R de Winter (1995) 'Judicial Activism in the Netherlands: Who Cares?' in R Bakker et al (eds) *Judicial Control: Comparative Essays on Judicial Review*, Metro.

Devlin, P (1979) *The Judge*, Oxford.

Diesel, N, 'Refugee Week Shame' (1996) 5(3) *Human Rights Defender*. <http://www.austlii.edu.au/au/other/ahric/Secondary/hrd/hrdindex.html>

Dixon, Sir Owen, 'Swearing in of Sir Owen Dixon as Chief Justice' (1952) 85 CLR.

Dixon, Sir Owen, 'Concerning Judicial Method' (1956) 26 *Australian Law Journal* 468.

Donaghue, S, 'Balancing Sovereignty in International Law: The Domestic Impact of International Law in Australia' (1995) 17 *Adelaide Law Review* 213.

Downey, C, 'The High Price of a Cashless Society: Exchanging Privacy Rights for Digital Cash?' (1996) 14(2) *John Marshall Journal of Computer and Information Law* 303.

Downey, PJ, 'Simplicity, Fairness and Reasonable Expectations' [1997] *New Zealand Law Journal* 147.

Doyle, JJ, 'Judicial Law-Making – Is Honesty the Best Policy?' (1995) 17 *Adelaide Law Review* 161.

Doyle, J (1996) 'Implications of Judicial Law-Making' in C Saunders (ed) *Courts of Final Jurisdiction – The Mason Court in Australia*, Federation Press.

Dworkin, R, (1986) *Law's Empire*, Belknap Press.

Ely, J and R Ely (eds) (1986) *Lionel Murphy: The Rule of Law*, Acron.

English, R, 'Judgment Days', BBC *Worldwide*, July 1994.

Equal Time, February 1999, New South Wales Anti-Discrimination Board Newsletter.

Etzioni, A, 'The Evils of Self-Determination' (1992-3) 89 *Foreign Policy* 21.

Evans, JG, 'Reintegrating the United Nations', *Peace and Disarmament News*, November 1994, Australian Government Publishing Services.
Evans, L, 'Tibet Expects Changes When Deng Dies', *The Australian*, 1 March 1995.
Evans, R et al (1997) *Our Future's Past*, Macmillan.
Fahnestock, K, 'The Loneliness of Command – One Perspective on Judicial Isolation' (1991) 30(2) *Judges Journal* 12.
Finkelstein, RA (1996) 'Procedural Fairness' in C Saunders (ed) *Courts of Final Jurisdiction – The Mason Court in Australia*, Federation Press.
France, E, 'Can Data Protection Survive in Cyberspace?' (1997) 8(2) *Computers and Law* 20.
Gaille, SS, 'Publishing by US Court of Appeals Judges: Before and After the Bork Hearings' (1997) 26 *Journal of Legal Studies* 371.
Gardner, JW (1990) *On Leadership*, Free Press.
Gibbs, Sir Harry, 'The Late Mr Justice Murphy' (1986) 160 CLR v.
Ginsburg, RB, 'Remarks on Writing Separately' (1990) 65 *Washington Law Review* 133.
Gleeson, AM, 'Who Do Judges Think They Are?' (1998) 22 *Criminal Law Journal* 10.
Glendon, MA (1994) *A Nation Under Lawyers – How the Crisis in the Legal Profession is Transforming American Society*, Farrar, Strauss and Giroux.
Goldman, S (ed) (1985) *Judicial Conflict and Consensus: Behavioural Studies of American Appellate Courts*, Uni Press Kentucky.
Gomez, M, 'Social Economic Rights and Human Rights Commissions' (1995) 17(1) *Human Rights Quarterly* 155.
Goodrich, LM and E Hambro (1949) *Charter of the United Nations: Commentary and Documents*, 2nd ed, Stevens.
Graham, K, 'Judges obliged to take a stand', *The Age*, 4 March 1997.
Greenleaf, G, 'Privacy and Cyberspace – An Ambiguous Relationship' (1996) 3(5) *Privacy Law and Policy Reporter* 88.
Greenleaf, G, 'Privacy Principles – Irrelevant to Cyberspace?' (1996) 3(6) *Privacy Law and Policy Reporter* 114.
Greenleaf, G, 'European Commission tests adequacy of our privacy laws' (1998) 4(8) *Privacy Law and Policy Reporter* 140.
Hamilton, A et al (1941) *The Federalist: A Commentary on the Constitution of the United States*, Modern Library, No 78.
Hannum, H, 'Rethinking Self-Determination' (1993) 34 *Virginia Journal of International Law* 1.
Harding, R (1970) *Police Killings in Australia*, Penguin.
Hassell, WR, 'High Court Must Know its Place', *The Australian*, 24 September 1997.
Hauptly, DJ, 'The Future of Judicial Education' (1996) 9(3) *Bulletin of National Judicial Institute (Canada)* 1.
HH The Dalai Lama (1990) *Freedom in Exile*, John Curtis.
HH The Dalai Lama, 'I Prefer Change in China without Total Collapse', *Tibetan Bulletin*, January/February 1995.
HH The Dalai Lama, 'True Expression of Non-Violence is Compassion', *The Asian Age*, 1 January 1995, reprinted in the *Tibetan Bulletin*, January/February 1995.
Hocking, J (1997) *Lionel Murphy – A Political Biography*, Cambridge.
Hughes, G, 'Nowhere to Hide? Privacy and the Internet' (1996) 29 *Computers and the Law* 21.
Hughes, T, 'Regulation of the "Net"' in Australian Law Reform Commission (1997) *Reform*, Issue 71, 23.

Human Rights Campaign, 'Human Rights Campaign Learns Pentagon Postponing Expulsion of Sailor with "Gay" in His America OnLine Profile', <http://www.hrc.org/feature1/mcveigh.html>.

Ioannou, S, 'Professor and High Court', *Australian Financial Review*, 14 October 1997.

Jackson, D (1996) 'The Role of the Chief Justice: A View from the Bar' in C Saunders (ed) *Courts of Final Jurisdiction – The Mason Court in Australia*, Federation Press.

Jacobs, S, 'Judge Warns of Short-Cut to Tyranny', *The Advertiser*, 26 March 1997.

James, C (1980) *Unreliable Memoirs*, Cape.

Joseph, GP, 'Judicial Imperfection and Judicial Independence' (1997) 23(4) *Litigation* 1.

Kadzielski, MA and RC Kunda, 'The Origins of Modern Dissent: The Unmaking of the Judicial Consensus in the 1930s' (1983) 15 *University of West Los Angeles Law Review* 43.

Kammen, M (1986) *A Machine That Would Go of Itself: A Constitution in American Culture*, Knopf.

Kaplan, RD, 'The Coming Anarchy' (1994) 273(2) *Atlantic Monthly* 44.

Kavanagh, L, 'Sentence Judges to Life on the Streets', *Courier Mail*, 14 June 1997.

Keal, RD, 'Stop Attacking the Judges', *West Australian*, 10 March 1997.

Kirby, MD (1983) *The Judges*, ABC Boyer Lectures.

Kirby, MD, 'Human Rights and Technology: A New Dilemma' (1988) 22 *University of British Columbia Law Review* 123.

Kirby, MD, 'The Bangalore Principles on "the Domestic Application of International Human Rights Norms"' (1988) 14 *Commonwealth Law Bulletin* 1196.

Kirby, MD, 'The Role of the Judge in Advancing Human Rights by Reference to International Human Rights Norms' (1988) 62 *Australian Law Journal* 514.

Kirby, MD, 'HV Evatt, The Anti-Communist Referendum and Liberty in Australia' (1990) 7 *Australian Bar Review* 93.

Kirby, M, 'HV Evatt, the Anti-Communist Referendum and Liberty in Australia' (1991) 7 *Australian Bar Review* 93.

Kirby, M, 'Current Topics' (1992) 66 *Australian Law Journal* 775.

Kirby, MD, 'Lionel Murphy and the Power of Ideas' (1993) 18(6) *Alternative Law Journal* 253.

Kirby, MD, 'The Australian Use of International Human Rights Norms: From Bangalore to Balliol – A View from the Antipodes' (1993) 16 *University of New South Wales Law Journal* 363.

Kirby, MD, 'Abolition of Courts and Non-reappointment of Judicial Officers' (1994) 12 *Australian Bar Review* 181.

Kirby, MD 'The Human Genome Project – Promise and Problems' (1994) 11 *Journal of Contemporary Health Law and Policy* 1.

Kirby, MD, 'Human Rights, the United Nations and Cambodia' (1995) 67(4) *Australian Quarterly* 26.

Kirby, M, 'Judicial Stress' (1995) 12(3) *Australian Bar Review* 101.

Kirby, MD, 'The Impact of International Human Rights Norms: A Law Undergoing Evolution' (1995) 25 *University of Western Australia Law Review* 1.

Kirby, MD, 'Civil Liberties: Early Days and Days Ahead' (1996) 28(1) *Australian Journal of Forensic Sciences* 3; (1996) 34(10) *Law Society Journal* 44.

Kirby, MD, 'Deakin: Popular Sovereignty and the True Foundation of the Australian Constitution' (1996) 3(2) *Deakin Law Review* 129.

Kirby, M, 'Sir Anthony Mason Lecture 1996: AF Mason – From *Trigwell* to *Teoh*' (1996) 20 *Melbourne University Law Review* 1087.

Kirby, M, 'Swearing in and welcome speech – 6 February 1996' (1996) 70 *Australian Law Journal* 274.

Kirby, MD, 'Challenges of the Genome' (1997) 20(3) *University of New South Wales Law Journal* 537.

Kirby, M, 'Judicial Activism' (1997) 27 *University of Western Australia Law Review* 1; (1997) 23 *Commonwealth Law Bulletin* 1224.

Kirby, M, 'Judicial Stress – A Reply' (1997) 71 *Australian Law Journal* 791.

Kirby, M, 'Judicial Stress – An Update' (1997) 71 *Australian Law Journal* 774.

Kirby, MD 'Julius Stone and the High Court of Australia' (1997) 20 *University of New South Wales Law Journal* 239.

Kirby, MD (1997) 'Lord Cooke and Fundamental Rights' in P Rishworth (ed) *The Struggle for Simplicity – Essays for Lord Cooke of Thorndon*, Butterworths.

Kirby, M (1997) 'Lord Cooke and Fundamental Rights' in P Rishworth (ed) *The Struggle for Simplicity in the Law*, Butterworths.

Kirby, MD, 'Teaching Australians Civics' (1997) 13 *Queensland University of Technology Law Journal* 149.

Kirby, MD, 'Attacks on Judges: A Universal Phenomenon' (1998) 72 *Australian Law Journal* 599.

Kirby, MD, 'Same-Sex Relationships: Some Australian Legal Developments' (1999) 19(1) *Australian Bar Review* 4.

Kirby, MD, 'The Future of Courts – Do They Have One?' (1999) 8 *Journal of Judicial Administration* 185.

Kneebone, S, 'Refugee Test and the "One Child Policy"' (1997) 4 *Australian Journal of Administrative Law* 173.

Koskemmiemi, M, 'National Self-Determination Today: Problems of Legal Theory and Practice' (1994) 43 *International and Comparative Law Quarterly* 241.

Kronman, A (1993) *The Lost Lawyer*, Harvard University Press.

Lane, B and L Slattery, 'Australia: Without Prejudice', *The Australian*, 20 April 1999.

Lau, S, 'Observance of the OECD Guidelines and the EU Directive in Asia' (1998) 4(8) *Privacy Law and Policy Reporter* 145.

Lee, Professor Hoong Phun, 'Why We Must Protect the Protectors', *Sydney Morning Herald*, 13 June 1997.

Leuchtenberg, WE (1995) *The Supreme Court Reborn*, Oxford.

Li-ann, T, 'An "i" for an "I"? Singapore's Communitarian Model of Constitutional Adjudication' (1997) *Hong Kong Law Journal* 153.

Lindell, G, 'Why is Australia's Constitution Binding? The Reasons in 1900 and Now and the Effect of Independence' (1986) 16 *Federal Law Review* 29.

Little, R and W Reed (1989) *The Confucian Renaissance*, Federation Press.

Liverani, MR, 'Mid-Life Crisis or Epiphany?' (1994) 32 *Law Society Journal* (NSW) 46.

Lloyd, CC, 'Not Peace But a Sword – The High Court under JG Latham' (1987) 11 *Adelaide Law Review* 175.

Marsic, S, 'Membership of a Particular Social Group' (1997) 22 *Alternative Law Journal* 97.

Mason, AF, 'The Role of a Constitutional Court in a Federation' (1986) 16 *Federal Law Review* 1

Mason, AF, 'The Use and Abuse of Precedent' (1988) 4 *Australian Bar Review* 93.

Mason, AF (1996) 'A Reply' in C Saunders (ed) *Courts of Final Jurisdiction – The Mason Court in Australia*, Federation Press.

Mason, A, 'Courts and Community Values' (1996) 6(9) *Eureka Street* 32.

Mason, Sir A (1997) 'Foreword' in P Rishworth (ed) *The Struggle for Simplicity in the Law*, Butterworths.

McCarthy, D, 'Superannuated', *Brother-Sister*, Issue 182, 15 April 1999, 7.

McClelland, JR, 'Criticism of Courts Unfounded', *Sydney Morning Herald*, 27 January 1997.

McHugh, MH, 'The Law-making Function of the Judicial Process – Part I' (1988) 62 *Australian Law Journal* 15.

McHugh, MH, 'The Law-making Function of the Judicial Process – Part II' (1988) 62 *Australian Law Journal* 116.

McKenzie, J, 'Super Boost for Equality Campaign', *Brother-Sister*, Issue 182, 15 April 1999, 3.

McNamara, L and T Solomon, 'The Commonwealth *Racial Hatred Act* 1995: Achievement or Disappointment?' (1996) 18 *Adelaide Law Review* 259.

Merritt, C, 'LCA Backs High Court', *Australian Financial Review*, 19 March 1997.

Middleton, M, 'Judges Told how to Deal with Stress' (1981) 67 *American Bar Association Journal* 1100.

Miller, J, '*John Fairfax Publishing Pty Ltd v Doe*' (1996) 20 *Criminal Law Journal* 288.

Miller, R, 'The Internet in Twenty Years: Cyberspace, the Next Frontier?' (1997) OECD Future Studies Information Base Highlight, No 14.

Miller, T, 'Law, Privacy and Cyberspace' (1996) 1(4) *Communications Law* 143.

Milne, G, 'Government Puts Judges on Good Behaviour Bond', *The Australian*, 9 June 1997.

Morgan, DG, 'The Indian "Essential Features" Case' (1981) 30 *International and Comparative Law Quarterly* 307.

Niebuhr, G, 'In US Pontiff to look to the new generation', *International Herald Tribune*, 26 January 1999.

Nussbaum, MC (1998) *Sex and Social Justice*, Oxford University Press.

O'Brien, J, 'The International Tribunal for Violations of International Humanitarian Law in the Former Yugoslavia' (1993) 87 *American Journal of International Law* 639.

Parkinson, P (1996) *The Principles of Equity*, Law Book Company.

Pearson, C, 'Saving not such a super idea for same-sex couples', *Australian Financial Review*, 3 May 1999.

Pennisi, E and W Roush, 'Developing a New View of Evolution', *Science*, vol 277, 4 July 1997, 34.

Perritt, HH and CJ Lhulier, 'Information Access Rights Based on International Human Rights Law' (1997) 45 *Buffalo Law Review* 899.

Peters, T, 'From Genesis to Genetics', *New Scientist*, 15 March 1997.

Pollack, SG, 'The Art of Judging' (1996) 71 *New York University Law Review* 591.

Poynder, N, 'Marooned in Port Hedland' (1993) 18 *Alternative Law Journal* 272.

Poynder, N, '"A" v Australia' (1997) 22 *Alternative Law Journal* 149.

Poynder, N, 'The Incommunicado Detention of Boat People: A Recent Development in Australia's Refugee Policy' (1997) 3 *Australian Journal of Human Rights* 53.

Pullin, C, 'From the President', *Australian Bar Gazette*, March 1997.

Ramsay, A, 'High Court Gets Short Shrift', *Sydney Morning Herald*, 8 March 1997.

Ray, R, 'Help is Available for Addicted Lawyers and Judges' (1991) 18 *Canadian Bar Association National* 26.

Reid, Lord 'The Judge as Law-Maker' (1972) *Journal of the Society of Public Teachers of Law* 22.

Renard, I (1996) 'Fair Dealing and Good Faith' in C Saunders (ed) *Courts of Final Jurisdiction – The Mason Court in Australia*, Federation Press.

Richardson, G, 'Oh, What a Tangled Web They've Weaved', *The Bulletin*, 4 February 1997.

Rosen, J, 'The Agoniser', *New Yorker*, 11 November 1996.

Rotenberg, M, 'Privacy Protection – A US Perspective: Data Protection in the United States – A Rising Tide?' in (1998) 14(1) *Computer Law and Security Report* 38.

Sackville, R (1996) 'Continuity and Judicial Creativity – Some Observations', unpublished paper.

Sallmann, PA, 'Life Beyond Caseflow Management' (1994) 3(2) *Journal of Judicial Administration* 143.

Sapolsky, RM (1994) *A Guide to Stress, Stress-Related Diseases and Coping*, Freeman.

Sarantakos, S, 'Same-Sex Marriage: Which Way to Go?' (1994) 24 *Alternative Law Journal* 79.

Sarantakos, S, 'Legal recognition of same-sex relationships' (1998) 23 *Alternative Law Journal* 222

Sarokin, HL, 'The Dangers of Judge-Bashing – Politicians are "Willie Hortonizing" the Bench', *Legal Times*, 27 October 1997.

Scutt, JA (ed) (1987) *Lionel Murphy – A Radical Judge*, McCulloch.

Sedley, Sir Stephen. 'Human Rights: A 21st Century Agenda' in R Blackburn and JJ Busuttil (1997) *Human Rights for the 21st Century*, Pinter.

Shakespeare, W, *Sonnet 30*.

Short, PJ, 'Who Speaks for the Judges?', *Australian Lawyer*, April 1997.

Showalter, CR and DA Martell, 'Personality, Stress and Health in American Judges' (1985) 69(2) *Judicature* 83.

Shukla, VN (1996) *Constitution of India*, Eastern.

Sidoti, C, 'Boat People and Human Rights' (1996) 31 *Australian Lawyer* 5.

Silva, SN, 'Interview' (1994) 19(1) *Dana* 5.

Skapinker, D, 'Gross Over-reaction', *Sydney Morning Herald*, 7 March 1997.

Smith, B, 'Craven Attack on Court Dubbed "Alarming"', *Australian Financial Review*, 17 October 1997.

Smith, GP, 'Judicial Decisionmaking in the Age of Biotechnology' (1999) 13 *Notre Dame Journal of Law, Ethics and Public Policy* 63.

Smith, Judge Anthony, 'Attacks by Senior Politicians on the Integrity of the High Court of Australia', *Judges' Forum Newsletter*, August 1997.

Smith, SB, 'The Constitution of Jurisprudence', unpublished.

Sorabjee, SJ (1996) 'Public Interest Litigation for Protection and Promotion of Human Rights: The Indian Experience' in *New Zealand Law Conference Proceedings*.

Sourdin, T, 'Judicial Management and Alternative Dispute Resolution Process Trends' (1996) 14 *Australian Bar Review* 185.

Starke, JG, 'International Legal Notes' (1989) 63 *Australian Law Journal* 497.

Steiner, HJ and P Alston, (1996) *International Human Rights in Context*, Clarendon.

Stevens, R (1979) *The Law and Politics: The House of Lords as a Judicial Body 1800-1976*, Weidenfeld and Nicolson.

Stevens, R (1995) 'Judges, Politics, Politicians and the Confusing Role of the Judiciary' in K Hawkins (ed) *The Human Face of Law: Essays in Honour of Donald Harris*, Clarendon.

Steyn, Lord, 'The Weakest and Least Dangerous Department of Government' [1997] *Public Law* 84.

Tay, AES (1981) *Teaching Human Rights*, Australian Government Publishing Service.
Thomas, JB, 'A Down-under Circuit: the Life of a Judge in the Remoter Parts of Australia' (1991) 74 *Judicature* 208.
Thomas, JB, 'Get Up Off the Ground' (1997) 71 *Australian Law Journal* 785.
Tobias QC, M, 'I Beg to Differ', *Sydney Morning Herald*, 30 October 1997.
Todd, B, 'From Village Pump to Superhighway: Internet and the Modern Law of Defamation' (1996) 1 *Media and Arts Law Review* 34.
Toohey, J, 'A Government of Laws, And Not of Men?' (1993) 4 *Public Law Review* 158.
Venter, JC, 'The Patentability of Genetic Discoveries' in BBV Foundation (Spain) *The Human Genome Project: Legal Aspects*, vol 2, 123.
Virtue, B, 'The Trial of a Gentle Man' (1993) 28(11) *Australian Lawyer* 8.
Wacks, R (1997) 'Privacy in Cyberspace: Personal Information, Free Speech and the Internet' in P Birks (ed) *Privacy and Loyalty*, Oxford.
White, BR, 'The Special Role of State Judges' (1991) 30(2) *Judges Journal* 6.
White, PJ, 'An America Without Judicial Independence' (1997) 80 *Judicature* 174.
White, RS, 'Self-Determination, Time for a Reassessment?' (1981) 28 *Netherlands International Law Review* 147.
Williams, G, 'Engineers is Dead, Long Live the Engineers!' (1995) 17 *Sydney Law Review* 62.
Williams, G, 'Attacks Undermine Role of High Court', *Sydney Morning Herald*, 9 March 1997.
Wintemute, R, 'Sexual Orientation Discrimination As Sex Discrimination: Same-Sex Couples and the *Charter* in *Mossett*, *Egan* and *Layland*' (1994) 39 *McGill Law Journal* 427.
Wintemute, R, 'Discrimination Against Same-Sex Couples: Sections 15(1) and 1 of the Charter, *Egan v Canada*' (1995) 74 *Canadian Bar Review* 682.
Wintemute, R (1995) *Sexual Orientation and Human Rights*, Clarendon.
Winterton, G, 'The Significance of the Communist Party Case' (1992) 18 *Melbourne University Law Review* 630.
Winterton, G (1996) 'Constitutionally Entrenched Common Law Rights: Sacrificing Means to Ends?' in C Sampford and K Preston (eds) *Interpreting Constitutions: Themes, Principles and Institutions*, Federation Press.
Wootten, JH, 'Creativity in the Law' (1972) 4 *Australian Journal of Forensic Sciences* 107.
Wright, H, 'Law, Convergence and Communicative Values on the Net' (1996) 7 *Journal of Law and Information Science* 54.
Wright, HGA, 'Sovereignty of the People – The New Constitutional *Grundnorm*' (1998) 26(1) *Federal Law Review* 165.
Wright, Lord of Durley, 'Section 92 – A Problem Piece' (1954) 1 *Sydney Law Review* 145.
Zimmerman, IM, 'Stress – What It Does to Judges and How It Can Be Lessened' (1981) 4(8) *Judges Journal* 20.
Zimmerman, IM, 'The Judge and Stress' (1984) 26 *Canadian Journal of Criminology* 6.

Documents and Reports

'Juror Stress: What Price Do Jurors Pay?' (1992) National Center for State Courts Report No 10.

American Bar Association (1997) Report of the Commission on Separation of Powers and Judicial Independency, *An Independent Judiciary*, American Bar Association.

Amnesty International, *Establishing a Just, Fair and Effective International Criminal Court*, Amnesty International, Amnesty International Index IOR 40/05/94.

Australia, Department of Foreign Affairs and Trade, Certified Agreement, 1998-2000.

Australian Human Rights and Equal Opportunity Commission *Superannuation Entitlements of Same Sex Couples* (June 1999).

Australian Parliament, Senate Select Committee on Superannuation (1997) *Parliamentary Contributory Superannuation Scheme and the Judges' Pensions Scheme*, 25th Report, Canberra.

Commonwealth Parliamentary Debates *(Senate)*, Senator Helen Coonan, 18 June 1997.

Convention on Biological Diversity, United Nations Environment Programme No. 92-7807, 5 June 1992.

Convention on the Elimination of All Forms of Discrimination Against Women, United Nations GA Res 34/180, 18 December 1979.

Convention on the Rights of the Child, United Nations GA Res 44/25, 20 November 1989.

Convention Relating to the Status of Refugees, 28 July 1951.

Cooney, B (1994) *Gender Bias and the Judiciary: Report by the Senate Standing Committee on Legal and Constitutional Affairs*, Senate Standing Committee on Legal and Constitutional Affairs.

Corell, H et al (Rapporteurs) (1993) *Proposal for an International War Crimes Tribunal for the Former Yugoslavia*, Council for Security and Cooperation in Europe.

European Union, *Data Directive* (Directive 95/46/EC).

Fernando, B (1998) *Problems Facing the Cambodian Legal System*, Asian Human Rights Commission.

Hansard, House of Lords, 5 June 1996, p 1254.

Hansard, Lord Bingham LCJ, House of Lords, 3 November 1997.

Hansard, Lord Irvine of Lairg, House of Lords, 5 June 1996.

Hansard, New South Wales Legislative Council, 18 November 1999, pp 28-29.

HH The Dalai Lama (1995) *On the Environment*, Department of Information and International Relations, Central Tibetan Administration of HH The Dalai Lama.

Homosexual Offences and Prostitution, Command paper 247, HMSO, 1957.

House of Lords Official Report, 15 June 1996, 572 Parliamentary Debates (Hansard) 1289.

ILO Discrimination (Employment and Occupation) Convention.

International Covenant on Civil and Political Rights, GA Res 2200A(XXI), 16 December 1966.

International Covenant on Economic, Social and Cultural Rights, United Nations GA Res 2200A(XXI), 16 December 1966.

New South Wales Parliamentary Debates (Legislative Assembly), Mr R Turner MP, 1 June 1999, p 741.

New South Wales Parliamentary Debates (Legislative Council) 13 May 1999, p 228; 26 May 1999, p 36.

OECD (1980) *Guidelines on the Protection of Privacy and Transborder Flows of Personal Data*, Paris.

OECD (1992) *Guidelines on Security of Information Systems*, Paris.

OECD (1997) *Guidelines for Cryptography Policy*, OECD Doc:C(97) 62/FINAL.

Report of the Commission on Global Governance (1995) *Our Global Neighbourhood*, Oxford University Press.

Report of the Special Representative of the Secretary-General for Human Rights in Cambodia (1996) UN Doc E/CN.4/1996/93.

UNESCO (1997) *Universal Declaration on the Human Genome and Human Rights.*

United Nations Diplomatic Conference of Plenipotentiaries on the Establishment of an International Criminal Court, *Draft Statute for the International Criminal Court*, UN Document: A/Conf. 183/C.1/L.76/Add. 1-12 (16 July 1998), Rome.

United Nations High Commissioner for Refugees (1998) *UNHCR by Numbers*, UNHCR, <http://www.unhcr.ch/un&ref/numbers/numbers.htm>.

Universal Declaration of Human Rights, United Nations GA Res 217A(III), 10 December 1948.

Wood, D (1996) *Judicial Ethics: A Discussion Paper*, Australian Institute of Judicial Administration.

World Conference on Human Rights, *Vienna Declaration and Programme of Action*, United Nations Document A/Conf/157/23 para 1/10, n 18.

Other Sources

Ahmadi, AM (1996) *Zakir Hussain Memorial Lecture.*

Attorney-General's Office, Press Release, 'Further Consultation on National Privacy Legislation', 30 November 1999.

Attorney-General Janet Reno (1997) Address to the American Bar Association House of Delegates, August.

Bitel, D (1998) 'Recognition of Same-sex Relationships in Australian Immigration Law', presented at the International Bar Association Conference, September.

Boutros-Ghali, B (1995) Address to International Peace Academy Conference on Peacekeeping.

Brennan, G (1997) 'The Third Branch and the Fourth Estate', Second Address in the Series *Broadcasting, Society and the Law*, April.

Brennan, G (1997) Address to the Twelfth South Pacific Judicial Conference, noted in *The Australian*, 15 April 1997 and *Sydney Morning Herald*, 15 April 1997.

Brennan, Sir Gerard (1997) 'State of the Australian Judicature', Address to the Australian Legal Convention, September.

Cowen, Sir Zelman (1997) Address to the Rotary Club of Richmond, March.

Craven, G (1997) 'The High Court: An Abuse of Power', 31st Alfred Deakin Lecture, noted in *Australian Financial Review*, 10 October 1997.

GLITF (NSW) (1997) *Same-Sex Couple Discrimination for Independent and Business Visa Applications*, submission to the Australian Human Rights and Equal Opportunity Commission.

Gryk, W (1998) 'The Recognition of Unmarried Relationships Under British Immigration Law – An Evolving Process?', presented at the International Bar Association Conference, September.

Kirby, MD (1996) 'India and Australia: A Neglected Legal Relationship and a Plan of Action', Address, New Delhi, India, October.

Letter from the Hon R Carr MP to the President, AIDS Council of NSW, 22 February 1995.

Moore, C, MP (NSW), Media Release, 20 October 1998.

Power, Bishop P (1998) 'Marginalised People: In Society and in the Church', address to the Oceania Synod of Bishops.

Robot Exclusion Standard, <http://web.nexor.co.uk/mak/doc/robots/norobots.html>.

Statement by HH The Dalai Lama on the 36th Anniversary of the Tibetan National Uprising Day, 10 March 1995, printed in *Australia Tibet Council News*, February/March 1995.

Statement to the Vienna Conference by the Singapore Minister for Foreign Affairs, 23 June 1993.

Williams, D (1996) 'Who Speaks for the Judges?', Address to Australian Judicial Conference, November.

Williams, D (1997) 'Judicial Independence, the Courts and the Community', Address to South Australian Chapter of the Australian Institute of Judicial Administration, February.

Wood, JR (1997) Address to NSW Police Academy by Royal Commissioner, May.

Table of Cases

Table of Legislation

Index